THE KABUKI THEATRE OF JAPAN

A. C. SCOTT

WITH ILLUSTRATIONS BY THE AUTHOR

DOVER PUBLICATIONS, INC.
Mineola, New York

Published in Canada by General Publishing Company, Ltd., 30 Lesmill Road, Don Mills, Toronto, Ontario.

Published in the United Kingdom by Constable and Company, Ltd., 3 The Lanchesters, 162–164 Fulham Palace Road, London W6 9ER.

Bibliographical Note

This Dover edition, first published in 1999, is an unabridged reprint of *The Kabuki Theatre of Japan,* published by George Allen & Unwin Ltd., London, in 1955.

Library of Congress Cataloging-in-Publication Data

Scott, A. C. (Adolphe Clarence), 1909–
    The kabuki theatre of Japan / A. C. Scott ; with illustrations by the author.
        p.   cm.
    Originally published: London : Allen & Unwin, 1955.
    Includes bibliographical references and index.
    ISBN 0-486-40645-8 (pbk.)
    1. Kabuki.   I. Title.
PN2924.5.K3S265   1999
792'.0952—dc21   98-43894
                                                                        CIP

Manufactured in the United States of America
Dover Publications, Inc., 31 East 2nd Street, Mineola, N.Y. 11501

PREFACE

DANCE, music, symbolism and colourful exaggeration have a universal appeal; they are indispensable to the Japanese heart as is exemplified in the old popular drama, the Kabuki. It is not without significance that some of the most enthusiastic admirers of this ancient theatre are to be found among the foreigners who throng Japan today, although the Kabuki is as far removed from the naturalistic entertainments of the West as it is possible to be. Perhaps its disregard for reality, and emphasis on imagination and make-believe, appeals to instincts deep within every man, but forgotten in the mechanical entertainments of an industrial civilization.

In learning to appreciate the Kabuki, it is rather like one of those toys common to one's childhood: a lid is removed from a gaily painted box revealing another closely fitted inside, and inside that yet another, and so on until one comes to the very kernel of all the boxes. The more knowledge gained of the background of the theatre, the more must be learned of the life of the Japanese people themselves and, in this way, the lid may be lifted from the first of the layers of boxes on the voyage of expectation and discovery.

I first came to the Kabuki by way of China and the classical drama of Peking. It taught me one lesson, that to gain a deeper understanding of the artistic background of Japan, and I include the theatre, too, it is a useful thing to have a prior acquaintance with China. To get beneath the superficial surface, the mere picturesque, which is too often the yardstick of Occidental interest, it is better to go first to China, the fountainhead of so much that has permeated Japanese culture. To know Japan only is to start at the wrong end of the stick, particularly today when that stick is busily engaged in stirring a melting pot. Unfortunately we no longer have the choice.

This volume is the result of two years spent working with the people of the Kabuki theatre of Tokyo, as well as with those from the Bunraku, or doll theatre of Osaka. It is hoped that it may serve as a useful handbook, not only for those fortunate enough to be able to visit this enchanting theatre for themselves, but for a wider circle of readers interested in Japanese artistic values which, regrettably, seem to be passing into the twilight of their existence.

A. C. S.

Tokyo/Hong Kong, 1953-4

ACKNOWLEDGMENTS

IT would require a great deal more space than is available to name individually all the people who have assisted me in writing this book, but among them I must mention some to whom I am particularly indebted.

I can only convey the most inadequate thanks to the management and staff of the Kabuki za, Tokyo, for the help and encouragement they have given me. From the first day I entered the theatre I was treated as a member of the 'family' and I cannot forget the many privileges extended to me by Mr T. Saito and his liaison officer. Everyone in the theatre spared no effort on my behalf, none more so than 'agemaku' who, from his domain behind the hanamichi, has proved a friend indeed.

I salute the actors one and all, without them this book could never have been written. I am beholden to Nakamura Utaemon, Ichikawa Ebizo, Onoe Baiko, Nakamura Tokizo, Ichikawa Shocho, and Ichikawa Arajiro, for individual services rendered to me.

To Yoshida Bungoro of the doll theatre and all his colleagues I pay tribute and offer sincere thanks.

Madame Azuma Tokuho and Mr Hanayagi Tokubei have given me assistance and offered me the hospitality of their studios on a number of occasions.

Dr Ueda Tatsunosuke, of the Japan Academy, has helped me in countless ways. As a lifelong friend of the late Fujinami Yohei III, he introduced me to the charming household of the master of kōdōgu, in whose workshops I have spent so many delightful and profitable hours. I am indebted to Dr Ueda for the anecdote concerning Danjuro IX and the lion mask related in Chapter VII, as well as for scrutinizing the draft of my original MS and making valuable criticisms. In this connection I am also most grateful to the distinguished Kabuki scholar, Professor Komiya Toyotaka.

Mr M. Matsuo, late secretary of the Japan branch of the IPR, has been a constant guide to me in matters Japanese, and first gave me an acquaintance with the Nō theatres of Tokyo. To him and to Mr Tsuda Masao of the Japan Newspaper Proprietors' Association I am indebted for an initial introduction to the Kabuki world.

I owe a great deal to Mr M. Yoshida of the Shochiku Company for his help in theatre matters, particularly for assistance in the Bunraku theatre and the many privileges I received there. I am also grateful to him for making available the Japanese acting scripts of a number of plays and for the photograph of Sakaya.

Mr Miura Tetsuo of Tokyo has given me invaluable advice and assistance in translations from the Japanese and has spared no efforts on my behalf and proved a patient mentor at all times.

I am indebted to the editor of the *Engekikai* magazine for the photographs of Ichikawa Ebizo, Nakamura Kichiemon, Ichikawa Ennosuke and *Masakado*. He has also helped in many other ways, while his assistant, Miss Ariyoshi, has rendered me services in connection with the Kabuki.

It is perhaps unorthodox to acknowledge a city, but I do, Kyoto. It is in her streets that I have been able to recapture a little of the essence of old Japan.

I am indebted to Mrs Chang An and Miss Lo Wai Lam of Hong Kong, and Mr T. Denvil Scott of London, for assistance in preparing the TS. Finally, I must acknowledge the patient assistance of my wife in the unenviable task of checking and proof-reading the MS.

A. C. S.

While this book was going to press, the author learned with regret of the death of Nakamura Kichiemon, the actor.

SELECT
BIBLIOGRAPHY

LE NŌ, Noel Peri, *Maison Franco-Japonaise*, Tokyo 1944.

NŌ TO NŌ MEN, *Kongo School*, Kyoto 1951.

THE NŌ PLAYS OF JAPAN, Arthur Waley, *Allen and Unwin*, London 1921.

BUNRAKU NINGYO ZUFU, Miyao Shigeo, Tokyo 1942.

SHIBAI NISHIKIYE SHUSEI, Yamamura Koka, Machida Hiroza, Tokyo 1920.

THE KABUKI, POPULAR STAGE OF JAPAN, Zoe Kincaid. *Macmillan*, London 1925.

JAPANESE DRAMA, Board of Tourist Industry, *Japanese Government Railways*, Tokyo 1935.

GEKIJO KUMMO ZUE, Shikitei Samba, Yedo 1803.

KABUKI BUYŌ NO HENSEN, Atsumi Seitaro, Tokyo 1941.

JAPAN, A SHORT CULTURAL HISTORY, Sir George Sansom, *Cresset Press*, London 1936.

A List of the Japanese Eras Relevant to the History of the Kabuki Theatre

KEICHO 1	*	1596	GENROKU 16	*	1703	KYOWA 1	*	1801
KEICHO 19	*	1614	HOEI 1	*	1704	KYOWA 3	*	1803
GENNA 1	*	1615	HOEI 7	*	1710	BUNKA 1	*	1804
GENNA 9	*	1623	SHOTOKU 1	*	1711	BUNKA 14	*	1817
KANEI 1	*	1624	SHOTOKU 5	*	1715	BUNSEI 1	*	1818
KANEI 20	*	1643	KYOHO 1	*	1716	BUNSEI 12	*	1829
SHOHO 1	*	1644	KYOHO 20	*	1735	TEMPO 1	*	1830
SHOHO 4	*	1647	GEMBUN 1	*	1736	TEMPO 14	*	1843
KEIAN 1	*	1648	GEMBUN 5	*	1740	KOKA 1	*	1844
KEIAN 4	*	1651	KAMPO 1	*	1741	KOKA 4	*	1847
SHŌŌ 1	*	1652	KAMPO 3	*	1743	KAEI 1	*	1848
SHŌŌ 3	*	1654	ENKYO 1	*	1744	KAEI 6	*	1853
MEIREKI 1	*	1655	ENKYO 4	*	1747	ANSEI 1	*	1854
MEIREKI 3	*	1657	KANEN 1	*	1748	ANSEI 6	*	1859
MANJI 1	*	1658	KANEN 3	*	1750	MANEN 1	*	1860
MANJI 3	*	1660	HOREKI 1	*	1751	BUNKYU 1	*	1861
KAMBUN 1	*	1661	HOREKI 13	*	1763	BUNKYU 3	*	1863
KAMBUN 12	*	1672	MEIWA 1	*	1764	GENJI 1	*	1864
EMPO 1	*	1673	MEIWA 8	*	1771	KEIO 1	*	1865
EMPO 8	*	1680	ANEI 1	*	1772	KEIO 3	*	1867
TENWA 1	*	1681	ANEI 9	*	1780	MEIJI 1	*	1868
TENWA 3	*	1683	TENMEI 1	*	1781	MEIJI 45	*	1912
JOKYO 1	*	1684	TENMEI 8	*	1788	TAISHO 1	*	1912
JOKYO 4	*	1687	KANSEI 1	*	1789	TAISHO 15	*	1926
GENROKU 1	*	1688	KANSEI 12	*	1800	SHOWA 1	*	1926

CONTENTS

ILLUSTRATIONS

PLATES

LINE DRAWINGS IN TEXT

THE KABUKI THEATRE
OF JAPAN

CHAPTER I

A BACKGROUND
TO APPRECIATION

THE Japanese and Chinese classical dramas have many points in common, yet differ widely from each other in a number of fundamental ways, apart from obvious variations due to national background and local colour. They have a kinship of spirit, however, in their conceptions. In outlining the essentials of the Kabuki it is helpful to consider briefly some of the important characteristics of the two theatres.

The Kabuki, like the Chinese theatre, lays great stress upon the virtuosity of the actor. He supplies the motive for the whole drama. He must play to an audience which knows the rules of the game and which is primarily interested in the way he recreates a stage character in a traditionally accepted mould. At the same time his performance must contain an individuality beneath the unchanging conventions, his symbolism must be something more than imitative repetition.

Women's parts are traditionally played by male actors, the *onnagata*, in the Kabuki in exactly the same way as on the Chinese stage. The convention has been more rigidly preserved in Japan than China for, whereas the actress has been common in the Chinese theatre within recent decades, women have never yet appeared on the orthodox Kabuki stage.

Two notable differences in the Chinese and Japanese theatres are found, first in the musical construction, secondly in stage presentation. In both theatres the orchestra is seated on the stage during a performance, but in the Kabuki the number of musicians varies much more according to the type of accompaniment required and their placing is a part of the general stage design, which in the Chinese theatre is ignored. These are perhaps superficial differences, although in both cases they add greatly to the individual characteristics of the two dramas. On both stages the orchestra is responsible for the control and timing of the actor's dancing, gestures and poses. In China the orchestra also accompanies the actor's singing which is an important feature of the plays, but in Japan the actor does not sing at all; it is done by the orchestra which, on occasion, speaks the actor's dialogue as well. This is an important feature of the music in the Kabuki theatre, it is known as *jōruri* and will be explained later.

The stage presentation of the Kabuki is unique. Unlike the Chinese stage, which is a simple platform bereft of all trimmings, in the Kabuki it is a complex affair using elaborate settings and effects which have been developed to a high pitch of artistry through the centuries. Today all the resources of modern stage lighting are skilfully incorporated to add to the attractions.

The proscenium opening of the theatre stretches the whole width of the auditorium, being very long in proportion to the height, which is roughly a quarter of the length. It allows groupings of actors, dancers and arrangements of sets which are peculiar to the Kabuki. In addition, all stages revolve, facilitating quick changes of time and place before the eyes of the audience.

The most celebrated feature of the Kabuki stage is the *hanamichi*, a raised gangway which connects the stage to the rear of the auditorium. On this the actors make entries and exits and perform dances; the action of the play is thus carried out into the body of the audience. Trap devices in both stage and *hanamichi* allow the actors to appear and disappear at will.

In the Chinese theatre, one of the primary requisities of a good actor is a fine singing voice in addition to his other accomplishments, on the Kabuki stage he is not required to sing, but he must with very few exceptions be a first class dancer. Dancing plays an exceedingly important part in the Kabuki drama. There are a large number of plays in the repertoire which are dance pieces pure and simple, others in which dancing is an underlying feature of construction, even in dialogue plays a dance passage is often introduced. The dancing element also shows itself in a great deal of formal posing and gesture, as of course in this sense it does in the Chinese theatre too. In the Kabuki drama, the actors, assisted by the musicians, carry the imagination along by a series of climaxes, which are very often obtained by pictorial effect. In every play there comes a moment when each actor on the stage takes his place in a kind of tableau, a common type of finale to most performances. Even in the more realistic type of plays this element is always present.

The *ukiyoe*, or wood block print artists of the eighteenth century, have undoubtedly left their mark on the Kabuki which has received inspiration in design from many of their masterpieces, while, in their turn, the *ukiyoe* artists drew upon the theatre.

The dialogue of the Kabuki actor may consist of archaic phraseology or relatively simple colloquial speech. Either type uses rhythmical metres and highly stylized intonation, which form a part of the general abstraction composed from music, dance and gesture. One cannot be separated from the other; they are co-related to form an art of exquisite fantasy and imagination.

The plays of the Kabuki may be broadly divided into three types: *jidaimono*, *sewamono* and *shosagoto*. The first named are plays with a historical background, even though the plots are far removed from actuality or have been changed to suit stage purposes. The *sewamono* plays deal with the domestic life of the people and human nature in its more plebian aspects, although they sometimes contain characteristics of the *jidaimono* plays as well. There is one class of *sewamono* play called *kizewamono*, which features the adventures of thieves, gamblers and the riff-raff of the underworld. The *sewamono* play belongs to the Genroku and Yedo eras and it is the background of those periods which they portray. The last of the three types are the *shosagoto*, which are dance plays only.

To tabulate these different types of plays on paper, and to see a performance, are two very different things. A general understanding of the social and psychological background of Japanese society in the past is a valuable aid towards a richer appreciation of the dramatic construction of the Kabuki.

The Tokugawa era, also called the Yedo (Edo) era, which covered approximately two hundred and sixty years, was the age in which the Kabuki was born and reached a flourishing maturity. It lasted from the establishment of the Shōgunate by Ieyasu at the beginning of the seventeenth century to the restoration of Imperial rule, known as the Meiji Restoration of 1868. It is the manners and customs of these times which colour the theatre throughout. Politically it was a period of long and undisturbed peace in Japan, never known before and never to be known again. Culturally and socially, it was an age of many changes and new developments.

Society was rigidly divided into classes among which the *samurai*, or warriors, were highest and held the reigns of govern-

ment. The *Shōgun* was the supreme head of the governing class
and beneath him came the *daimyo*, feudal chiefs directly responsible to the *Shōgun*. Beneath them came a lower class, the
hatamoto, and below them a number of various ranks of lesser
degree. They were all *samurai* nevertheless. The *Shōgun, daimyo*
and some of the *hatamoto* class drew incomes from fiefs and
estates, but the *samurai* class as a whole received an annual
allowance in rice fixed according to their rank. A *daimyo*, for instance, would probably draw a minimum of 10,000 *koku* per
annum, a *koku* being 4.96 bushels.

The distinguishing badge of the *samurai*, from the highest to
the lowest, was the right to wear two swords, a custom which
became mandatory at the beginning of the Tokugawa era. No
other persons were allowed this privilege, although at certain
times other classes were allowed to carry a single blade. The two
swords worn by the *samurai* were known as the *daito* and *shoto*.
The *daito* has a squared end to the scabbard and was taken off
whenever entering a residence or castle, the *shoto*, shorter in
length than the other, was always carried in the belt and had a
rounded end to the scabbard, which was considered to mean the
wearer had no hostile intentions.

The sword in old Japan was something very much more than a
weapon. It was a symbol of family honour and possessed a sacred
quality, so that the most precious dowry a wife could bring to a
samurai was the sword of her ancestors. Time and time again in
Kabuki plays, it will be found that an underlying theme is the
quest of a stolen sword. Forged by master craftsmen, these old
blades were works of art which, with their pedigrees, were
handed down from generation to generation. The theft or loss of
these family heirlooms was one of the greatest disgraces any man
could suffer, redeemable only with his life. It is understandable
that the Kabuki utilizes these factors in its plays and naturally
the sword is an exceedingly important stage property.

The *samurai* prided himself at all times on adhering strictly to
rules of conduct which were rigidly laid down, and to break them
constituted a disgrace. In his personal etiquette he was adjured
to be meticulous in correct dress for ceremonial occasions, always
wear his swords and carry a fan in his girdle. His hair had to be
dressed daily and the forehead shaved as was the custom. A bath
every day was a necessity and in every single movement, whether

Kamishimo—Samurai's costume

in repose or action, he had to preserve an attitude befitting his rank.

The first principle on which the *samurai* based his living was the fact that he must always be ready to face death, for life is impermanent and the path of the warrior doubly uncertain. Bearing this fact in mind, he was considered capable of living in accordance with the principles of filial duty (*kōkō*), and loyalty to his lord (*chūgi*), two basic concepts. As in China, filial piety was an ethical principle which no Japanese ever questioned. The claims of the family came before the claims of the individual. Beyond family loyalty lay yet another principle, real and compelling, known in Japanese as *giri*, and this was identified as the cardinal virtue of the *samurai*. It has been a central theme in a number of Kabuki dramas. *Giri* extends beyond loyalty to immediate relations, it is the debt of honour a man owes to the comrades of his own class and, beyond that, the supreme debt to his lord and superior. Nothing could stand in the way of this debt, which was only repayable with a man's own life, or that of a member of his family. The expression of this code leads to a number of tense and tragic situations on the stage. Suicide by *seppuku*, sometimes called *harakiri*, or the killing of a member of one's own family as a substitute for another, are two common themes in such cases.

Samurai, who lost their position through the disgrace of their lords, or because of the liquidation of their master's estates, became *ronin*, literally 'men adrift', a class which increased in great numbers in the latter half of the Tokugawa era. The most celebrated examples of this class are the famous forty-seven *ronin*, who figure as the heroes of the Kabuki classic, *Chushingura*.

At the other end of the social scale from the *samurai* were the *chonin*, a general class which was subdivided into *shonin*, merchants and tradesmen, *shokunin*, artisans and craftsmen, and *hyakusho*, farmers and peasants. The *chonin* were looked down upon by the *samurai*, who considered it beneath their dignity to associate with them. The *chonin* in turn were not allowed to participate in the cultural pursuits and pastimes of the ruling classes. It was this which was directly responsible for the development of the Kabuki, the theatre of the *chonin* who, denied access to the privileges of the *samurai*, created their own cultural background in spite of the ruling classes.

The long reign of peace during the Tokugawa era, and changing conditions of life, gradually brought about the decay of the *samurai* and, proportionately, the increased prosperity and therefore the influence of the *chonin*. There was little use for the services of the warrior in times of peace but the *samurai's* love of luxury increased although their allowance remained stationary in spite of the rise of living costs. They fell into debt and had to rent their houses, pawn their goods and, greatest disgrace of all, even their swords to the merchants and tradesmen. Besides this, the numbers of the *samurai* class were far greater than the posts available for them. Hereditary income in a *samurai* family was only transmitted to the eldest son, and this made it even more difficult for the other sons, especially as no member of the *samurai* class was fitted by upbringing for any form of trade or labour and traditional pride would not allow them to forsake their principles.

While the long peace saw the decline of the *samurai*, the merchant class rose to prosperity and as they grew wealthier their social importance increased and it was they eventually who, through their money, held the real power in social life. They began to live in luxury and style and to surround themselves with a pattern of culture of their own. Kyoto, the ancient capital, pro-

Theatrical wig:
'Chō-mage'

vided them with the things they demanded, the high class products of clothing, lacquer, ceramics and furnishings, which were
the mark of the refined background of the Imperial Court.

Eventually the *samurai* found it impossible to ignore the
chonin and in many cases was constrained to swallow his pride
and even don the costume of the once despised merchant. On the
other hand, the *chonin* began to emulate the ideals of self-
sacrifice and loyalty which had been the feudal virtues of the
samurai. Long oppression from the latter class had already developed special characteristics in the *chonin*, a ready wit and
humour, a fearlessness in criticizing their rulers and a readiness
to help the weak and downtrodden, traits immortalized in the
characters of the Kabuki stage. In old Yedo there were friendly
associations of brave *chonin* who were sworn to stand by each
other through thick and thin, without inquiring into their comrades' antecedents. Their mission was to help the oppressed and
fight the oppressor. They were known as the *otokodate* or 'chivalrous men of honour', and Banzuin Chôbei, the head of the Yedo
otokodate, is a famous Kabuki character.

It was against such a background that the theatre rose to prominence. Young and old, men and women, were all welcome and

the Kabuki became the centre of the public and social life of the town. The theatres were segregated in special quarters by the authorities and forbidden to the *samurai* class, but that did not worry the *chonin*, it was their gain and the *samurai's* loss. Their spirit is best summed up in a popular song of old Yedo: 'In Yedo there is nothing to be seen but Danjuro and the cherry blossoms in March.'

Other recreations of the people were the numerous *matsuri*, or feast days and religious festivals, which are still observed and are the occasion, as they were then, for everyone to indulge in that love of dancing which comes as second nature to the Japanese people. The colourful dances and gay music of the *matsuri* have been woven into many a Kabuki play to make a merry stage scene. Another popular entertainment was *sumo*, the traditional wrestling of Japan, and tournaments were notable events in the amusement calendar, and indeed still are, in spite of baseball. The *sumo* champion was a popular hero and wrestlers appear in a number of Kabuki plays. There were three public idols in Yedo times, the Kabuki actor, the *sumo* wrestler and the *tobi* or fireman.

In a country whose building construction was wholly of wood, fire formed one of the greatest scourges and the history of Yedo is marked by some of the greatest conflagrations of all times. Standing companies of firemen were maintained by the *daimyo*, they wore their own livery and held a special parade at the New Year festival. There was great rivalry among the different companies and quarrels often took place over setting up their *matoi*, or standard, to mark the extinguishing of a particular blaze. The *tobi*, with his hot temper and dashing style, adds spice to many Kabuki plays.

Here it may be fitting to say something about a public figure of a different type, the *oiran* or courtesan, who is the subject for many important roles in the Kabuki and constantly figures in many kinds of plays. A great deal of nonsense has been written on the subject which does nothing to clarify an understanding of her significance as a theatrical character. The *oiran* is enshrined in the Kabuki as a nostalgic symbol of the romantic ideals of a past age. She long ago disappeared. The ancient quarter of Yoshiwara, where she flourished, still exists, but only as a district for the ladies of the night, which is neither better nor worse

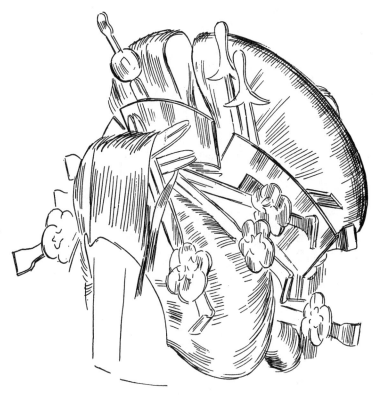

Hyōgo Mage: A theatrical wig for courtesan roles

than similar quarters in other great cities of the world. Before making judgment from a Western standpoint, it is necessary to take a number of social factors into account in considering the position of the *oiran* in former times, together with the respect and favour which she received.

Gay quarters like Yoshiwara were a centre of pleasure and gaiety for the ordinary citizen, a world of excitement in which he moved about at will, an escape from the tyranny of feudal life as well as a means to satisfy the more romantic aspects of human nature. In the latter case it has to be remembered that 'romantic' love was completely absent from Japanese domestic life. Marriage was an affair arranged by parents whose sole purpose was the continuance of the family line, it was unthinkable that anyone should question parental decisions in these matters, any straying from the path of filial conduct was a grave offence with

Komurasaki the courtesan:
A typical onnagata pose

severe penalties attached. There was no ideal which regarded love and marriage as identical, and while a man was expected to preserve the most formal relations with his wife, it was no offence against public opinion if he sought his romantic pleasures in the officially recognized gay quarters.

The *oiran* herself, that is the great *oiran*, true to tradition, was something more than a mere purveyor of physical charm. She received a strict training and was talented and accomplished in musical and other arts, she was versed in witty andintelligent conversation and adopted a rigid etiquette, originally based on the old court, which had to be observed at all times. It was an etiquette which extended its formality throughout the quarter and had to be practised by visitors as well, if they wished to be received. The Yoshiwara of olden days stood for gay elegance as well as the embodiment of the sentimental ideals of the *chonin*. At certain times of the year there were public processions of the *oiran* resplendent in all their elaborate costume and this provided a spectacle to delight the community at large. Even when she walked abroad by herself and not in procession, she still deported herself with dignified ceremony, as may be seen in the plays of the Kabuki.

The model *oiran* was a woman of poise and graciousness with a trained mind, and what may sound paradoxical enough, high principles; her favours were not to be had for the asking. To the houses of the most prominent *oiran* came writers, artists and other distinguished members of the community. They were the centre of the social and artistic life of the times in which the *chonin* reigned supreme, where the *samurai* was forbidden, and, if he wished to share the privileges, could only enter as a member of the despised class. It is in epitomizing such a background that the *oiran* takes her place in the gallery of Kabuki characters, a figure of wistfulness around whom has developed a symbolical stage technique, which charms the eye with its delicacy and grace.

Marriage, it has been said, was a purely formal family arrangement in old Japan. The wife went to live with the husband's family, she was asked to devote herself to the needs of her husband and regard his parents as her own. The traditional devotion, faithfulness and modesty of the Japanese wife form important background elements in Kabuki dramas. At a time when marriage was so prearranged, divorce unknown and elopement a major crime, and where even the unfaithfulness of a husband was often a factor impelling greater wifely ministrations, it is not surprising that the theatre used such facts to create themes for some of the more celebrated plays; the supreme qualities of the

Japanese wife and mother colour some of the most powerful stage roles.

Buddhism, Shintoism and Confucianism had a profound effect on the Japanese philosophy of life and this in its turn is reflected in innumerable ways in the Kabuki drama, and directs sentiments expressed through the characters of both historical and domestic plays. There is, for example, a favourite Kabuki technique in which a dying man recalls his past, regrets past misconduct and reveals his inner thoughts. It is an extension of the Buddhist principle that man is fundamentally good, that on death his sins are expurgated and he returns to his original innocent state. Or again in the ever popular *michi yuki* dance play, the young lovers, victims of fate, go on their way to commit a double suicide and so achieve reunion in another world. This shows the strong influence of Buddhist thought as it coloured the minds of the people.

Such influences are seen in more material aspects. There is that strange figure the *komusō*, who appears in several plays and is used to gain a particularly dramatic effect in the ninth act of *Chushingura*. The *komusō* wears a large basket-like head covering completely obscuring his face and plays on the *shakuhachi*, a flute with a plaintive tone. The *komusō* was originally a wandering priest of a Buddhist sect, who until recently was still occasionally seen, although the order was supposedly dissolved in 1871. The name *komusō* was that of a follower of the Buddhist priest Kakusha, who returned from China in A.D. 1254, and was said to have introduced the *shakuhachi* from there, his pupils after that carrying it when preaching Buddhism. In the Tokugawa era lordless *samurai*, seeking vengeance, began to adopt the *komusō* costume as a disguise, often carrying a flute made of much stouter bamboo as a weapon. This is typical of the background which lies behind so much Kabuki stage usage.

In certain plays, the Japanese sliding doors at the rear of a stage set are decorated with a bold blue and white pattern called *manjitsunagi*, a pattern adopted from Buddhist symbolism. Based on the Buddhist cross, this piece of traditional stage decoration is another small example of the varied type of influence which contributes towards the general pattern of stage production.

Japanese people in the past lived in a manner strikingly different from that of other countries and satisfied their requirements for housing, clothing and furnishing in an astonishingly simple, economical and decorative fashion, which is reproduced in the sets, properties and costumes of the Kabuki.

Houses were made entirely of wood and plaster, great attention being paid to window space. Instead of glass, paper of various thicknesses and quality was used on screens and windows and to cover the sliding doors separating the rooms. Floors were covered with finely woven mats made of reed or rush on top of a bed of rice straw, tightly bound together, surfaced and bound with a broad black or dark blue strip at either end. Floors were laid in sections, each piece of matting being six feet by three feet by two inches deep. Known as *tatami*, this still serves as the standard flooring for all Japanese style dwellings today, and the size of a room is measured in terms of *tatami*, i.e. a six *tatami* room or a ten *tatami* room and so on. The main decorative feature of any room, whether it belonged to a rich or a poor man, was the *tokonoma*, or alcove, in which was placed a single hanging scroll and a flower arrangement, both of which were changed with the seasons. Woodwork was not painted but left in a natural state with a dull polish. Furniture as the West knows it was conspicuous by its absence. People did not sit on chairs but upon the *tatami* itself, *zabuton* or silk cushions being used. There were no beds, people slept on the *tatami* in thick padded quilts and eiderdowns which were rolled up and stored away in built-in cupboards during the day. The main furnishings used were folding screens, lamps, low tables and chests of drawers, all of which were executed with supreme good taste, great attention being paid to design and quality. Built-in cupboards were an integral feature in the design of any room harmonizing with the simplicity of the general decoration, besides serving as useful yet unobtrusive storage space.

Interiors were spotlessly clean, for the Japanese remove all footwear at the outer entrance before going into a house, wearing only their *tabi*, the Japanese style sock described later, when indoors. Heating was by means of charcoal, the *hibachi*, or firebox, being a feature of every room as was the *tabako bon*. The *tabako bon* was a small wooden tray with a handle, carrying a container of burning charcoal for lighting the minute bowled pipes which everyone carried; it is one of the most characteristic of the stage properties seen in *sewamono* plays. Lighting was by means of candles and oil lamps and here again the exceedingly decorative *andon*, or low standard lamps, which stand on the *tatami*, are typical of stage decorations.

Roofs of houses were of thatch in the country and of grey curved tiles in the cities. An architectural feature of the towns was the merchant's *dozō*, or warehouse, a squat building made of stone covered with white plaster and a decoratively tiled roof. It can still be seen dotted here and there in the older quarters of cities in Japan, and is to be found painted on many a Kabuki stage set particularly in dancing plays.

Clothes were made of cotton, linen and silk. Great attention was paid to the quality and design. There were certain patterns, and styles of clothing worn by the different classes according to their status, for ceremonial occasions as well as the seasons, and this etiquette was most strictly adhered to by Japanese people. So, too, with the many ornate hair styles of both men and women; these also signified their rank and status in society. Theatrical costumes and wigs, therefore, are vital elements when considering the symbolism of the Kabuki theatre.

An important article of clothing is the *tabi*, or Japanese sock. It has a reinforced sole and is made of white cotton although for men's outdoor use it is sometimes black; it is made with a separate division for the big toe, is of ankle length and secured with fasteners above the heel. Sandals and clogs are worn with the *tabi* but are removed indoors. There is an exception in that courtesans never wore *tabi* and this is seen on the stage, for the actors in *oiran* roles always go barefooted. It used to apply to the *geisha*, too, although they all wear *tabi* today. *Tabi* are extremely important to the actor from a purely practical point of view, for all Japanese dancing is performed wearing *tabi* only, and those for actors and dancers have to be specially made for them. Good fitting *tabi* are vital and the quality of those worn by stage people must be of the best. A recognizable feature of stage *tabi* is that they have four fasteners above the heel instead of the normal three. Apart from its theatrical use, the *tabi* is a part of the correct formal dress for the upper and middle classes. To go barefooted signifies poverty or distress, or an inferior status in society.

One interesting fact worthy of note is the very small basic difference in the ways of living of both rich and poor. The richer man would have better quality clothing, finer material used in the construction of his house, and possess more furnishings and

The Japanese Tabi

goods of high quality, but his fundamental ways of life were the same as his poorer brother. His methods of eating, sleeping and general living, together with the clothes he wore, were in principle much the same and this provided a remarkably similar etiquette between the various strata of society in spite of the wide class distinction. This is noticeable in the Kabuki drama where it even makes a certain unity of design.

The staple food of the people was rice. With this were eaten innumerable kinds of dishes, which varied according to material circumstances. Most important was fish in great variety, raw, dried or fried. Vegetables of many kinds including large radishes and beans were put to different uses. Seaweeds, eggs, chicken and fruit formed the other important items in the popular diet. Animal flesh such as beef and mutton was never eaten. Drinks consisted of tea of different qualities and flavours, and *sake*, rice wine.

Each item of food would be served on separate lacquer dishes and eaten with chopsticks, or *hashi*. No article used in cooking and serving was without its intrinsic design or pattern, and, even among the poorer classes, such things were rarely inartistic.

There is a Japanese proverb which says, '*Sake* is a jewelled broom that sweeps away your worries.' It is true that on informal occasions Japanese men shed all inhibitions in drinking and give way to carefree indulgence in the pleasures of the wine cup. But, as with most other things, wine drinking has a certain etiquette, and is a custom that may not be omitted between host and guest,

without showing a disregard of the normal standards of behaviour. Formalities are less rigid today, but in the past drinking
wine was governed by severe rules, not only as to who might offer
the first cup, but how the cup should be held or received, the
wine poured and thanks expressed for it.

Besides the etiquette stipulated for normal social gatherings,
there were ceremonial and even religious occasions on which the
drinking of *sake* was a form of ritual. This was seen in the old
marriage ceremony in which the bride and bridegroom had to
seal their pledge by drinking three cups of *sake* three times (*san
san kudo no sakazuki*); it made the nuptials valid and was a solemn
performance which may sometimes be seen enacted on the
Kabuki stage. In many plays, the drinking of *sake* is seen performed by the actors, both as a form of ceremonial etiquette or
mere jovial quaffing which is often not without its humorous
implications, particularly in many dance pieces.

Formerly, everything and everybody in Japan was bound by a
strict code of etiquette. There were correct ways of eating, drinking, wearing clothes and moving about according to time and
place. The daily lives of everyone from the married lady to the
oiran, the *samurai* to the shopkeeper, were regulated by etiquette. This fact, coupled with their characteristic manner of
living, such as for instance sitting, dining and sleeping on the
tatami, created gestures and movements which were individual
in style, and these translated into terms of stage technique have
developed a very special visual effect, both in the case of the
single actor or group composition. The European sometimes fails
to realize that an apparent lack of action is due to the unhurried
formality with which Japanese people conducted themselves in
daily life, emphasized for dramatic effect. Display of emotion between the opposite sexes was never shown outwardly as it would
be between Europeans, and if a particularly emotional passage in
a Kabuki play may seem lacking in such a quality to the foreigner,
it is because he fails to understand an approach which is very different from his own.

An old maxim for Kabuki playwrights advised them to write a
play as if drawing a picture, not as if writing a Chinese character,
for in that case women and children could not understand it. This
sums up the Kabuki drama in a way that nothing else does. A
Kabuki play is not meant to be a literary work in itself, it is con-

sidered in the first place as stage effect. It is primarily visual in appeal and everything else is subordinate to that. Fact and fantasy are intermingled without reserve, realism and logic are ignored whenever necessary, human nature is painted with bold and vivid strokes, but there is no attempt to go beyond the conventional concepts of human behaviour within a certain pattern of society. The Kabuki is not concerned with any particular message, it is first and foremost entertainment, designed solely for the ordinary citizen; everything is devoted to making a vivid appeal to the eye and creating atmosphere by all possible artistry to keep the audience enthralled. In short it is superb theatre.

To achieve its ends it ignores no possible source, and the legends, customs, habits, religion, loves and hates of the Japanese people are drawn upon freely and woven into the pattern of construction of this colourful drama. What has been outlined here emphasizes salient points of Japanese life, a knowledge of which is useful towards a deeper understanding of that pattern as a whole.

CHAPTER II

THE HISTORICAL BACKGROUND

THE history of the Kabuki ended with the Meiji Restoration of
1868 from the point of view of the purist. The passing of the old
feudal order in Japan abolished the segregation of the theatre in
special quarters and with this the old types of audience disappeared. The drama moved into a wider community, there was
a reformation in the theatre as in other walks of life, which
meant far reaching changes in many of its aspects including the
plays. The Kabuki from now on was to match its hallowed traditions in an increasing struggle with new styles and new ideas
imported from the West, a struggle which is still going on, for
the Kabuki has lived on into the twentieth century and even
survived the vicissitudes of the last twenty troubled years.
Whether this is the final phase, as its most severe critics conspire
to agree, is a question discussed elsewhere. The fact that it still
survives signifies a continued popularity, if not development, and
to accept 1868 as an arbitrary finis is to ignore a long line of very
distinguished actors who came after the Meiji Restoration. They
in themselves are a part of Kabuki history.

Whether we accept 1868 or 1953 as the boundary, the life of
the Kabuki theatre is a short one by the standards of Oriental
history, although its development owes a great deal to sources
which extend back into very early times. The origins of the
Japanese drama, like those of the Chinese drama, lay in sacred
dances, religious ceremonials and folk dances of ancient days.
These eventually resolved themselves into separate techniques,
from which the Kabuki proper drew its first inspirations.

The oldest type of dance was known as *kagura* and was religious in form and associated with the legend of the Japanese sun
goddess. In the seventh century there arrived from China a dance
known as *gigaku*, in which masks were used and this was incorporated as part of the Buddhist services. Some time after
gigaku there appeared another form, *bugaku*, which was of
Chinese, Hindu and Korean origins and became popular as a
court entertainment, as well as a Buddhist ritual dance and so

superseded the *gigaku*. The *bugaku* holds a unique position, for it is still preserved today by the Music Department of the Imperial Household, which gives special performances on certain occasions. The *bugaku* achieved its highest point of development in the Heian era (781–1185). At the end of this period it suffered a decline and was replaced by *dengaku*, a simpler and more acrobatic form of entertainment, devised for the amusement of the general public. At the same time there arose another form, the *sarugaku*, which from being a comic, mimic dance developed into more serious forms. *Dengaku* and *sarugaku* were refined each in its own way, but the latter finally became the basis of the Nō drama, which was perfected by the Buddhist priest Kwanami (1333–84) and his son Zeami (1363–1444). With the perfection of the Nō theatre a solid foundation was laid for the future development of the Kabuki.

It is to a woman, O Kuni, that credit goes for the beginning of the Kabuki. Accounts of her personal history are conflicting, but she is said to have been a ceremonial dancer from the great Izumo shrine. One thing seems certain, about the eighth year of the Keicho era (1596–1614) she gave a performance on the dry bed of the Kamo River in Kyoto. She danced the *nembutsu odori*, a Buddhist ceremonial dance, but adapted it to variations of her own and became an immediate success. She began to expand her performance, using a flute and drum accompaniment, and her lover, Nagoya Sanzaburo, is said to have joined her. In any case she quickly drew a group of pupils, both men and women, around her and formed a company. A stage was built based on that of the Nō, new dances were created, the theatre ritual of the Nō being adopted to the needs of more popular entertainment. The new theatre, which became known as O Kuni's Kabuki, was a development which received a great welcome and paved the way for the modern Kabuki.

As O Kuni's theatre flourished many other troupes sprang up in imitation and these were often composed of women of easy virtue. After O Kuni's death, the date of which is uncertain but generally given as about 1610, her successors flourished in a form which became known as the Onna Kabuki, Women's Kabuki. During this period the *samisen* began to be used as a musical instrument for dramatic accompaniment.

The Onna Kabuki became popular to such an extent that

theatregoing was fashionable among all classes of towns-people, but in 1629 the Shogunate issued a decree prohibiting all women on the stage, because of their adverse effect on public morals. It was an edict which was to remain in force for long years to come.

With the disappearance of the Women's Kabuki what was called the Wakashu, or Young Men's Kabuki, took its place. Handsome youths had already been a feature of the Women's Kabuki, but now they became the sole occupants of the stage. They eventually proved as great a source of attraction as the women, until the Shogunate once more decided that the physical charms of the boys were an equal menace to the community, and in 1652 the authorities issued a decree which suppressed the Wakashu Kabuki too. After this actors were compelled to shave off their front hair to lessen the charms of their appearance. The drama was now in thoroughly bad odour with the governing authorities, who from then on maintained a strict surveillance and made it the object of many petty as well as major restric-tions, which survived in one form or another throughout the Tokugawa era.

After the disappearance of the Wakashu or Young Men's Kabuki, the people were without a theatre at all for the period of about two years until the Yaro Kabuki came into being. This was the beginning of profound changes in the actual form of the Kabuki drama itself. The word *yaro* meant a man or fellow, and the implication was that the Kabuki was now being performed by robust men of adult age. In this new entertainment all the players of both male and female parts were men who had to hold the attention of an audience by dint of skill alone; they could no longer rely on mere physical charm as in the past. They were under close scrutiny by the authorities and if they wished to keep the favour of their public, it was obvious that there must be new and interesting advances in the contents of the entertainment. During this period the Kabuki steadily developed, new methods of acting were invented, scenarios which previously had been nothing more than a type of revue created by the actors began to take an orthodox pattern and plays divided into acts became the custom. This was due to the coming of the independent play-wrights, the pioneer of whom is thought to have been Heibe Tominaga in about the year 1680, his exact dates being uncertain.

Stage construction, settings, costumes and music also made rapid strides until the Kabuki by the Genroku era (1688–1703) had reached a pinnacle of achievement as a mature art, the theatre of the common people. It was a rapid and significant advance; from being a primitive entertainment, within the space of less than fifty years it became a drama of technical perfection.

The Genroku era is regarded as a golden age in Japanese cultural and social history, a period which left its hallmark on all that was considered the apogee of perfection and refinement. In the history of the Kabuki it is vital, for the theatre developed forms in that period which were to be the criterion for all future advances. Although bounded by the dates 1688–1703, its period of influence is actually covered by the last quarter of the seventeenth century and the first quarter of the eighteenth.

Three actors deserve mention at this point for their achievements played a vital part in the development of the Kabuki. They are Ichikawa Danjuro I of Yedo (1660–1704), Sakata Tojuro of Kyoto (1645–1709) and Yoshizawa Ayame (1673–1729). Ichikawa Danjuro I initiated a school of acting noted for its symbolism and robust bravado and made many innovations in stage technique. He was the forerunner of a long and distinguished line bearing his name in unbroken succession until the death of Danjuro IX in 1903. The name of Danjuro is one of the most famous in the Kabuki.

Sakata Tojuro was an actor of a different type; he was distinguished for his playing in social and romantic drama and was noted for his skill in love scenes and his name became synonymous with this type of drama, which eventually became the prerogative of the Osaka and Kyoto theatres. He was, however, more than a mere actor on the stage, he was gifted with rare artistic insight.

Yoshizawa Ayame was regarded as the greatest *onnagata* or female impersonator of his time and was an artist of ability, who developed the unique technique which was to be a model for the actors of the future. His ideas and secrets were written down in a book called *Ayamegusa*, which was afterwards regarded as the Bible of the female impersonator. These three actors, all distinguished in widely different ways, left a lasting mark on generations of actors who followed them.

In surveying this period of great advance in the Kabuki

drama, it is imperative to consider another exceedingly important factor, the development of the *ningyo shibai* or doll theatre. The story of the Kabuki is inextricably bound up with the *ningyo shibai*, and although they both commenced as independent entertainments, they were eventually destined to have the closest connection with each other. The doll theatre as a public entertainment existed before the days of O Kuni's Kabuki, but it was not until around the early years of the Kanei era (1624–43) that a permanent puppet stage was evolved, and the dolls were made of wood instead of clay as formerly.

A milestone in the history of the *ningyo shibai* was the establishment of a theatre in 1684 by a famous *joruri* singer, Takemoto Gidayu (1650–1714). This was the Takemota za in Dotombori, Osaka. He was joined there by the great dramatist Chikamatsu Monzaemon (1653–1724). Chikamatsu had been working as a Kabuki playwright and had written many dramas for the actor Sakata Tojuro. His decision to collaborate with Takemoto Gidayu and devote his time to working for the doll theatre was a significant event both for its future and for that of the Kabuki. The Takemoto za was destined to be a centre of theatrical activity from which sprang much of the Kabuki's finest drama.

For a period of about eighty years after the establishment of the Takemoto za, the *ningyo shibai* reached such heights in public favour that it completely eclipsed the Kabuki, which it replaced as the theatre of the people. After this it ceded its position to the Kabuki once again and the theatre of the human actor reigned supreme. It was a period unique in the annals of theatre history, and the *ningyo shibai* at the height of its fame influenced the Kabuki to such an extent that a new technique and a new repertoire were added, which were to have a lasting effect.

The Kabuki, pushed into the background by the rise of the *ningyo shibai* as the popular theatre, depended more and more on its rival and almost became a puppet theatre by influence, for it was not only supplied with themes for plays, but also borrowed a great deal of the doll theatre's technique of production. This was seen particularly in the case of the Kabuki actors who emulated and adapted the movements and gestures of the dolls in their own performances. The results had a permanent effect on the technique of Kabuki acting. Besides this a large new repertoire was added, and it would be true to say that the number of plays of doll theatre origin acted on the Kabuki stage now far exceed the plays written for human actors.

The dependence of the Kabuki on the doll theatre gave rise to great changes in the Kabuki itself, which, prior to the merging, had been more realistic in comparison with the symbolism of the doll theatre. The harmonizing of their different characteristics did much to further stage technique and the Kabuki owes a great deal of its fantasy to the *ningyo shibai*. In a later chapter the doll theatre is considered in more detail.

From being overshadowed by the doll theatre the Kabuki passed into a second creative period, and, utilizing the formal beauty and literary values adopted from the *ningyo shibai*, it largely replaced the last named in the affections of the public. The doll theatre was a product of Osaka and Kyoto, but with the revival of the Kabuki the dramatic centre shifted to Yedo, the present Tokyo. It became a period of many distinguished actors who added to the lustre of the Kabuki stage; they were the idols of the townspeople who flocked daily to see them.

The salaries of actors rose to unheard of heights. They surrounded themselves with luxury, their clothing and the smallest articles of daily use were of the finest quality. This state of affairs did not make the play a cheap entertainment and prices rose higher and higher as a result, but people did not mind as it was an age of increasing prosperity and the theatres were always packed to capacity.

A writer of the times remarked pointedly that, whereas before the actors who played women's roles had emulated the manners of high-born ladies, now the ladies imitated the actors. It was a fact that the kimonos, coiffures and all the many little articles of dress used by famous *onnagata* on the stage were avidly noted and copied by the women of Yedo; the actor became the leader of women's fashion. The Government frowned upon this state of affairs, but they were unable to do anything for some time. The period of flamboyant luxury into which the theatre passed at the end of the eighteenth century was the climax before a period of decadence, both in the tastes of the audience and the condition of the theatre in general.

In the early years of the nineteenth century audiences tended to look for novelty and abnormality in their drama, which is reflected in many of the plays and dance pieces of a period marked by some of the least worthy productions. Other factors also contributed towards the decline of the Kabuki. The continued hostility of the governing classes, who brought increasing pressure to bear, was a thorn in the flesh of the theatre. Added to this were natural disasters with which it had to contend.

Between 1804 and 1844 there were thirteen fires in the major theatres of Yedo, which placed the owners in severe financial difficulties and the Kabuki passed through a period of bankruptcy. In 1841 there was a great fire which completely destroyed the two main theatres, the Nakamura za and the Ichimura za. Mizuno Echizen no Kami, a powerful executive in the Yedo Government at this time, attempted to take this opportunity to abolish the Kabuki once and for all by saying that the actors and their plays were harmful to the moral interests of the people as well as being a dangerous source of fire. However he did not succeed, the theatre was too deeply rooted in the lives of the people. Other counsel prevailed, Mizuno was overruled and the Kabuki survived yet one more crisis in its history. The only result of it all was that the theatre quarter was changed to another part of the city.

The Meiji Restoration of 1868 saw far-reaching changes in everything, and the influence of the West became apparent in the theatre as in other things. It appeared that at last the Kabuki might be relegated, as there was an outcry against it in many quarters on the grounds that it was an anachronism in a changing world. The Kabuki was facing a bleak future again, although this time there were grounds for pessimism which had not been present before. In the past there was nothing to replace the Kabuki had it been abolished, nor did the people consider there ever could be any other drama than the Kabuki of Yedo. Now it was surrounded on every side by a flood of new ideas in the drama which threatened to engulf and destroy it. It is possible that had it not been for certain great actors, the Kabuki would have succumbed. As it was it survived to enter on a new period of greatness.

The Meiji era was fortunate in having Ichikawa Danjuro IX who carried on the traditions bequeathed him by his distinguished ancestors. A supreme artist, whose dramatic skill earned for him a reputation as the greatest actor of all time, he was a broadminded man of rare intellect and generous character. He brought a new spirit to the Kabuki and did a great deal to change the social position of the actor and place the Kabuki theatre on a higher plane of respect. He revised the artistic contents of the drama and created new forms in an attempt to contain a fresh intellectual appeal within the boundaries of traditional technique. It was natural that a man of Danjuro's character should respond to the spirit of the times and as a result he performed a series of plays specially written for him known as *katsureki geki*, or plays of living history, in which historical incidents were performed in correct detail based on accurate research. They never proved really popular and only the supreme acting of Danjuro sustained them at all. They have long since been relegated to a forgotten yesterday. It is as a great actor in the field of pure Kabuki that Danjuro's memory lives on.

Onoe Kikugoro V (1844–1903) was another great figure contemporary with Danjuro, his friend and rival. His dramatic talents were of a different order, he excelled in domestic plays and dramas dealing with the ordinary people and his realistic style was a model of its type. Kikugoro was also drawn to many experiments in the theatre which lasted only during his lifetime.

Both these men left a lasting influence on the traditional Kabuki; with their deaths which were separated by only a very short space of time, Japan mourned two of her greatest actors. Their going symbolized the complete break of the old world with the new, for both were born and had their training in what was still the Yedo period, against whose background the Kabuki had risen to prominence as a theatre.

The Taisho era (1912–26) was marked by the great earthquake of 1923 which interrupted all developments in the arts for a time, including the Kabuki, and swept away the last of the old theatres and with them many old customs. It was in this period that the Kabuki passed under its present form of monopoly control. The Otani brothers acquired interests in the Kabuki in the second year of Taisho and this eventually culminated in the registration of the Shochiku as a limited company in 1923, which today controls all the Kabuki theatres and actors of major importance throughout Japan.

Taisho was an era in which further innovations in the theatre were to the fore, innovations which gained the attention of a noted Kabuki actor, Ichikawa Sadanji II (1880–1940), who introduced a considerable body of new style plays into the Kabuki repertoire. Whilst he never forsook the genuine traditions of the old theatre, he is remembered as a progressive and energetic force in the theatrical world of modern times. In using the term 'progressive' it should not be read in the light of the confused political application customary today.

With all the new developments both inside and outside the theatre, the Kabuki still remained an ever popular entertainment and retained its hold on the affections of the people. This state of affairs continued until the outbreak of the last war. The period was marked by a body of distinguished actors, who carried on the great traditions with a skill and artistry that endeared them to the public, upholding the Kabuki as a significant element in the artistic background of Japan. Among them were Nakamura Utaemon V, Matsumoto Koshiro VII, Onoe Kikugoro VI and Ichimura Uzaemon XV, all of whom died in the years between 1940–9. Their loss closed another chapter of Kabuki history.

The destruction of the Kabuki za in Tokyo by bombing in May 1945 was to many symbolical of the destruction of the Kabuki, and there were those who wondered if it could ever be resuscitated. Within recent years, however, it has undergone a complete revival in spite of greatly changed conditions and difficulties not present in pre-war Japan.

To the superficial observer the Kabuki seems to be as firmly ensconced in Japanese life as ever. The theatres devoted to it play to full houses, most of the older dramas continue to be performed and the actors, if not receiving the admiration accorded to baseball players, still remain popular idols to a great number of people. It is obvious that the Kabuki can never again hold the same position. It was unique among all theatres, except perhaps the Chinese theatre of former years, in that it was a vital part of family life. It was the entertainment of everybody; young and old alike shared it as a common love. The present century saw it recede, it had to take its place among many new developments, but it was always there firmly in the background; whatever else they did people still went to the Kabuki. The war changed all this, old patterns of life disappeared and with them the Kabuki as a family entertainment. It is a new Kabuki which has taken the stage since the war.

One of the first things Japanese people will tell the visitor today is that the Kabuki is now an expensive luxury entertainment that the ordinary man cannot afford; it is no longer a family recreation but an occasion for company outings, tripper parties and so on. Even from a Japanese point of view, therefore, it has become a kind of tourist attraction. As this type of audience replaces the genuine theatregoer of the past there is a tendency for the people who run Kabuki to cater for the new tastes, so that programmes become increasingly devoted to productions which are not true Kabuki at all.

The art of the actors suffers in this, and a common criticism heard in Japanese circles is that standards of acting have deteriorated so much today that real theatre lovers find little pleasure in the performances of the younger school of actors. This is perhaps not always fair to the actors, who have to face difficulties of a type never experienced by their forefathers. The fact remains that the future of the Kabuki lies in the hands of the younger actor, and his position is not exactly a happy one. First, the Kabuki circuit is much smaller than in pre-war days, acting opportunities are considerably fewer, and younger people do not get the chances they might in a system which overworks the stars to a pitch detrimental to both actor and theatre in general. No young Kabuki player can expect to fill his rice bowl from the Kabuki alone today, and he must needs turn to more lucrative sources such as the cinema, with adverse effects on his Kabuki technique. Some promising young actors have already been spoilt by film work.

Economic conditions prevent the Kabuki from being the theatre of the people any longer; at the same time the younger actor is unable to make his living by his profession. But the man in the street and the young actor are essential, without these two people the Kabuki theatre can no longer exist. The difficulty becomes serious when we consider that there is an increasing majority of the younger generation in Japan who take no interest in the Kabuki, and this poses a problem to which it is very difficult to find an answer. The Kabuki has been recurringly faced with grave threats to its existence throughout its history, but this time the odds seem pitted against it in rather a different fashion. Previously, the hold it had on the people had always been too strong for extinction and the Kabuki has survived to go from strength to strength. That hold is greatly reduced today and the

true Kabuki actor is a dying race. These two things alone constitute a threat that is the sword of Damocles over an ancient
and well beloved theatre.

CHAPTER III

THE NŌ DRAMA

❧

A BRIEF outline of some of the more important physical aspects of the Nō drama is useful in providing a clearer picture of dramatic forms which have had a lasting influence on the Kabuki theatre, not only in the matter of plays, but in stage construction and technique.

The texts of Nō plays contain little original matter but might be described as a patchwork composed of fragments drawn from all kinds of sources, popular historical works such as the Heike Monogatari, poetical writings like the Genji Monogatari, accounts of temples and shrines and both Japanese and Chinese odes. Old phrases and poetic expressions were utilized in order to give significant ideas as briefly as possible and to make them easier to commit to memory by the audience. Nō plays are partly in prose, *kotoba*, and partly in verse, *utai*. The language of these is now archaic, being that of the upper classes of the fourteenth century and is expanded for dramatic purposes by the use of a great number of honorific expressions in repetition. In the verse portions punning is frequently resorted to for the purpose of enriching the text.

The actor intones his words in what may best be described as a form of chant, he is accompanied by a chorus who sit at the side of the stage and sing the actor's part while he is dancing, as well as narrating the course of events throughout the play. The orchestra sits at the rear of the stage; it is known as *hayashi* and the instruments comprise flute, *kan*, stick drum, *taiko*, and two hand drums, *kotsuzumi* and *otsuzumi*. These are described in the chapter on music. The instruments of the *hayashi* supply a background for the recitation, song and dance of the Nō, control the timing of the actors' movements and the flute, which has a high shrill pitch, is used both before a play commences, at the climax of a performance and towards the end.

The essential features of a Nō play are a dance with preceding dialogue and song that describes and explains circumstances of which the dance is the ultimate expression. The Nō dance relies to a great extent on mime, but it is mime far removed from any realistic imitation being idealized to the extreme limit of symbolism. Weeping is simulated by merely touching the eyes with the hand, for instance. The word *mai* is used for a dance performance and there are many variations such as *jō no mai*, i.e. woman's dance, according to the speed of motion and the character of the dance. In general, *mai* are characterized by slow steps and solemn dignified gesture and movement; even the more vigorous forms contain a deliberate quality unlike that seen in any other type of dance technique.

Five different positions are used and form the elements of any Nō dance, standing erect, moving left, right, forward and backward. The primary position is standing erect, and from this the actor introduces his variations through the other positions in rotation. To assist him in his movements, he generally carries a fan which is used to express symbolic ideas in a number of different ways. It may represent the heavens or the elements, or, going to the other extreme, more material objects such as a wine cup or a sword. The folded fan is held in front of the dancer in such a fashion as not to deviate from the centre between the eyes. The sleeves of the dancer are also used symbolically, covering the head with the sleeves, for example, signifies looking far into the depths. Every motion of the hands and feet is controlled by set rules; changes of movement have special names used in connection with the different kinds of *mai* to which they apply. An important element in *mai* is a stamping movement called *hyoshi* used to define the beats.

The principal actor on the stage is called *shite* and the secondary player *waki*, both have supporting actors. When the *shite* reaches the final part of his performance, including the dance, *waki* usually assumes a purely passive part and remains on one side, the chorus chanting the words for *shite*. Child actors, *kokata*, are used in Nō plays to take the parts of princes, young emperors and so on. There are no women players.

A distinguishing feature of the Nō drama is the use of masks by the actors. They are worn by *shite* and his supporting actor, *tsure*, or companion actor, *tomo*, but not by *waki* and his supporting players. The masks are made of painted paulownia wood, and many of them have been handed down for hundreds of years and are works of art in themselves. Their beauty and subtlety can only really be appreciated when seen in the round, particularly when worn on the stage. There, the inclinations of the actor's head seems to imbue them with a living quality, again it is not brazen reality which is seen, but the essential of some human spirit, the calm beauty of a young girl, the grief of an old woman or the fierce snarling of a demon. The masks can be broadly divided into five types, *rojin*, the aged; *otoko*, male; *onna*, female; *shinbutsu*, deities and Buddhas; and *henge*, monsters; besides these there are many masks which are confined to special plays and of course several variations on the principal types already named.

The wearing of the masks is a difficult art which requires years of long experience. The actor's face is completely covered and the eye openings are small; it is no mean feat to throw the voice and execute a dance while wearing one, apart from the fact that it is an extremely warm process. The art of carving these masks has been lost today; many of the well known actors have had copies made of their family treasures, but skilful though they be, they lack some quality of the originals which are almost fiendishly subtle in their forms. The ten most celebrated mask makers were at work in Japan between four and eight hundred years ago, and the next most celebrated artists produced masks between three and four hundred years ago. The masterpieces of some of these carvers rank as national treasures.

The costumes worn by Nō actors were derived from the official dress of former times but adapted for dramatic purposes. The main object is to give bulk, grandeur and increased stature to the actor on the stage; they are rich in colouring and design, but it is a richness that is restrained in quality, there are no lurid contrasts. Made of silk and intricate embroidery elaborately woven, many of the robes belonging to actors are family heirlooms which have been handed down from generation to generation. Costume can be divided into five main classes, *uwagi*, outer garments; *hoi*, garments worn indoors or without any other covering; *hakama*, lower garments in the nature of a divided skirt or elongated trousering worn in ancient Japan; and finally, *kaburimono*, or head dresses of various descriptions. There are several different kinds of dress within these four main branches which have their own special names. No expense is spared in the weaving and making of this stage costume, but on the other hand, there is a certain economy in them as one particular type of robe may be worn in several different kinds of roles. In common with every other aspect of the Nō there is no attempt at realism. Before passing on it should be explained that the Nō actor like both the Kabuki player and classical dancer wears no kind of footgear, only *tabi*.

The influence of Nō stage costume and head dresses is easily discernible in the Kabuki theatre, many of the *kaburimono* were adopted direct, while in the case of the costume, changes were made in colour and pattern and a certain gaiety and boldness, lacking in the originals, was adapted into those of the Kabuki. No make-up is used by Nō actors, but the masked players always wear wigs which are nothing like as numerous as the varieties seen in the Kabuki theatre. One wig, the long, flowing mane worn by demons and spirits in the Nō and called *kashira*, is used more or less in the same form in Kabuki dance plays.

Stage properties in the Nō are extremely simple and highly conventionalized. Perhaps the simplest, although the most important, is the fan used by the actor, who also on occasion may be armed with sword, pike or spear. An article often seen is a wooden stand, three feet by six feet by one foot high, called the *ichijo dai*; it may represent a palace, the foot of a mountain or a bedchamber among other things. A boat is symbolized by a framework of light bamboo carried by an actor who represents a sailor. Another article commonly used on the Nō stage is a cylindrical, black, lacquered tub called a *koshioke*; it serves as a seat or throne for the actors and in the *kyogen*, or comic interludes, the lid is often used as a wine cup of an extra large size!

The traditional Nō stage is square in shape, made of highly polished and specially seasoned cypress. It is nineteen feet square and built with a slight decline towards the front; pillars at each corner support an ornate roof which is an integral feature even though today stages are customarily built within an auditorium. This roof has remained a part of the Nō theatre since the days when stages were built out of doors, it was adopted by the early Kabuki and, as will be seen later, it was centuries before the last traces of it disappeared from the younger theatre. The pillars at the corner have special names, the one by the entry to the stage being called *shite bashira*, the next *metsuke bashira*, followed by *waki* or *daijin bashira*, and lastly *fue bashira*. The pillars serve as direction points for the dancing. On the wall of the recess at the back of the stage, a conventional pine tree is always painted; some authorities say this tradition had its origin in the sketch of a pine found in the Kasuga temple at Nara. At the right of this is a small sliding door called the *kirido*, through which the chorus and stage assistants make their entry and exit. There is a balustraded extension of the stage beyond *waki* and *fue bashira*, i.e. to the right of the audience, and here the chorus sit. The orchestra sits immediately in front of the painted pine tree in the space known as *atoza*. At the front of the main stage there is a small flight of steps down to the auditorium, now purely ornamental, but a relic of the times when an actor was summoned to speak to high authority. The actors make their entry along the *hashigakari*, a roofed and balustraded passage which connects the stage platform with the greenroom. Its length is not uniform but it is set at an angle to the main stage with a slight incline towards it. At the side of the *hashigakari* are planted three small pine trees standing in a pebbled walk, which runs the length of the structure and along the front of the main stage. The entrance to the *hashigakari* is covered by a curtain, the *agemaku*, which is patterned in broad vertical stripes of green, ochre, purple, dark red and orange, with a large, braided, silk orange-coloured tassel on a looped cord at each side. On the inner side of the curtain two poles are attached at the bottom; attendants seize these and lift the curtain high with a swift movement when an actor comes on and goes off the stage. Behind the curtain is a room called the *kagaminoma*, or mirror room, so named because there is a large mirror in front of which the actors adjust their wigs and costume and have their masks fixed before making their entry.

The Nō stage is built out into the auditorium so that the audience actually sit on two sides of it; the performance is not seen like a picture in a frame on a single plane, it is a part of the audience. The Kabuki theatre, which lays such emphasis on obtaining a pictorial effect on the stage, was nevertheless profoundly influenced by this three dimensional quality, and, in adapting the *hashigakari* to stage construction so that it eventually developed into the celebrated *hanamichi*; the Kabuki found its own method of identifying the action of the play with the audience itself.

A formal programme of Nō plays usually consists of five pieces though sometimes today it may be three and in times past was seven or more. Programme arrangement follows set patterns and takes into consideration factors like the seasons and the purposes for which the entertainment is given. A five-act programme is arranged in the order of *shin, nan, jo, kyo* and *ki. Shin* is a god play. The principal theme lies in praising the noble virtues of a god. In the first scene the god will appear disguised in some other form, often an old man, and talk with another character and in the second part he reveals himself in his true shape. *Nan* is a battle play. The chief characters in such dramas are the spirits of dead warriors, such as the great ones of the Heike or Genji class who first of all appear as ordinary men, and then assume their real shape and narrate pathetic accounts of the tragedies of the great battles of the past.

Jō is the woman's play, often called *katsura mono* in view of the fact that the principal characters, i.e. women, always wear wigs on the stage. A common feature of such a play is the introduction of a beautiful young woman who dances a graceful dance, but on occasion it may be an aged woman. Lyrical expression is the outstanding feature of these dramas.

Kyo, a mad play, in general shows the tragedy of a demented woman, a mother who has lost her child or a girl her lover. Under this class also fall plays which have as a main theme the emotions of revenge and hostility, a woman towards her unfaithful lover, or the ghosts of men and women unable to escape from their earthly passions.

Finally *ki* means supernatural beings, demons, *oni*, and goblins, *tengu*. The *tengu*, or long-nosed goblin, is celebrated in Japanese literature. He can shake mountains or rivers with his powers, and possesses all kinds of fearsome attributes. The famous stage hero, Yoshitsune, was supposed to have been taught fencing as a boy by a large *tengu*. On the Nō stage the *tengu* first of all appears as a *yamabushi* or wandering priest of the mountains. Under this heading also come plays which have as principal characters gods, who though not possessed of high virtues, have some mysterious power. There is one other class of play which is called *genzai mono*, or earthly play. In this group of dramas the principal roles deal with living people as against the majority of plays in which the ghosts of the dead are the principal characters.

There are other ways of arranging programmes besides the one described here and many variations under the main headings of the different styles of play. In a formal play there are two scenes, *mae* and *noti*. In the first or *mae*, the principal actor enters as a character whom he continues to portray in the second half, or *noti*, although in this case he wears a different costume signifying a change of rank and position. In other dramas the actor may play a new character in each scene, while in some, the principal actor is on the stage all the time, there being no change.

The dance or *mai* of the principal actor is generally performed in the second half of a play, but when a play contains an important piece of choral singing, i.e. the *kuse*, or theme song of the drama, it occurs in the second half of the first scene. In plays which contain a great deal of action, or *mai*, the chorus singing stops and instrumental music only marks the timing. There is a double appeal to the ear and eye in a Nō drama, the emphasis may be on one or the other according to the type of play.

Besides the formal kinds of dramas described, another feature of a Nō programme is the *kyogen*, or comic interlude, which takes place between the main plays. The *kyogen* depends purely on humorous dialogue, there is no musical accompaniment of any kind and the actors, who are distinct from the Nō actors, are usually two in number, though on occasion three or more, their act generally concluding with one of them chasing the other off the stage shouting, 'Yarumai zo', which may be translated as, 'You will not get away with that'. The characters most often seen are the *daimyo* and a comic servant, Kaja Taro, but there are many others besides. The effect of these depends on their humorous quips, coupled with a certain amount of dumb show, while the movements of the actors are also carried out to a strictly formal pattern. The *kyogen* provide comic relief to the seriousness of the main items on a programme, being enacted in the intervals when the orchestra and singers have withdrawn from the stage. Many of them were drawn upon by the Kabuki in the nineteenth century and some extremely witty and light hearted dance plays were the result.

The Nō play is not concerned with action, it expresses a situation in lyrical form; its characters are passive in the fact that they are directed by external influences over which they have no control, they are the ghosts of past memories, and this the Nō dance epitomizes. Reality in any form is shunned, and construction is stylized to an extreme degree; the Nō drama in its entirety presents a distilled grace and beauty of form, appealing to the senses through qualities which can only be called unearthly in their effect.

CHAPTER IV

THE NINGYO SHIBAI, OR DOLL THEATRE

꘠

THERE are records of puppet entertainers in Japan in the Heian era (781–1185), a crude form of doll manipulation known as *kugutsu mawashi* was practised by wandering entertainers, and from this time, puppets in one form or another survived as a street entertainment through the centuries. It was during the Keicho era (1596–1614) that developments took place which were to lead directly to the creation of the *ningyo shibai*, or doll theatre, that is still in existence today and has been of such supreme value in the moulding of the Kabuki drama.

Certain musical innovations were primarily responsible for the rise of the doll theatre. The reciting or chanting of stories, popular histories and Buddhist legends to the accompaniment of the stringed instrument called the *biwa* had been a popular art in Japan before the doll theatre began to develop. Towards the close of the sixteenth century, the arrival of another stringed instrument, the *samisen*, from China, profoundly affected this style of playing, the new instrument replacing the *biwa* as accompaniment to recitations.

One of the recitations of the period was Zoshi Junidan, which dealt with the adventures of the famous warrior Yoshitsune and his love Joruri Hime, the daughter of a wealthy family. The story proved so popular with the new style of accompaniment that afterwards the entire class of music, consisting of recital chanted to a *samisen* accompaniment, became known generally as *jōruri* music after the heroine of the story.

During the Keicho era, the art of working puppets to *jōruri* music was first devised by Hikita, a puppet showman, and Menukiya Chozaburo, who was a famous *samisen* player of Kyoto. The new technique soon became popular and puppet shows of this kind flourished and even attracted the attention of the Emperor himself. In the mid-seventeenth century a skilled *jōruri* chanter of Kyoto, Satsuma Joun, developed a technique which earned for him high approbation from the Shogun, who twice summoned him to his palace to perform; he had many pupils who carried on his art after his death. It was in this period that the dolls were first made of wood instead of clay. A pupil of Satsuma Joun, named Toraya Gentayu, founded a school of *jōruri* which produced a number of famous chanters. Among them were Inoue Harima and Uji Kaga, who gave lessons to a man who was to become the most famous of them all, Takemoto Gidayu (1650–1714), founder of the school of *jōruri* which bears his name still. Takemoto Gidayu possessed a voice of uncommon quality, and by using it in special interpretations of his master's styles, he developed a musical form which became so popular that people referred to it as *toryu jōruri*, *jōruri* of the present age, and to all other schools as *ko jōruri*, or *jōruri* of the past. Eventually *jōruri* as a term became synonymous with the *gidayu* style, whilst other schools were compelled to rely less on the narration and more on the singing.

In 1685 Takemoto Gidayu established his famous doll theatre, the Takemoto za at Dotombori, the theatre quarter of Osaka. He was assisted by a *samisen* performer, Takezawa Gonnemon, and two doll handlers, Tatsumatsu Hachirobei and Yoshida Bunsaburo. The year after saw the commencement of a partnership which was to be a momentous one in the history of the theatre, for Chikamatsu Monzaemon joined his friend Gidayu and started to write plays exclusively for the performances at the Takemoto za. The fame of the theatre spread far and wide and Takemoto Gidayu's technique made such an impression on the public that a school was born, founded on his methods, which became the leading *jōruri* henceforth never to be separated from the doll theatre. The names *jōruri* and *gidayu* were afterwards used expressly to indicate the doll theatre. Other schools of *jōruri* disappeared or else turned their attention towards the Kabuki where they began to lay emphasis on melody rather than the descriptive effects of the doll theatre music, but this is rather anticipating events.

In 1702, another theatre sprang up in rivalry to the Takemoto za, called the Toyotake za, run by Toyotake Wakatayu (1680–1764), who was a pupil of Gidayu. He also gathered many able men around him, and the keen competition between the two theatres did a great deal to foster new developments and preserve a high standard of performance. During this period the mechanics of the dolls also underwent changes and passed through many stages before they assumed the complex and artistic form in which they exist now. Originally the doll consisted of a head only, hands and feet were added later when the art of the *ningyo shibai* began to develop. In the early stages, one man only was used to handle the doll and he was hidden from the view of the audience, but after the middle of the Genroku period, the handler performed in sight of the audience and this is the method in operation today, called *de tsukai shiki*. It requires three men to handle one doll; they are called *omozukai*, the leader, who manipulates head and right arm; *hidarizukai*, the assistant who manipulates the left arm, and *ashizukai*, the third handler, who operates the feet.

Records show that in the fourth year of Empo, 1676, the dolls first learned to dance, and two years later they acquired feet to assist them in this art. In 1730 the mechanism which enabled them to move their eyes was invented, and three years later, articulated fingers were added to their construction. In 1734, it became the practice for three handlers to manipulate a single doll in the manner described above. Naturally enough, increased ingenuity in the construction of the doll's anatomy gave rise to all kinds of new techniques, which were loudly applauded by the public who encouraged the doll handlers to further heights. Shortly after acquiring movable heads the dolls also learned to move their eyebrows, thus achieving new feats of facial expression, later to influence the Kabuki actor's technique. In the first year of Gembun, 1736, the dolls were deemed too small to meet the requirements of the rapidly developing entertainment, so that they were made twice as large as before, assuming the standard proportions they take today.

In 1715 movable stage settings were invented for use in the doll theatre, together with landscape and architectural features which helped to provide greater realism combined with qualities of decoration. After 1727, the *jōruri* chanter, who until then had always sat at the front of the stage, was moved over to the left side, i.e. the right side of the audience, and six years later, the combination of musicians with the doll handlers on the stage together in full view of the audience was seen for the first time. The *ningyo shibai* now went from strength to strength and reigned supreme as the theatre of the people for a period of about eighty years.

After 1780 the fortunes of the doll theatre declined, overshadowed by the Kabuki, and remained at a low ebb until about 1803. During this time there were no *jōruri* chanters or doll handlers of note associated with it. A renaissance of the doll theatre was brought about by Uemara Bunrakuken, a *jōruri* chanter who came from Awaji and who with his successors paved the way for the foundation of a theatre, the Bunraku za, at Osaka in 1871. This theatre became famous and survives in name to this day, the present structure having been rebuilt after a fire in 1929. It is the only doll theatre in Japan and the training ground of many famous doll handlers and *jōruri* chanters. The title Bunraku has now come to mean the doll theatre as a whole.

The Bunraku passed under the control of the Shochiku Company early in the century and they have since been responsible for its continued existence. Public interest in the doll theatre has declined throughout recent years and this delightful drama was in danger of succumbing completely at the end of the last war. To counteract this a Bunraku Supporters' Club was founded, by which the financial moguls and company directors of Tokyo have been induced to pay an annual subscription, which assures the Bunraku of a regular sum towards its upkeep. Twice a year now, in winter and summer, the Bunraku comes up to Tokyo to perform and on these occasions the supporters have a certain number of privilege tickets which, if they do not use themselves, they can always give to friends. The system has certainly ensured full houses though it is hard to say the percentage of them that are true lovers of the doll theatre; the charitable viewpoint would be to hope that if they are not, such opportunities go far to converting them. Among a younger generation surfeited with cinema and all the more sophisticated types of entertainment, it is difficult not to feel that schemes such as this to save the Bunraku are but voices crying in the wilderness.

If ever there was a case for State support it is that of the Bunraku. It is a tragedy that one of the great folk arts of the Orient, indeed of the world, preserved through so many vicissitudes and for so long, should be allowed to disappear. But the great artists and craftsmen of the Bunraku are old or ageing men, and what incentive is there for the younger men to carry on their art? They will carry on, of course, for they are true artists and their theatre is their only world, they live only for their dolls; if their theatre dies they go with it. Their future is an uncertain one, and financial stability, in the meagre form that it takes, is artificial. The men of the Bunraku should be ensured of an adequate living and stable conditions, which would allow them to train their successors and so enable the doll theatre to be saved as a living entity for Japan and the outside world. State support offers the best solution in this case.

The art of manipulating the Bunraku dolls requires a rigorous training which would appal any but the most single-minded artists and the men of the doll theatre are confined to a life so rigid and austere that the Japanese critic, Miyake Shutaro, likened it to that of Trappist monks. The training of the doll handler commences in boyhood and he graduates by learning to manipulate the feet of the dolls first, an art which takes about ten years to master perfectly. After that, he masters the technique of the left arm, which takes him another ten years, and finally, the head and right arm, which requires yet another ten years. By the time he reaches middle age he may count himself a fully matured artist. During all these long years he must be constantly observing, practising and assimilating the technique of the masters and there is no respite for him, no reaching a point where he may stop. Every day of his life must see him just a little better than the one previously, until by the time he becomes an old man, he may feel that he is just ready to begin.

The artists and craftsmen of the Bunraku are men of sterling quality and worth who commanded the deepest admiration for their integrity. Honoured leader of the troupe is Yoshida Bungoro, a delightful old man of eighty-seven, who carries on one of the most famous names of the *ningyo shibai*. He was recognized officially in 1948 by being made a member of the Geijutsuin, or Art Academy, a nominal distinction which of course does nothing to better his standard of living, great national honour though it is. Bungoro is now deaf, nearly blind and failing in body, but when he steps on the stage with his dolls, physical infirmities are forgotten and his art remains as perfect as ever; he is still the master doll handler and great actor. He specializes in the feminine roles; the courtesan, the housewife, the high lady or the servant girl all spring to life beneath his magic touch. To him they are living be-

Portrait of Yoshida Bungoro of the Doll Theatre

ings, and indeed this applies to all the people of the doll theatre
for whom the dolls are alive and possess souls, they judge others
by the respect shown to their charges. Bungoro's favourite doll
never leaves his side, sleeping or waking she is always with him.
What memories must she evoke in the mind of the octogenarian
artist as he sits dozing away the hours in his dressing room between the acts of the plays, for he has lived through a long period
of changes, the like of which a modern world cannot imagine.

  Bungoro is accompanied by Toyotake Yamashiro Shojo, aged
seventy-six, the leading *joruri* chanter. He, too, was made a
member of the Art Academy, and his rich and resonant voice has
a power unequalled. A vigorous, hale old man, like Bungoro he is
an artist unrivalled in his accomplishments. Behind the stage,
'unheralded and unsung', sits an artist of another kind. Yurikame II, aged sixty, is a maker of dolls; tucked away in his corner
he carries out repairs necessitated by the wear and tear of stage

Scott/53 . Tokyo

Yurikame II
Bunraku Bunkashi Gekujō July/53

Yurikame II, the doll maker

life, under the soft touch of his loving hands they are restored
once more to their normal activity. In between the routine work
he creates new dolls, sighing because he cannot devote at least
three months to the carving of a single head without interrup-
tion. He is one of the few craftsmen of his kind alive today.
Quietly he deprecates the dolls he makes now, saying that his
colleagues are kind enough to be satisfied with them. By the
time he reaches eighty, he expects to be able to look forward to

creating dolls with souls and character of the kind found in those made by the masters of the past, whose work he admires so much. A simple, modest, penniless craftsman, he sits with his dolls year in year out; his life is dedicated to them, their existence is his reward.

There are many others besides these men, doll handlers, *jōruri* chanters and craftsmen, old and young, who without exception are striving for a common ideal and in this they achieve their greatness.

The Technique of the Ningyo Shibai

Ningyo jōruri, i.e. the acting of dolls to the accompaniment of narration and *samisen* music, requires the collaboration of three kinds of performers, the *ningyo tsukai*, or doll handler, the *jōruri* chanter and the *samisen* player himself. As previously explained, each doll requires three men to manipulate it. The *samisen* player and the *jōruri* chanter sit together on a raised dais at the right of the stage to the audience; this combination of instrumentalist and chanter is referred to as the *chobo*, whilst the name *tayu* is applied to the chanter. The *chobo* controls the timing of the dolls' movements, provides their dialogues and describes time, place and action to the audience. *Gidayu jōruri* and the *chobo* are described in further detail in the chapter on the music of the theatre; here we are concerned only with the dolls and the stage technique of the doll handlers.

The *ningyo*, or dolls, vary in size according to the character portrayed, but, in general, are between three and four feet in height. The dolls are classified under six main divisions, *tateyaku*, *fukeyaku*, *oyama*, *koyaku*, *chari* and *tsume*. The *tsume* are mere dummies used for minor roles and the *chari* are for the comic parts. *Koyaku* means child roles and *oyama* those of women. *Fukeyaku* signifies the parts of the aged and *tateyaku* the principal males. The dolls have a complex mechanism which allows them to move eyes, mouth and eyebrows. The arms are jointed at the elbows and the hands articulated. These technical features are found either singly or combined in most of the larger dolls according to their importance and their character, the *tsume* excluded.

There is one marked difference between the male and female dolls; the latter do not have feet or legs, an impression is created by moving the hem and drape of the *kimono* with the fists of the handler simulating the knees. The head and right arm of a doll is manipulated by the handler called *omozukai*, he is the leader; next comes *hidarizukai*, who takes the left arm, and lastly, *ashizukai*, who looks after the legs and feet, or as in the case of the female dolls, simulates them. The dolls are supported in an upright position from behind.

The heads, which are called *kashira*, are removable from the neck sockets and mounted on wooden grips known as *dogushi*, in which are set various levers on springs for moving the eyes, mouth and eyebrows, there being separate mechanisms for each. The left hand of *omozukai* controls the *dogushi*. A pivot arrangement at the top of it allows for general movement of the head as a whole. There are more than thirty basic types of heads, which are greatly increased in number if all the variations in size and degrees of mobility of facial features are taken into account. There are also heads made for special purposes, such as the *gabu*, in which the pull of a string changes the face of a beautiful woman into that of a grimacing fiend.

The *kashira* are made from paulownia wood, the head and neck being constructed separately and fitted together. They are exquisitely carved and painted and have wigs of real hair, *busho*, which are dressed in all the elaborate styles of the past in the same way as the human actors of the Kabuki stage. In the Bunraku company, there is one member behind the scenes whose work it is to prepare, dress and renovate the *busho*; there are scores of different styles all demanding accurate knowledge and correct handling in every detail.

The body of the Bunraku doll is surprisingly simple. In the case of the male dolls it consists of a hollow trunk at the right of which is attached a bamboo rod, called the *tsukiage*, for supporting it against the manipulator. The jointed arms and legs are suspended from the shoulders by strings and the right arm has no upper part as it is supported in the right hand of *omozukai*. The left arm, however, is complete and has attached to it a wooden control known as the *sashikane* with which *hidarizukai* directs the movements of the hand and arm. The right hand of the doll has a leather thong, the *yubikawa*, attached beneath it, and through this the doll handler must simulate the action for gripping an article. There are nine different basic types of hands and twenty-four special kinds, in addition they are classified under nine different colourings according to the character depicted. Hands are carved from Japanese cypress and play as important a part in the movements of the dolls as do the heads.

The feet and legs are classified in three basic kinds, besides specialized types of limbs. There is an angular metal or bamboo grip fixed above the heel of each foot and this is held by *ashizukai* as he moves the limbs in time to the arms and head. If the doll wears *geta*, the Japanese clog or wooden sandal, they are attached to the grip. The majority of the female dolls have no lower limbs and when walking, the *ashizukai* inserts his fingers in the skirt and moves it, the thumb and forefinger of the left hand and the forefinger and middle finger of the right hand grip the *kimono*. To handle the *kimono* of a female doll is considered a difficult task and though *ashizukai* is the junior of the three handlers, his task is one which requires great skill and is regarded in essence as important as handling the head. Those female dolls requiring a shortened *kimono* have legs and feet like the male dolls, but these are the exceptions to the rule.

Ashizukai must practise a special technique known as *tokoton o fumu*, in which he stamps the floor vigorously with his feet to represent the movement of the dolls and provide dramatic emphasis. The noise of *tokoton o fumu* is quite peculiar to the Bunraku theatre, which it symbolizes in a fashion that nothing else does. It is said that after forty no man can play *ashizukai*, because he then lacks the youthful vigour necessary to perform this technique. It is certain that *ashizukai* leads a physically strenuous life, for nearly the whole time he is performing, he is in a half sitting position with his head thrown back to observe every movement of the doll.

Omozukai, in contrast to his two assistants must stand in a higher position, both to give him dignity and to assist in the manipulation of the dolls; he therefore stands on *geta*, or wooden clogs, the largest of which is a foot high and called *umanori*. They are box-shaped with straw soles fixed to the bottom and are also used for stamping on the stage at certain moments for dramatic effect.

The stage of the doll theatre is long in proportion to its height, and in general is partitioned off from front to rear in three levels in which the handlers perform, although these divisions will depend on the nature of the play. All kinds of stage settings and properties are used in the plays and there are many tricks and grotesque effects which never fail to appeal because of their ingenuity. *Kazari*, or scenery, is changed before the eyes of the audience, the sets being placed in layers behind each other and dragged right and left off stage as a new set is moved up. There is one kind of stage set called *hikidogu*, which is mounted on runners and pulled slowly off stage so that a doll can be made to appear moving whilst remaining stationary. The scenery and sets of the Bunraku are named *odōgu* and a special staff is responsible for their construction, upkeep and use. The small properties are known as *kodōgu* and cover everything from a butterfly to a bun; they are the responsibility of one man who has his headquarters to the left of the stage.

When the curtain is drawn at the beginning of a Bunraku performance, an announcer appears on the stage. He is clad in black from head to foot and over his head and face wears a hood. This costume is worn by all stage hands and also the assistant doll handlers, *hidarizukai* and *ashizukai*. The announcer holds two oaken clappers, called *kine*, and beats them together. Then he cries in a loud voice, 'Tozai, to-zai, tozai, to-zai', literally, 'East and West', or 'calling the four corners of the earth'. After this, he announces the title of the play and the names of the *ioruri tayu* and *samisen* player. His announcement is called out in a specially pitched tone and again, this preliminary is an event which personifies the doll theatre to those who are familiar with it.

Omozukai, the leader of the doll handlers, in contrast to the other members of the trio, wears *kamishimo*, the ceremonial dress of the theatre, to show his rank as a master performer; his face is therefore visible to the audience. His two assistants are dressed in black cotton clothing with the hood kept clear of the face by a wire frame. A flap at the front of the hood can be turned back to show the face as sometimes happens if *omozukai* wears it. This costume is the working dress of the men of the doll theatre and is also seen on the Kabuki stage where it is worn by the *kyogen kata*, the stage assistants, who perform so many different duties. The hoods of the Bunraku men vary slightly in pattern according to the two leading schools of doll handling. The leader of all the handlers in the theatre is called *zagashira* and he occupies a special room backstage. The chief of the whole company is called *todori* and he too has his special room; his work is to look after the arrangement of the plays and programmes, assign parts and supervise the general administration of the performance. Both these people have opposite numbers in the Kabuki theatre, where they are called by the same name.

The names of *zagashira* and *todori* appear on the show bill, together with the names of the *omozukai*, and are written in special positions according to rank. *Hidarizukai* and *ashizukai* do not appear on the main show bill, but a special bill in the theatre itself gives their names in conjunction with the various *omozukai* with whom they are to perform.

There exists an old manual of doll handling which was prepared in rhythmic stanzas, so that beginners could assimilate the rules easily. In it are given all the various directions for stance and movement in the handling of dolls of every description. A male doll steps forward with the left foot, a female doll with the right. A general looks back when he stands up, other dolls only when they leave the stage. In fear a doll turns its face left and right; to make a request it steps forward, to refuse, retreats. The courtesan wipes her tears away with paper, the hero with his hand. A man moves his shoulders when laughing, but a woman bends downwards holding her sleeves before her mouth. There are many different kinds of bows, methods of holding a fan or carrying a sword, and all must be mastered and strictly adhered to. The doll handler who makes an error in these matters is disgraced. Whatever the season of the year the fan must not be forgotten, when the doll takes off its sword it must also discard its fan. The fan is taken up before the sword and always carried in the right of the *obi* or sash. Details such as these are important in preserving the correct pattern of movement on the stage.

When a doll is directed by its master it must look at his knees; it is wrong for a doll to remain idle after it has spoken, but it is worse for it to move unnaturally. The great doll handler does not move the doll when there is no occasion to do so, and to avoid artificiality he must be thoroughly at home with the contents and emotions of the drama whose tempo dictates the poses of the doll.

Finally, after being exhorted to master by heart all the rules set down, the apprentice is told that if he wishes to achieve great-

PLATE I

A child actor. Kamesaburo as Sankichi, the pack horse driver

PLATE II

A Bunraku Tayu. Yamashiro Shojo

A sewamono play in progress. A scene from 'Sakaya'

ness in his craft, the cardinal principle is to forget himself and become as one with the doll he handles, and this, perhaps, explains better than anything else why the doll theatre achieved such depths of feeling in its performance that it proved a lasting inspiration to the human actors of the Kabuki.

CHAPTER V

THE MUSIC OF THE THEATRE

THE history of the music of the Kabuki theatre is closely related to two main factors, the rise to popularity of the doll theatre and the introduction of the *samisen* into Japan from China. A characteristic feature of Japanese music is the importance of narrative and recitative, which brings to it a literary function that marks it apart from music in a more occidental meaning. The predominance of the spoken word in musical forms received a new impetus when it was first realized that there were dramatic possibilities in puppets. The doll theatre made great advances with the introduction of the *samisen*, which proved to be the ideal instrument for its purpose; the combination of the narrative and recital of the doll theatre with a *samisen* accompaniment was responsible for the rapid development of that type of music which is known as *jōruri*.

In the theatre today the term *jōruri* in its strictest sense is applied to one particular form of music only, but in actual fact, *jōruri* is an element which is found underlying all kinds of music used in the Kabuki, to a greater or lesser degree. There are four main types of Kabuki music. They are named *gidayu*, *nagauta*, *tokiwazu* and *kiyomoto*. Two other types are heard on special occasions, *shinnaibushi* and *katobushi*, the latter being restricted to one play only, the famous *Sukeroku*. The term *bushi* is a generic one originally signifying a melodic form but now applied generally to a musical style. It is used for *gidayu*, *tokiwazu* and *kiyomoto*, though not for *nagauta* whose name has a special connotation. In all these styles the *samisen* is the only musical instrument used, with the exception of *nagauta* which has adopted other instruments as well.

The *samisen* or *shamisen*, the latter being a popular pronunciation of the same word, is the key instrument in theatre music. Like so many Japanese musical instruments, the prototype of the *samisen* originally came from China, but was adapted and transformed into something which is so characteristically Japanese that it long since ceased to have any connection with its early origin. It is interesting to note that an instrument, the *san hsien*, is still occasionally used in the Chinese theatre orchestra; it is a descendant of the same instrument from which the *samisen* developed and one has only to compare the two to see how utterly different the *samisen* has become.

Opinions vary as to the date when the *samisen's* ancestor was first introduced, but it is generally accepted as being sometime during the Eiroku era (1558–69). It came in from the Loo Choo Islands through the port of Sakai, south of Osaka. The body of the original instrument was faced with snake skin, as the *san hsien* of China still is, and was at first called the *jamisen* in Japan. It was quickly taken up by the musicians of the time, who played the current popular songs on it, and later used it to accompany the rapidly developing art of *jōruri*. Through its popular use the structure of the instrument was modified considerably, new methods of playing were devised and new music composed. The first innovation was that instead of snake skin, cat or dog skin was used for the face of the *samisen*, which was enlarged, while instead of the small plectrum patterned after the fingernail as used in the prototype, a much larger accessory known as the *bachi* was quickly adopted, made of wood and later ivory.

The *samisen* has three strings, hence its name, and belongs to the lute family, but it differs from other string instruments in that not only is the string plucked, but the plectrum, or *bachi*, is also simultaneously brought into contact with the skin surface of the instrument, thus producing a drumming sound in addition to the string effect. The resonating body of the *samisen* is a hollow wooden frame with convex sides, slightly greater in length than width. Cat skin or dog skin is stretched tightly over the back and front of the frame, which is known as the *do*, the skin face being termed the *kawa*. Cat skin is used for the best *samisen*, dog skin for practice or cheaper models. The strings are of braided silk, not gut, and the wooden arm which carries them is called the *sao*. This is long in proportion to the size of the *do*. It tapers towards the neck, which is curved backwards from the *sao*. In the neck are set three long pegs of ivory or hardwood, two left and one right. The strings are attached from the base of the *do* over an ivory bridge, the *koma*. At the upper end of the *sao*, i.e. the neck, is the *kamikoma* or upper bridge. A peculiar feature of the *samisen* is that the heaviest and thickest of the three strings does not rest on this *kamikoma*, but on the neck itself, to produce a tone known as *sawari*, which possesses a subtle quality of great importance to the ears of the Japanese listener.

The general size of the *samisen* differs according to the type of music it is used for. These sizes are defined according to the thickness of the *sao*, or arm, there being *futozao*, thick or heavy arm; *chuzao*, medium arm; and *hosozao*, thin or light arm. The sizes of other parts of the instrument vary slightly in proportion to these different sizes of the *sao*. The *samisen* is played with the seated performer holding the *sao* diagonally across the body to the left and the *do* resting against the right side of the waist. The *bachi* is held in the right hand to pluck the strings and to produce *bachi oto*, the drumming of the *bachi* against the surface of the skin. The downstroke of the *bachi* is the basic stroke, but the upstroke is also used to secure a softer tone, whilst a combination of the two in *tremolo* form is constantly used. The fingers of the left hand stop the strings to give the correct pitch and also perform a sliding movement on the strings to merge one tone into the next. The strings, too, are occasionally plucked with the finger to obtain a *pizzicato* effect. The combination of the right and left hands is used to obtain a variety of subtle tonal effects which are all important. The three basic tuning methods are known as *honjoshi*, *niagari* and *sansagari*.

Honjoshi is the first tuning position, whilst in *niagari* and *sansagari*, the second string is tuned a complete note above and below *honjoshi* respectively. These tunings are important in the expression of mood in *samisen* playing. *Honjoshi* is often used as the basis for dignified and solemn music, *niagari* for light cheerful effects and *sansagari* for melancholy or tranquillity, although these must not be accepted as rigid in application.

In analysing the structure of *samisen* playing it is necessary to remember that it is primarily designed to be used as accompaniment to the human voice, a factor which emphasizes the fundamental difference between Western and Oriental instrumental music. *Samisen* music is constructed so as to precede or follow, but not to intrude on, vocal expression and it also serves to bridge the intervals in which narrative ceases altogether. It embodies complex changes of tempo during the playing of a composition to emphasize emotions.

Vocal music itself may be broadly divided into two kinds, *utaimono* and *katarimono*. The former is largely concerned with the rhythm and melody of the music itself, while in the latter the interest lies more in the text, or the spoken instead of the sung word; recitative is as important as musical effect. These factors have a great bearing on the composition of *samisen* music, as evidenced in the various styles already named and described later.

In *samisen* music set phrases are used to build up a complete composition. It was by the rearrangement, modification and varying uses of these phrases that new works were created; in other words, the inclusion of existing musical phraseology rather than the creation of completely new forms. For instance, a phrase may be used to depict a certain emotional or atmospheric effect and by analogy, the use of such a theme in a completely new arrangement would automatically call to mind identical emotion or atmosphere. The phrases are therefore bound up with the narrative of the music, but there are also some known as *tegoto*, which bear no relation to the narrative and are played independently to add variety to the performance and serve as a relief between the passages of narrative. The term *aikata* is also used in *samisen* playing to indicate a certain passage inserted in the middle of dialogue or narration to emphasize dramatic effect, e.g. it may be to give an instrumental version of sounds such as the chirping of cicada. Variations on the phrases are obtained by the use of alternating scales, special instrumental techniques and various combinations of these adapted to the narration of the different musical types. The phrases, which form the weft and warp of musical composition, go by certain names, many of them literary and descriptive in their relationship to the music.

Nagauta. It has been said that vocal music divides itself into two, *utaimono* and *katarimono*. An important branch of theatre music, *nagauta*, evolved from a form of *utaimono* popular in

Kyoto and known as *jiuta*. From *jiuta* came a Tokyo version called *edo nagauta*, this form adopted other musical styles in the course of its development and finally became known simply as *nagauta*. The name *nagauta* literally means long song as opposed to *kouta*, short song. *Kouta* were songs popular before the eighteenth century, many of them were incorporated in *kyogen*, the comic interludes between the main plays in the Noh drama. *Kouta* were adapted for *samisen* playing and in the early years of the eighteenth century began to be used in Kabuki dances. The adoption of *nagauta* as Kabuki music was largely through the efforts of an old theatrical family, members of which began to specialize in *samisen* music. The name of this family, Kineya, became synonymous with *nagauta* and is still borne by the head of the school today. *Nagauta* was created entirely to meet the requirements of the Kabuki theatre and became a musical style which served a number of purposes on the stage. A notable feature of its development lay in the fact that it received a great deal of inspiration from the music of the Nō theatre and the *yokyoku*, vocal music of the Nō, was adopted into *nagauta*, but was used with the *samisen*, an instrument completely foreign to the Nō orchestra. The latter, known as *hayashi*, consisted of *kan* or flute, *taiko*, a drum beaten with two sticks, *kotsuzumi*, a small drum played on the shoulder, and *otsuzumi*, a slightly larger drum played at the waist. These instruments were taken into the orchestra with the *samisen* and the special music they gave rise to marks *nagauta* apart from all other styles. *Nagauta* may be described as the general purpose music of the Kabuki theatre. It is popular for dance plays but it serves many other needs as well.

On every Kabuki stage, to the left of the audience, may be observed a black wooden structure with a horizontally slatted façade. Sometimes this is concealed behind a stage set, in which case the set is always pierced with a series of vertical apertures. It is called the *kuromisu* or *geza* and behind sit a group of musicians who are invisible to the audience, but themselves have an uninterrupted view of the stage and auditorium from their vantage point. *Kuromisu* literally means a black rattan blind, while *geza* means lower seat. In the early days of the Yedo period, the *kuromisu* was merely a blackboard on the stage covered by a rattan blind, hence the name. The *kuromisu* is manned by a number of musicians whose work is specialized, but who are, in fact, *nagauta* players. The music of the *kuromisu* is referred to as *gegi ongaku*, or music of the play. It is also sometimes referred to as *kage no narimono*, literally instruments of the shadows, and *ohayashi*. This should not be confused with *hayashi* used previously in describing the instruments of the Nō; the meaning is basically identical, but the term *ohayashi* is only used when describing the particular form of music named here, i.e. the music of the *kuromisu* or *geza*.

The *kuromisu* is situated directly opposite the *hanamichi* and one of its main functions is to control the entrance and exit of the actors from there, and also time running or walking and provide atmospheric effect according to the nature of the situation and the particular character who is appearing. The music of the *kuromisu* is also used during the course of a play if some special accompaniment is required. For example, the instruments of the Nō *hayashi* are often played at a particularly solemn or dignified moment. In *sewamono* plays, which are primarily dialogue dramas and have no musical settings, the *kuromisu* provides the only music. From it, too, come all sound effects, rain, wind, snow, the sea, the galloping of horses or the cry of a bird and a dozen others; also the various sounds which by tradition mark the opening or closing of a play. A sound effect for snow may sound peculiar to Western ears, but in the Kabuki when snow is falling a rapid but very light tattoo is played on a large drum in the *kuromisu*. It is called *yukioroshi* and conveys an atmosphere of intensity and sadness in quite an unusual fashion.

In addition to the *samisen* and *hayashi* instruments already named, other instruments which are important in the *kuromisu* can be listed as follows. *Otaiko* is a large barrel-shaped drum set horizontally on a stand. Many different effects can be obtained on this from a light and delicate beat to a powerful resounding boom. There is also a smaller drum of this shape known as *okedaiko*. *Tsurigane* is a hanging bell, used among other things to mark the passing of the hours of night. The Oriental bell does not have a clapper as in the West, the reverberation is caused by a striker which is rammed against a certain point on the exterior of the bell, and this produces a deep characteristic vibration. *Rin* is a tiny hand bell used in Buddhist religious services, whose tinkle is utilized to provide a religious atmosphere on the stage. *Mokugyo* is a hollow red wooden shell-like instrument, used by

Buddhist priests in chanting the *sutras*, also heard with the *rin*. *Dora* are the gongs and *shinbari* are cymbals, whose use provides a livelier and more metallic background when required. The *tsuzumi*, the small drums of the *hayashi* previously mentioned, merit fuller description as they are so characteristic of Japanese music, and are constructed in the oldest shape devised for the drum.

The bodies of both *kotsuzumi* and *otsuzumi* are shaped like an hour glass with the discs for the skins at either end. The skins, horsehide, are tightened by laced silk cords which connect the two discs. The *kotsuzumi* is gripped with the left hand holding the hour glass shaped body, the instrument being supported on the right shoulder. The palm and fingers of the right hand are used to play the drum. The *otsuzumi* is held by the left hand, supported against the left side of the waist and played with the fingers of the right hand which are thimbled. The laced cords on the drums are manipulated to tighten the skins and so vary the tones; these are very different in the case of the two instruments. The *kotsuzumi* is soft and rich and the *otsuzumi* high pitched and almost metallic in quality. The *taiko* is a flat drum which is fixed on a low support and tilted at a slight angle towards the player. The skins of this drum are also tautened by silk cords laced through the rims of the hoops which support the skins and then taken zigzag fashion round the body of the drum. The *taiko* is played with two wooden cylindrical sticks of even thickness, held in either hand.

Two important types of flutes, or *fue*, are used in the *kuromisu*, the Nō *kan*, which is played transversely and has a high shrill tone, and the *shakuhachi*, which is played vertically and might be described as a pipe rather than a flute. It is made of a single piece of bamboo whose standard length is one *shaku* eight *sun*, about 1.8 feet, and this gives it its Japanese name. It was the instrument carried by the wandering *komusō* described in Chapter I. It has a plaintive note which is used with great dramatic effect in the Kabuki.

The *kokyu* is a stringed instrument also heard on occasion in the *kuromisu*. It has three strings with a large bow attached for playing. The *kokyu* is held in an upright position resting on a prong and is tuned while being played, the string to be sounded facing the path of the bow which remains constant. This instrument has a melancholy tone which is sometimes used to emphasize an emotional passage on the stage.

A sound effect often heard in conjunction with *kuromisu* music, although it has an important independent function as well, is the use of the *hyoshigi*. These are two stout, quadrangular sticks of hardwood, which are held in each hand and clapped together in a *crescendo* effect. They are sometimes called the *ki*. The *hyoshigi*, or *ki*, are always heard at the opening of a performance when the curtain is drawn and again at the close of the play. There is another use of the *hyoshigi* known as *tsuke*. In this an attendant at the right of the stage to the audience beats the *hyoshigi* rapidly on a thick, rectangular wooden board on the floor. *Tsuke* is used to emphasize and accentuate the posing of the actor. There is one instance where it is combined with the *kuromisu* music, to create a special effect called *idaten*. This expresses the hurrying steps of one bearing an urgent message or gives an atmosphere of hustle and is played on the *samisen* with strings high pitched, *tsuke* being performed simultaneously. Another effect is *ekiro*, which reconstructs the noise of a busy highway in former times, and is based on the tinkling of bells worn by pack horses and the songs of the horsemen. The feeling of back streets is symbolized by a song called *yotsudake bushi*, which requires two sticks of bamboo as timebeaters as used by street musicians in the past.

The Nō *hayashi* instruments in the *kuromisu* are used to play music known as *tennodate* in scenes of great solemnity. *Samisen* music goes by the general name of *aikata* when it is used on the entry or exit of an actor, when the curtain is drawn, or when it is a special accompaniment to dialogue and action, but not singing. The music of the *kuromisu*, therefore, is used to obtain better dramatic effect rather than anything else and it is part and parcel of the fabric of the plays. Whilst *nagauta* had its origins in *utaimono*, the other types of theatre music belong to the form known as *joruri*, which in turn is a branch of that second division of vocal music known as *katarimono*. But although the musical types such as *gidayu*, *tokiwazu*, *kiyomoto* and the two less used forms *shinnai* and *katobushi*, all come under the broad heading of *joruri*, it is to *gidayu* only that this term refers if used by itself today. The reason underlying this is that *gidayu* is used primarily for narration, while the other types are chiefly used to provide the musical background for dance plays. In making such a generalization, it should be borne in mind that the term dance is used in the broadest sense to cover gesture and posture, as well as more vigorous movement. The element of *jōruri*, i.e. narration to a *samisen* accompaniment, is always present even in the types of music just noticed, which are used chiefly in dance plays, and in *nagauta* already described, literary quality is at times so stressed that there is little difference from *jōruri* as such. To make matters more complicated, *gidayu* is sometimes used for dance plays and there is nothing more stirring than to hear a full *gidayu* orchestra from Osaka perform one of the celebrated dance pieces of their repertoire. This begins to appear a little involved, but a clearer understanding of the true relationship between *gidayu* and the other types of music may be obtained from the descriptions which follow.

Gidayu. *Gidayu* was named after Takemoto Gidayu (1650–1714), details of whom are given in Chapter IV. *Gidayu* is the original music of the doll theatre, and in the Kabuki it is without exception used in all plays of puppet origin, although there are also plays written in more recent times with *gidayu* accompaniment.

During the heyday of the doll theatre, *gidayu* became so popular that it rapidly pushed all other *jōruri* music into the background. The result was that other forms began to develop in new directions and concentrated on the sung rather than the spoken word, emphasis was laid on the melody and the music, rather than on pure narration, as in *gidayu*. This was the underlying factor responsible for the eventual creation of schools of music like *tokiwazu*, *kiyomoto* and the others. Owing to the supremacy of *gidayu*, the other types of music had to devise a new appeal in order to survive, but they shared a common origin with *gidayu* and the fundamental principle of *jōruri* was never completely absent in their construction. *Gidayu* might be described as the head of the musical family in the theatre.

Except in the case of some dance plays, there are two musical performers in a drama with a *gidayu* accompaniment, a *samisen* player and a *tayu*, or narrator. This combination is referred to as the *chobo*. To see a *gidayu* narrator, or *tayu*, performing is a revelation in itself. While he is in action he is one with the characters on the stage, who are expressing their feelings and emotions through him. The *tayu* smiles, weeps, starts with fear or sits back in astonishment. Every movement of his face is expressive of the progress of the play, his voice rises and falls to a set pattern of rhythm, which is yet capable of many shades of expression. Watching a master *tayu* perform, it is possible to conjure up in the mind's eye a vivid picture of everything that is happening, without seeing the stage. The *samisen* player provides an undercurrent of musical emphasis to it all, supplements the voice of the *tayu* and, at times, accentuates with special passages on the strings.

The *chobo* performs a number of important functions in relation to the proceedings on the stage. One is to describe when and where. In the famous tragedy, *Terakoya*, for example, the *chobo* opens the play with the following prologue: 'It is worth one thousand or even two thousand gold coins to learn each character well, it is of untold value in the present and the future. The teacher encouraged his pupils with these words, among them was Kanshushai. Genzo Takebe and his wife guarded him well as though he were their own son. Genzo moved to Seriu village and gathered many boys as pupils, some were skilled in handwriting and some were not, some daubed the faces of other boys and some their hands, instead of writing in their copybooks. . . .'

While this is being played, the curtain on the stage is drawn to reveal a village school of calligraphy. The pupils are at their desks, their faces smeared with ink. A little apart from them all, Kanshusai sits working quietly; he is the disguised son of a nobleman. In this fashion the *chobo* describes to the audience the scene which is revealed to them.

The *chobo* also explains and describes individual characters who appear on the stage. In *Terakoya* again, the schoolboys are being examined by the lieutenant of a nobleman who is anxious to secure Kanshusai in person. The fathers of the schoolchildren are ordered to call up their sons one by one before the examining authority: 'The boy whom his father calls out with such precautions has an oval face, dark skinned. Gemba takes him saying: "This cucumber! His skin is quite dark, especially at the neck. I do not know whether it is due to ink or some blemish, but anyway he is not the one for whom we seek. . . ." '

Or again in the play *Moritsuna Jinya*, a messenger appears at a famous general's camp, the reason for his coming is not immediately clear to the general: 'Instead of armour he wears ceremonial dress and walks with long strides, he carries the sword of a dandy although he is a rough and ready character.' The subject of this description appears on the *hanamichi* while he is being explained to the audience.

The movements of characters on the stage are also announced to the playgoer. A good example of this occurs in yet another passage of *Terakoya*. Genzo, the village schoolmaster, has been ordered to behead Kanshushai, his noble ward, and produce the head as proof. He substitutes another of his pupils instead and produces his head in an atmosphere of great suspense, with the examining officials gathered round ready to kill him at any sign of treachery. 'These words were spoken at the risk of his life. Behind him stand the guards, in front Gemba with watchful eyes. He is thinking there is no escape, when Matsuo draws the box towards him and takes off the lid.' (The head of the victim is in the box.) 'It is the head of Kotaro, so if he says it is false, I will kill him at a blow, thinks Genzo. He is about to draw his sword. Tonami with staring eyes prays within herself to the Gods to help them. After carefully looking at the head this way and that, Matsuo says . . . ' The *chobo* helps to build up suspense by describing the movements, both real and intended, of the various characters. It also expresses the thoughts of a stage personality, his mental reactions to a certain situation. In a famous scene from the play *Chushingura*, Kampei, a figure of tragedy, exclaims through the *chobo*:

'Good God, what, was it my father-in-law who was killed by my gun last night?' And the *chobo* continues: 'He had more pains in his breast than if he had been shot by a gun himself.'

The audience watches the movements of the actors and listens to the descriptions simultaneously, so that there is a double effect in the scene on the stage. The *chobo* acts as a conductor's baton to the actor, it sets his timing and dictates his movements and gestures. In effect, it turns him into a puppet and then explains him to the audience. This is the fundamental principle of *gidayu* music.

Tokiwazu

Tokiwazu as a school of music was founded by Miyakoji Mojidayu (1709–81), who was a disciple of a famous musician, named

Miyakoji Bungonojo, the leader of a school known as *itchubushi*. From the *itchubushi* school came another school, *bungobushi*. *Bungobushi* achieved great popularity and its melancholy and wistful tones had such a profound effect on people, many cases of double suicide resulting from its influence, that the Government issued an ordinance forbidding it to be performed. This caused the suicide of the leader of the school, Miyakoji Bungonojo, but several years after his death, his disciple Mojidayu obtained permission to found another school, which became the present *tokiwazu*. *Itchubushi* developed in Osaka, parallel with it in Yedo was *katobushi*, mentioned earlier in the chapter in connection with the play *Sukeroku*. *Shinnaibushi*, the other musical form described as being used only occasionally in Kabuki, was a branch of *itchubushi*.

A characteristic of *tokiwazu* is that melody and verse are regarded as equal in importance and neither the one nor the other is overstressed. An interesting feature of its construction is the use of a certain type of musical phrase known as *kudoki*, which might best be described as a combination of grieving and wistful recollection of passion spent. Not all *tokiwazu* music is melancholy, however, and there are gayer and livelier tunes. In the Kabuki theatre *tokiwazu* is used only to accompany dance plays. A better idea of the use of a certain type of music for stage purposes may be obtained, if a famous play is explained in relation to its musical setting.

In *tokiwazu bushi*, there is a tune which takes its name after the famous dancing play, *Masakado*, which it accompanies. The formal title of both play and tune is actually *Shinobiyoru Koi wa Kusemono*, but the shorter version is invariably used. In speaking of a tune, in this case it implies a long, complex composition, which contains many different arrangements of the types of musical phrases already spoken about.

The story of the play is based on a legend concerning the celebrated Masakado of the Taira or Heike clan, who was killed in battle against the Genji or Minamoto clan. He has a daughter, Takiyasha, who disguises herself as a courtesan and being imbued with supernatural powers, secludes herself in a ruined mansion intent on the revenge of her father's death. Here she is found by Oya Taro Mitsukuni of the Genji clan, who is searching for the remnants of the Heike clan and has been ordered to investigate the presence of the suspicious character reported hiding in the old mansion.

Takiyasha, as the courtesan Kisaragi, tries to lure him to destruction; she employs all her wiles to make the suspicious Mitsukuni succumb to her purposes. While she is dancing for him, a silken pennant of the Heike clan drops from her sleeve accidentally. Mitsukuni's suspicions are now confirmed and the play finishes with a vigorous scene in which he calls his men to arrest her. Kisaragi transforms herself into a supernatural being and destroys the mansion with her occult powers before the eyes of her opponents.

This play is a fantasy which pays no heed to logic, it is first and foremost a vehicle for the actors' dancing, which is all important. The music is designed to control the dancing and to provide atmospheric background and in the latter, it is assisted by the musicians of the *kuromisu*.

The curtain is drawn to the sound of the *ki*, or wooden clappers, combined with the beating of a drum in the *kuromisu*. The intermingled tones of both increase in tempo and finish with a quick, short beat. The auditorium is in complete darkness, while the stage set represents a deserted mansion, whose façade presents an air of mystery with its drawn rattan blinds. No actors are visible.

After a very short *samisen* passage, the leading singer commences a solo, which is known as an *oki*, a prelude to the entry of the actors. The singing is in a key which adds to the general air of mystery, and towards the end, the other singers join in unison. Then comes a notable scene in the play. The figure of Kisaragi appears slowly through the *suppon*, the trap door in the *hanamichi*. She is spotlighted against the darkened house and there is something unearthly about her motionless figure, with an open paper umbrella over her shoulder. Her appearance is accompanied by the rapid beating of a drum in the *kuromisu*. On either side of her, on the *hanamichi*, kneel two *kyogen kata*, stage assistants, each grasping a long handled holder in which is set a large candle, whose flickering light adds to the dramatic effect. These holders are known as *sashidashi* and date back to the days when modern lighting effects were unknown in the theatre; such a procedure was used to gain a special emphasis in illumination on the stage. It has been retained as a traditional feature in the first scene of *Masakado*. The *kyogen kata*, in their black hooded costume, are practically invisible against the darkness of the theatre.

Kisaragi at first remains posed for a few moments and then comes to life, closes her umbrella, gestures and unrolls a long letter and dances slowly on the *hanamichi*. Letters in former times were written on a long scroll of paper, which was unrolled from right to left.

With the appearance of Kisaragi the musicians play once more and there is a sung passage which is known as a *dewa*, entry of a character. A famous line commences, '*Koi wa kusemono . . .*' and the gist of what follows might be translated as: 'Love knows no reason and even a courtesan is possessed with true passion and weeps for her fickle life. She writes letter after letter but finds no answer to satisfy her love.' Literal rendering of the words fail to convey the real character of Japanese singing. It is the special accentuation and merging of the words in a particular rhythm, pronunciation at times being distorted to meet this rhythm, which gives the song its individual effect.

Kisaragi proceeds from the *hanamichi* on to the stage, the lights go up and the blinds of the mansion are rolled up to reveal Mitsukuni sitting sleeping inside. He awakes and there follows what in music is known as a *monso*, which begins: '*Oya no Taro wa me wo samashi . . .* Oya no Taro wakes up.' It goes on to relate who he is and why he is there. Next comes what is called *kudoki*; it is an important musical form, in this particular play it is regarded as a model of its kind in *tokiwazu* playing. *Kudoki* expresses a woman's yearnings, her recollections and regrets, and is chanted in a lyrical tone marked by wistfulness. The *Masakado kudoki* commences: 'Saga ya Omuro . . . At Saga and Omuro see the cherry blossoms in full bloom. The flitting butterflies come from afar to accompany the courtesans like flowers, who visit the beautiful mountain of Arashi. Do you remember, my lord, you wore *hakama* of *oborozome* and you were gallant, not distant in your manner.'

In the Japanese original, there is a play on the double meaning of the word *oborozome*, which it is quite impossible to translate. This playing on words, punning in fact, is a marked feature of dramatic dialogue and the narrative of musical accompaniment. It is responsible for a vocal pattern which finds no parallel in

English. *Hakama* is a kind of divided skirt worn by men as ceremonial dress and *oborozome* was a special kind of dyed cloth.
The word *oboro* means misty, dim and vague. Kisaragi, in the
song, says that although her lover wore *hakama* of *oborozome*
yet his manner was not *oboro*, i.e. distant and cold, but gallant;
of course the bare English cannot convey the real effect of the
Japanese. The *kudoki* continues ' "You fascinated me completely,
how I loved you, how I yearned for you. It was then that I knew
you were Mitsukuni Sama. How happy I am that I am here
with you at last." She clung to him saying, "Believe me, do not
doubt me," and blushing covered her face with her sleeve.' Note
how the singer not only speaks the words of Kisaragi, but also
describes her actions; this is *joruri* technique. After the *kudoki*
comes *monogatari*; in this the actor tells the story of past events
in mime with no dialogue, using only his fan in a number of
symbolical forms. *Monogatari* is not so much a musical form as
an acting technique, but in these cases, it refers to the music
which accompanies the actor, and which indeed is very important, as it times his every movement and acts as a control. In
Masakado, the *monogatari* commences '*Satemo Soma no Masa-
kada wa* . . . Now Masakado of Soma', and proceeds to relate a
heroic tale of battle and how Masakado, father of Takiyasha, was
killed. During the recital, Kisaragi, the disguised Takiyasha,
weeps and a change of mood is introduced as a contrast to the
brisk *monogatari*. This comes in *uta*, a song passage, '*Honobono to
suzume saezuru* . . . The sparrows twitter in the dim light'. *Uta*
passes into *sōodori*, which accompanies a dance duet by Kisaragi
and Mitsukuni with the refrain, '*Sore, sore, sore sokko de sei* . . .
Now listen all of you. One night . . .'. During this dance, Kisaragi
drops the Heike pennant and there is a sharp passage called
miawarashi, commencing, '*Satekoso, satekoso, Soma no nishiki no
kono hata o shoji nasu karawa* . . . So! since you have with you
this silk banner of Soma . . .'. Next comes *chirashi*, a movement
in quick tempo, which contains an aggressive quality. *Chirashi*
is a general term used in dancing and *samisen* playing to indicate
a final passage. The song here opens with '*Ikareru omote tachi-
machi ni* . . . Being flushed with anger . . .'. The play ends with
dangiri, a concluding paragraph which slackens the quick tempo
of *chirashi*, as all the characters pose in a spectacular tableau on
the stage. Kisaragi, turned into a fiend, strides the roof of the

mansion with a monstrous frog beside her and the Heike pennant held aloft. The curtain is drawn to the sound of the *ki* once more and the performance ends with the drum and flute of the *ohayashi*.

Kiyomoto bushi

Kiyomoto bushi is a school of music which developed out of *tomimoto bushi*, which again was an offshoot of *tokiwazu* previously described. The founder of the *kiyomoto* school was Kiyomoto Enjudayu (1777–1825), who began as a disciple of the *tomimoto* school. He broke away from the leader of the school to found the *kiyomoto* school in 1814. It became so popular that it completely replaced its parent school *tomimoto*, which has now almost disappeared. *Kiyomoto* introduced innovations in its construction, including popular songs of the period. Melody is stressed as more important than anything else in *kiyomoto* and it is characterized by a lightness which caused many people to rate it as vulgar, when it first achieved popularity. It, too, is used in the Kabuki for accompanying dramas in which the dance element predominates.

In the Kabuki, the players of the various schools of music are always seated on the stage in full view of the audience. There is a great deal of formality in their arrangement, quite unlike the happy-go-lucky placing of Chinese theatre musicians, who also sit on the stage. The various schools by long tradition occupy special positions during a performance. *Nagauta* players sit at the rear of the stage facing the audience. *Kiyomoto* and *tokiwazu* players sit at the left of the stage to the audience and *gidayu* players to the right. The positions may sometimes vary if certain circumstances require it, but these are the accepted places for the musicians while performing.

All stage musicians, of whatever school, wear *kamishimo*, the ceremonial dress of the *samurai* in former days. The costume consists of two parts, *kataginu* and *hakama*; the latter, a form of divided skirt, is worn above a *kimono* over which are fitted stiff horizontal shoulder pieces, the *kataginu*. They are in different colours and bear family crests. The custom of wearing this costume is said to date back to the time when Takemoto Gidayu received an honorary title from the governing authorities of his day, in recognition of his achievements in *joruri*.

There is a strict formality about the movements of the musicians of the stage, who sit motionless and upright when not performing. In the case of *gidayu*, both musicians bow on first appearing before the audience, and the *tayu* lifts the script from the small reading stand in front of him and places it to his forehead as a mark of respect. They sit on a dais, which is known as the *degatari dai*, it is built on a revolving base divided from the backstage by a screen, against which the musicians sit. In the middle of a play, the *degatari dai* can be swung round to reveal two more musicians on the other side and in this way, the performers are relieved in the speediest fashion without interfering with the course of the drama on the stage. Sometimes the *gidayu* musicians are seated in a small alcove, known as the *misu uchi*, which is situated above the stage entry to the right of the audience. When it is in this position, the *chobo* is concealed from the audience by a rattan blind which covers the front of the alcove.

The dais on which the performers of the other schools of music sit is known as the *yamadai*, if it has two tiers it is called *hinadan*. It is always covered with a scarlet drape, which adds a characteristic splash of colour to the stage in all dancing plays. The orchestra composed of *nagauta* players is known as *debayashi* and that composed of players from the other schools as *degatari*.

As the reader will have gathered, the music of the theatre depends on a complex, interweaving process in its construction which has developed through the years. Composers adhered rigidly to traditional forms, which were passed on from generation to generation, although there were changes as some disciple of a school would tire of his limitations and branch out into new forms. A school of music would remain pre-eminent for a period, then there would be another break away and a new school would come into being. The old schools did not die out completely, but continued to exist alongside the new, and this gave rise to the rather involved musical relationships already described.

This chapter outlines some technical aspects of the more important branches of Kabuki music, but of course, it is impossible to convey the true nature of any type of music by the written word alone. The significant thing is that music in the Kabuki theatre cannot be isolated as an independent feature, it is not incidental, it is a branch of dramatic technique which is vital to the staging of a play. Without it the actor could not function.

CHAPTER VI

THE DANCE IN THE THEATRE

DANCING is the essence of the Kabuki theatre. In a sense the history of the dance is the history of the Kabuki, which owes its origin to sources that, in turn, developed from dance forms which were the earliest dramatic expressions of the Japanese people.

An ancient Chinese writer said: 'If you want to dance, first move your feet.' It neatly sums up the fact that as soon as there is controlled movement there are the beginnings of dancing. When speaking of the Kabuki it is advisable to forget the more rigid meaning of the word dancing. The formal posturing and conventional gestures of the actor are as much dancing as more active movement. To the Occidental mind the ballet possibly provides the closest parallel in Europe, but there are wide divergences of approach on both sides and the term 'Japanese ballet' sometimes applied to Kabuki dance plays, is misleading.

The Japanese people have a long tradition of dancing. The dance has always been the means by which all classes of society celebrated ceremonial and festive occasions and gave expression to their emotions. It is hardly surprising that this ingrained characteristic has exerted a profound influence on the theatre. The art of the classical and traditional dance is still vigorously alive, in spite of modern encroachments, its continued hold in the life of Japan is perhaps one of the more happy omens for the survival of the Kabuki.

A knowledge of the names used in describing the various forms of dancing is a useful aid towards a better understanding of the construction of the dance in the theatre. There is a term, *buyo*, which is used of the dance in general, thus the Japanese speak of Nō *buyo*, Kabuki *buyo* or just *Nihon buyo*, i.e. Nō dancing, Kabuki dancing and Japanese dancing. The word *buyo*, however, is really the pronounced form of a Chinese character compound whose components give the two words, *mai* and *odori*, both of which mean dancing. There is another term, *shigusa*, to consider with these two. *Mai, odori* and *shigusa* are separate techniques which are used singly or together in dancing, forming three distinct divisions into which the dance as a whole, i.e. *buyo*, can be classified.

Mai is based on the technique of the Nō theatre, it is a general term and there are many different types of *mai*. Usually *mai* in *Nihon buyo*, or Japanese dancing, consists of slow, dignified movements and the use of a special foot technique known as *suriashi* or sliding step. In this the foot is moved along the ground without lifting the heel. *Mai* also makes use of a deliberate stamping movement known as *hyoshi*. *Odori*, on the other hand, is characterized by more gay, rhythmical movement and swift footwork. There are different gestures of the hands and head for character types, and character portrayal is an important feature of this type of dancing. The name *odori* is sometimes used in a much wider sense and covers dancing which also contains qualities of *mai*. *Shigusa* implies gestures such as weeping, or laughing; emotions are portrayed by dancing technique, mime in other words.

The dancing of the Kabuki embodies all three in its general form which is referred to as Kabuki *buyo* or Kabuki *no odori*. There is another name used when speaking of Kabuki dancing, it is *shosagoto*, an inclusive term which defies any brief description. Translated very literally, *shosagoto* means a 'thing of posture' and is now a classification under which fall most of the important dancing plays of the theatre. Again it must be emphasized that the term dancing, in this case, embraces the extremes in techniques.

The development of *shosagoto* is closely related with that of the musical forms discussed in the last chapter. The rapid progress of these in the eighteenth century brought about many innovations in stage dance music, with the result that the professional choreographer came into being and became an essential member of the staff of every theatre. New dance forms began to be created expressly for Kabuki purposes and a *shosagoto* was a prerequisite of every programme. At that time however they were not designed as independent dance numbers, but intended to be fitted in between the scenes of the main drama. It was not until the nineteenth century that the independent *shosagoto* was staged.

The professional choreographer, or *furitsukeshi*, was responsible for commencing the *iemoto* system, which has remained a feature of all Japanese dancing. An *iemoto* was a leader who established his own school and granted a licence to his pupils when they reached a certain state of efficiency. Training was severe and a high level of accomplishment was not easily obtained. Many schools came into being and the successors of some of them still carry on the names today. The various schools gained their theatrical supremacy through their popularity with the leading actor and the personalities of the chief choreographers, rather than though any marked differences in idea. Fundamentally they were all related, disciples of one school for instance might, and did, become the *iemoto* of a rival school.

Women were trained in dancing and became teachers, but if the succession of a dance school passed to a female heir, it debarred the school from direct connection with the theatre, for the Kabuki forbade the use of women in any form. This factor was sometimes responsible for the decline of a school of dancing in the theatre.

The Shigayama school, still active today, dates back to the early years of the eighteenth century when it was founded by Shigayama Mansaku of the Nakamura theatre in Yedo. During the Tenmei era (1781–8), two schools arose which overshadowed the earlier one, they were the Nishikawa and the Fujima schools; both are active today and the Fujima school ranks as the premier school in Kabuki choreography.

The Nishikawa school fell into a decline at one period, but it was taken over by Kansuke, a pupil of the Fujima school, who adopted the Nishikawa name and became Nishikawa Senzo IV, choreographer to Ichikawa Danjuro VII, the two being responsible for the great dancing play, *Kanjincho*. Nishikawa Senzo IV had two pupils, one of whom went to Nagoya and founded a branch of the Nishikawa school, whilst the other adopted the name Hanayagi Jusuke, founding the Hanayagi school which is still famous today. In 1903, a pupil of the Hanayagi school founded yet another school, known as the Wakayagi, and that too is still active.

The Fujima school, being without a male successor for a period, lost its place to the Nishikawa and Hanayagi schools. A pupil of the Fujima school, one Fujima Kanemon, restored it to prominence at the end of the Tokugawa era, being encouraged by Ichikawa Danjuro IX, to become a Kabuki choreographer, and the school has retained an important position in the Kabuki world ever since. The adopted son of Fujima Kanemon was the celebrated actor, Matsumoto Koshiro VII (1879–1949), who became the leader of the school. Through him the succession passed to his son, the modern Kabuki actor, Onoe Shoroku II, and he is the present leader. Fujima and Hanayagi are now the two main schools of Kabuki choreography, but mention must be made of a third, the Bando school, whose leader is the veteran Kabuki actor Bando Mitsugoro VII. Mitsugoro is regarded as the premier dancer on the Kabuki stage, the school, of which he is leader, being founded by a pupil of his ancestor, Bando Mitsugoro III, in the latter part of the Tokugawa era.

There are several other famous schools of dance in existence besides those named, such as the Inouye and Azuma schools, which have no direct connection with the theatre, although actually they all have a common bond with the Kabuki. Formerly the Kabuki and the Japanese dance were as one, but later the dance became an independent movement, particularly after the great earthquake of 1923 when progress in the theatre was completely interrupted, causing many professional dancers to develop along their own lines. Although the Kabuki lost the monopoly of the dance, it received many contributions from the new developments in choreography, and the link between the theatre and the independent dance has never really been severed. Every actor is instructed in dancing from the earliest age, teaching commencing at seven and even earlier. Training and practice is never relaxed from then on throughout his career. Early training has three stages, first, basic hand movements are taught, next, dancing with a fan and the sleeves to musical accompaniment, i.e. spoken as well as instrumental, and finally *yariyako*, dancing with weapons such as spears and lances. Students are first taught the feminine forms in dancing, as these are considered the necessary foundation for delicacy and rhythm of a more subtle kind. Male dancing with its greater vigour is regarded as easier to acquire and instruction in this form comes last.

The cardinal principle in Japanese dancing is natural movement with no straining of form. The aim is to represent the beauty of the clothed body either in costume or ordinary dress. Dancing in ordinary dress, known as *su odori*, is considered the most difficult art and is looked upon as illustrating the finest points in dancing in the most subtle way. A great dance master has said: 'All you need to do is to dance as your heart dictates; attempts to display your skill, however well meaning, will deform your dance. Dance innocently with no cloud in your heart. If in your mind you are expecting applause, your dance will fail.'

Posture is one of the first things to consider in the technique of dancing. While standing, there should be a perpendicular line running from the neck to the heel. The line of the shoulders and line of the feet must be diagonally placed to the audience. A diagonal is regarded as fundamental and the dancer sets his whole body to the corners of the stage. A centre of movement, known as *idokoro no fudo*, is also important in dancing, e.g. if moving three steps to the right, the dancer returns to his former position whilst continuing his dancing. Movements up and down the stage must limit their distance, this is known as *ashi jun*, good order of steps, which is a principle either in solo or group dancing. Frame of mind is also regarded as an essential, all dancing is accompanied by verbal description at some point and it is necessary to know what the words are expressing, concentration on form at the expense of this deprives the dancing of soul. The dancer must know *what* he is dancing besides how he is dancing.

The three elements of *mai*, *odori* and *shigusa* form the basis of dancing technique; two other things important to this technique are costume, or *ishō*, and small properties or *kodōgu*. Naturally all stage dancing is in costume and the dress of actors has been developed to add a certain brilliance and novelty to the dance itself. A particular feature of Kabuki dancing is the *henge*, or variation dance, and plays which embody this technique are sometimes called *hengemono*. In *henge*, the actor dances several characters continuously, or it may be several different moods of the same character, all with changes of costume. The interest centres in the different forms of dancing that go with the various changes in costume. This style of dancing was experimented with in the early days of the Kabuki, but later it became so popular with audiences that it developed on a wide scale and became a necessary part of all stage dances, and has remained so until today.

Two special features of stage costume are used in the *henge* dance, they are called *hikinuki* and *bukkaeri* and will be discussed in detail in a later chapter. In *hikinuki*, different dresses are worn one over the other and sewn together by loose threads which can be ripped off quickly to allow the under garment to show. In *bukkaeri*, the personal appearance of the actor is changed by lowering the upper part of the costume and letting it hang from the actor's waist, revealing a new garment beneath.

Kodōgu, or to give them their full title, *odori no kodōgu*, consist of a variety of articles used by the actor while dancing and include the special head dresses. The article may be a sword, a pipe or a lantern, but the two most fundamentally important are the *ogi*, or fan, and the *tenugui*. The *tenugui* is commonly described as a towel, but in ordinary life serves a multitude of purposes, being used as a headband, a scarf, or a souvenir for presentation on special occasions. It is usually a white cotton strip patterned with a bold design in indigo. On the stage it is made of silk and carries the actor's or dancer's crest as a pattern. Many theatre fans collect actors' *tenugui* which are treasured as precious possessions. Sometimes at the end of a dance movement in a play a famous actor will hurl several *tenugui* gracefully into the audience, and a mad struggle ensues to secure the prizes. This is a traditional custom.

The fan may be used to depict riding on a horse or shooting a bow from an arrow, it may symbolize the rising moon or opening a sliding door, it can represent the falling cherry blossoms or the waves of the sea. Both the fan and the *tenugui* are indispensible to the Japanese dancer in performing various symbolical movements during the course of his performance.

Besides costume and properties, the peculiarities of stage construction contribute in no small measure to the originality of the Kabuki dance. Features like the *hanamichi*, *suppon* and *seriage* are important to the choreographer in creating his dance patterns, providing dramatic and spectacular effects. *Shosagoto* developed in relation to the work of the *furitsuke shi*, or choreographer, first as a necessary element in other plays, later as an independent form. As a result *shosagoto* exist in a wide variety of forms. There are *shosagoto* which belong to *nagauta* music, including some of the most familiar on the stage, *shosagoto* of *gidayu*, *tokiwazu*, *kiyomoto* and so on. Others are adapted from Nō and *kyogen* plays, in which case they are often referred to as *matsame mono*. This relates to the conventional pine tree painted on simple boarding which is always used as a background to the stage setting for plays of Nō origin. The décor is adapted directly from the older stage. Some *shosagoto* are merely a type of dramatic dance, with emphasis on the music and movement rather than theme or story, others are merely a combination of mime and gesture to *jōruri* accompaniment, others yet again are complete dramas in dance form with a consistent plot. There is a type which is put into a programme merely for technical effect and has now lost connection with its original background, a point that applies to most of the older *shosagoto* used only as one-act plays today. To sum up, *shosagoto* is dancing designed solely for the Kabuki stage and dependent for its technical effect upon its co-ordination with the rhythm of the song and narrative of the music.

It is impossible to point to one particular dance play and say 'that typifies Kabuki dancing'. So many different factors have gone to the making of the stage dance through the centuries, each period making its own individual contribution, that today there are a wide variety of styles in existence. Within this variety, however, there are consistent patterns of technique and recurring forms which strike the observer, and it is possible to analyse the Kabuki dance play by tracing the development of these common features from the earliest days.

The earliest Kabuki provided its audience with entertainment which was largely based on dancing and from this time, evolved many independent styles which were to influence the actor's technique in later years. Besides these there were independent dances, which were used solely for ceremonial and commemorative occasions. One was a dance which in the Kabuki became known as *Sambaso*, and which exists in many forms today.

The Kabuki drew a great deal upon the Nō drama and one of the things it took direct was a ceremonial dance known as *Okina*, which later became the *Sambaso* named above. *Okina*, in the Nō theatre, was a sacred dance always performed at the very beginning of the main performance; its purpose was to pray for the peace of the world and the safety of the realm, as well as a good harvest. There were three principal characters in the dance: Okina, an old man wearing a mask, symbolizing longevity and good luck, and Senzai and Sambaso, also old men, signifying longevity and felicity. They originally symbolized heaven, earth and man, joining together in prayer for the peace of the world.

In the Kabuki, this was danced at the opening ceremony of a new theatre, at the New Year, or opening of the theatrical season in November. Like everything which the Kabuki adopted, the *Sambaso* dance was transformed and many different types came into existence, whose emphasis is on entertainment rather than any ceremonial significance. In the Kabuki versions, Sambaso becomes important as a figure of comedy, who is the centre of various dances created for different schools of *samisen* music. Okina appears as an old man and Senzai a young man in the prologues to these *Sambaso* dances.

There is a popular version called *Ayatsuri Sambaso*, in which Sambaso does a dance emulating the movements of a marionette on strings. It was first performed in 1853. Another called *Shita Dashi Sambaso*, or Sambaso putting out his tongue, was first performed in 1812. The dance is so called because Sambaso shows his tongue in the course of it. Other important variations of the dance are *Shiki Sambaso*, four seasons, *Ninin Sambaso*, two men, *Shiki Sambaso*, ceremonial *Sambaso* and *Hinarazu Sambaso*, the young crane.

Sambaso is always colourfully dressed, a feature of his costume being the high hat, known as *konsaki eboshi*. It is about fifteen inches high, with broad gold and black stripes and a scarlet roundel on each side, it tapers to a point at the crown and is set back at an angle from the head and tied beneath the chin with strings, a distinguishing mark of Sambaso. There were other independent ceremonial dances in the old Kabuki theatre, but *Sambaso* is the most important one to have survived.

After the ban imposed on women in the Kabuki and the development of the Yaro Kabuki (see Chapter II), the actor was compelled to concentrate on technique and not physical attraction. It was the period when the *onnagata*, or female impersonators, became common, and as they were not allowed to take a variety of important roles in the plays, the dance was a branch of stage art in which they came into their own and they were constantly searching for new material for dance plays. Until the Tenmei era (1781–8), the dance remained the privilege of the *onnagata* actors, who were responsible for many innovations and developments. It was then that the *tateyaku*, or male role actors, began to devote themselves increasingly to dancing, while at the same time, the *onnagata* began to play more important roles in the main dramas. Nevertheless, some of the most popular roles in Kabuki dancing plays have remained those created by the *onnagata* actor and dancing is still the most important feature of the *onnagata's* art.

A notable development in Kabuki technique was *aragoto*, originated by Ichikawa Danjuro I (1660–1704). *Aragoto* is a technique of exaggeration, which emphasizes the power of the hero or the evil of the villain by extremes in costume, dialogue and movement. It was received with loud acclaim by the audiences of the time and became a characteristic of the Yedo theatre as against the romantic quality of the Kyoto and Osaka theatres, which preferred plays dealing with the gay quarters. The technique of *aragoto* has been handed on and survives in many plays. Its bold display of rhythmical, emphasized movement and gesture mark it as one manifestation of the dance, which exerted a great influence on the Kabuki stage.

Two dance plays which incorporate *aragoto* are *Yanone* and *Kusazuri Biki*, the theme of both being based on the Soga brothers whose story is related in Chapter IX. *Yanone*, 'Arrowhead', is one of the *juhachiban*, or eighteen best plays (see Chapter IX). The plot is brief. Soga no Goro, while sharpening an arrow head, has fallen asleep. His brother Juro appears to him in a dream and begs him to save him from danger. A peasant passing by, his horse loaded with large radishes, or *daikon*, is stopped by Goro who seizes the horse after a struggle and rides off using a long *daikon* as a riding switch. Goro is attired in colourful costume typical of *aragoto* with a bizarre painted make-up known as *kumadori*. As the curtain is drawn he is revealed grasping a monstrous arrow. He awakes slowly and his deliberate movements with the arrow result in a series of vigorous poses, which finally terminate in swifter movement as he goes off on the purloined horse. *Yanone* was first performed in 1729.

Kusazari biki also has a slight theme. Soga no Goro is about to depart, carrying his armour, to go and join his brother in battle. An official, Kobayashi no Asahina, tries to detain him by seizing hold of a portion of the armour, the *kusazari*; the dance consists of a series of postures and poses by the two characters. Asahina is a fantastic figure with exaggerated painted make-up, whilst that of Goro represents the young hero of *aragoto*.

In 1731, a *shosagoto* was staged in the Yedo Kabuki, which was to be the prototype of a dancing play that has remained outstanding in the Kabuki repertoire. *Keisei Dojoji* was based on a theme from the Nō drama; the plot concerns Katsuragi, a courtesan who comes to make an offering to a new temple bell and, after dancing, climbs into the bell as a spirit. It was danced by Segawa Kikunojo I, an *onnagata* actor, and it became so popular that many versions were produced from the original, with different musical settings.

The legend which originally gave rise to the various dramatic versions was as follows. In former times there lived the beautiful daughter of a feudal lord in Kishu province. Once a year a young priest stopped at their mansion on his annual pilgrimage to the Kumano shrine. The lord told the girl one day that she was betrothed to the priest. Parents in those times, of course, arranged marriages for their children. The maiden believed her father and began to make advances towards the priest. To avoid temptation and fearing for the salvation of his soul, the young priest fled by night and hid in the bell of the Dojoji temple. The maiden followed him but was stopped by the flood waters of the Hidaka River. Thereupon she changed into a serpent, crossed the river and coiled herself seven times round the temple bell. The bell melted under her venomous fire and the priest was destroyed.

In the Kabuki version of *Dojoji*, the play commences with the priests of the temple holding rites for the new bell. A beautiful maid, attired as a *shirabyoshi*, arrives at the temple gate and begs to be admitted. The priests at first refuse, but eventually allow her to join them, when she promises to perform sacred dances for them. She dances and dances, but eventually turns into the spirit of a serpent and leaps on to the bell before the terrified priests.

A *shirabyoshi* can be considered an early precursor of the *geisha* and dates back to 1115, when the daughters of two high families, Suma no Senzai and Waka no Mae, are said to have attired themselves in the white garb of noblemen, wearing the high hat known as *tateboshi*, and danced with swords. In the beginning, the *shirabyoshi* danced a form of ceremonial dance, but later it developed into less virile and more elegant forms, which were used by these entertainers waiting upon the great at their banquets. The legend is shrouded in the obscurity customary in these cases, but at any rate, the *shirabyoshi* were accomplished women who in the past entertained others with singing, dancing and playing.

In 1752 the actor Nakamura Tomijuro I danced a version of *Dojoji* in Kyoto and the next year in Yedo. In it, he attempted to outshine the performance of *Keisei Dojoji* by Segawa Kikunojo I in 1731, which, up until then, had remained supreme, Tomijuro succeeded, his *Dojoji* became so popular that the other version was relegated and the *Dojoji* of today, *Kyokanako Musume Dojoji*, has come down from Tomijuro's version. Several other versions came from Tomijuro's, but none of them remained successful and were inferior in standard. *Musume Dojoji*, as it is generally referred to, is one of the classical pieces of dancing repertoire. Any dancer who wishes to rise to fame must graduate by way of *Dojoji*. The outstanding feature of it is that beauty is expressed in a large variety of moods, being the interpretation of the feelings and movements of a pretty maiden in love, joy, hate and fury. Many different techniques are embodied and a series of dances performed within the main play, which come under the category of *henge*, mentioned previously. In *Musume Dojoji*, the dancer makes no less than nine changes of costume.

There is another version of *Dojoji* sometimes performed, known as *Ninin Dojoji*. It is different from the main version, in that two maidens appear and dance together and then alternately. In former times, there was also *Gonin Dojoji*, in which five maidens danced, but *Kyokanako Musume Dojoji* is the accepted version which now holds an honoured place in the esteem of all true lovers of the theatre and the dance. It is such an outstanding play that it merits a more detailed description of the stage procedure.

The stage setting is colourful and typical. When the curtain is drawn, a huge bell in green and gold is seen suspended above the right of the stage to the audience and a long red and white rope trails from it to the left. Above the proscenium, long sprays of cherry blossoms are hung, a technical device known as *tsuri eda*, common to the Kabuki. The background of the set consists of a curtain in broad red and white horizontal stripes, traditional decoration for festivals in Japan. To the rear left of the stage is a small wooden signboard, which informs people that a *kanekyo*, bell festival, is being observed. Beyond this, in the centre of the stage, is a low portable wooden gate, technically known as *shiyorido*, a typical stage prop. Early in the play, the red and white curtain at the rear is dropped to reveal the *nagauta* orchestra, seated against a set which depicts a mountain landscape covered with cherry blossoms.

The play opens with a row of *bozu*, Buddhist priests, filing down the *hanamichi* chanting a *sutra* in quick time and finally lining up on the stage. There is some comic dialogue and one produces an octopus from his robe and another a bottle. The octopus is a delicacy in Japan, but it is also associated with a certain type of ribald jest. The point is that this scene is a light-hearted prelude to the great events to come. Then Hanako, the maiden, appears on the *hanamichi* and performs a graceful posture dance. This is called *michiyuki* and represents a young maid's emotions in love, and at her toilet, as she pauses in her journey to the temple. In the course of her dance, she screws into a ball the piece of soft paper known as the *kaishi*, which is the equivalent of a handkerchief in Japan. It is customary for the actor to throw this ball of paper into the audience and there is always a wild leap to secure the souvenir from the hand of a famous actor.

Hanako wears a colourful *kimono* and *obi*, together with the decorative hair style of a young maiden. This part of the dance is, incidentally, performed to a *gidayu* accompaniment, although the rest of the play has a *nagauta* setting. Hanako finally goes on the stage and up to the gate of the temple, where she begs for admittance. After questioning her, the priests eventually let her in and bring a gold *tateboshi* on a ceremonial tray. She takes the hat and disappears behind the red and white curtain at the back. Another comic scene occurs with a great deal of humorous by-play and dialogue between the assembled priests, in which contemporary references are often inserted. The priests then file off to the sound of the drum, flute and *rin*, the small sacred hand-bell, and reappear to seat themselves at the extreme right and left of the stage. There are often one or two child actors among the priests and it is common to read in an actor's biography, 'made his first stage appearance as a *bozu* in *Dojoji* at such and such a time'.

Next occurs a passage of dancing which is full of great dignity and depth of dramatic appeal. The red and white curtain at the rear is drawn to reveal the full *nagauta* orchestra in two tiers, and in front of them Hanako, posed with a fan in her hand. She wears the high, gold *tateboshi* on her head and a scarlet and golden *kimono*. This portion of the dance uses *mai* and is performed in slow tempo, a drum and vocal accompaniment in the *kuromisu* being the only music; the main orchestra is still silent. It is an extremely fine opening, as Hanako moves slowly forward to the famous chanted line: '*Hana no hoka niwa, matsu bakari, hana no hoka niwa, matsu bakari.* . . . Besides the cherry blossoms only a single pine, here and there. . . . *Kure somete kane ya hibikuran.* . . . The sound of a bell resounds through the twilight. . . .' Hanako advances on to the *hanamichi* and there is a famous scene where she stops short, grasping her fan in her left hand and gives a swift glance back over her shoulder at the bell. It is the climax to this part of the dance. Then she goes back on the stage, her fan pointed towards the bell, under which she dances to the accompaniment of the *nagauta* players. In the middle of the dance she suddenly takes off the *tateboshi* which is flung across the rope of the bell by the *koken*, the stage assistants to the actor. At the end of this she poses, kneels to discard her fan, rises and dances again, and there is a swift change of costume once more by the *hikinuki* method. She is now in a pale blue colour scheme and performs a dance which symbolizes bouncing a ball while on her bended knees. It is a graceful passage, followed by a quick dance to music and she goes off.

Two of the *bozu* now come forward and perform a short dance, until two stage assistants run in from the left, holding a scarlet cloth behind which is Hanako. They suddenly take it away to show her in another change of costume. The top half of her *kimono* is lowered, showing another colour beneath, and on her head she wears a large, circular, ribbed hat, about fourteen inches in diameter and slightly concave in the crown. It is crimson in colour and tied round the chin with a ribbon of the same hue, which is turned up to fasten in a bow across the mouth. In either hand the actor holds what are known as *furidashigasha*, which are miniature replicas of the hat that Hanako wears, but consisting of three which fit inside each other by a hinged device, enabling the actor to fling them out as a trio in each hand while dancing. It will be noticed that in *Dojoji* great use is made of *kodōgu*. After this scene, Hanako retires once more and the *bozu* all come on with their robes tucked up, exposing tight yellow trousers and carrying *hanagasa*, paper umbrellas decorated with cherry blossoms. The priests dance, opening and shutting their umbrellas and bobbing up and down in turn, after which they depart and a pair of *bozu* only, do an acrobatic dance. Finally, all the priests go back to their positions at the sides of the stage. Hanako appears on the stage again, her entry concealed by the red cloth. This technique is used to give an element of surprise to the audience. She appears this time in a *kimono* of lilac colour patterned in white, and holding a white *tenugui* with the indigo crest of the actor. An expressive type of dance, known as *furi*, is now performed. It has a slow and melancholy opening movement in which the *tenugui* is used to the refrain: '*Koi no tenerai tsui minaraite*. . . . I have learned to love. . . .' This passage concludes with the dancer beneath the bell, the upper part of the body leaning right over backwards, followed by a quick dance with the full orchestra, and it is here, very often, that the actor throws *tenugui* to the audience. Hanako goes off once again and there is a short interval of instrumental music, after which she quickly reappears in yet another patterned *kimono*, with a small ornamental drum, known as a *kakko*, fastened on her chest. First she dances a quick movement, then a slow, kneels and beats a quick tattoo on the *kakko*, stick in either hand, in time with the *samisen* music. Next, she poses, drumsticks held before her. She goes off stage and there is a passage of *samisen* music, she reappears in a different patterned *kimono*, dances, and takes a pair of *suzudaiko*, a kind of tambourine, from the *koken* who assists her to make another change in her costume by the *hikinuki* method. There is a rhythmical dance, in which at one point she beats the floor with the *suzudaiko* in alternating time with the *nagauta* playing. At the end of it she suddenly rises, the huge bell drops to the stage. Some priests rush in behind it, others kneel in prayer, Hanako disappears behind the bell and reappears on top of it in her final change of costume. The upper part of her *kimono* is flung back, to show a black and white garment beneath, her hair hangs down in two long strands at either side as she poses on the bell, the spirit of the snake. There is an alternative finale to this. After dancing with the *suzudaiko*, Hanako disappears from the stage, while on the *hanamichi* appears the fantastic figure of Terutake Samaguro, a supernatural character, who has a painted face, bizarre costume and high *geta* on his feet and clasps a heavy stake from a bamboo tree in one hand. He poses and is followed by a troop of what are called *hanayoten*, a type of guard who come to seize characters on the stage. There is no suitable name to describe them in English, as they are quite peculiar to the Kabuki; they have a comic twist to their actions, wear bright clothing and carry sprigs of cherry blossom.

Hanako returns to the stage with her face made up in fierce fashion in blue and black. It represents an *oni*, or demon, and is a terrifying contrast to the maiden of the preceding scene, but of course it is always the same actor in both parts. She fights with her opponents and there is a finale in which she is astride the top of the bell, with Terutake Samagoro posing at the front of the stage and the *hanayoten* lying on their backs in a long serpentine coil from the bell to the left of the stage. This, in brief, describes the stage procedure for *Kyokanako Museme Dojoji*, a Kabuki dance masterpiece.

The technique of *henge* described in this play was one which became more and more popular with audiences. At first, the *henge* dances were the privilege of the *onnagata*, and because these actors were limited in their stage parts, *henge* plays retained a certain similarity in form. During the Bunka period (1804–17), Bando Mitsugoro III, the most perfect dancer of his time, changed this convention, and became responsible for many changes in this type of dance. He perfected the technique known as *hayagawari*, or quick change, which was so fashionable that it became one of the principal features of the Kabuki dance.

The *henge* dance eventually reached such heights in public favour that actors and choreographers were hard put to it to satisfy the demands of the audiences, who, tiring of historical backgrounds, demanded humorous or witty dances. A comical dance devised for this period is typified by *Oharame*, danced by Nakamura Utaemon III, in 1810. It is also interesting as an example of a *henge* dance with only one change instead of several. *Oharame* depicts a shopwoman of Kyoto, who, in the second part of the dance, transforms herself into a *yakko*, or *daimyo's* attendant, with a spear, bearded face and top knot. *Hikinuki* is used in this transformation. In the first part, Oharame wears a comical mask which is often seen in Japanese dancing, known as *Otafuku no men*, or more commonly, as Okame. It came from an older dance, the *kagura*, and represents a woman's snub-nosed face, with bulging cheeks and a happy grin, which gives a most amusing effect when worn in the dance. *Yakko* were the bodyguards who used to walk in a procession when a *daimyo* travelled abroad and executed a special dance as they went along. They were powerful bewhiskered fellows and are always shown on the stage with red faces and black markings, to represent side whiskers, and their dance has for long been incorporated in the Kabuki repertoire.

Eventually, theatre people in their search for new materials for the *henge* dance, began to adapt the performances of street entertainers and the manners and customs of every kind of peddlar, beggar or tradesman, who made up the bustling life of the city highways and byways. A new type of dance was born which henceforth was to form an integral part of all Kabuki dancing. A good example is the *Echigo Jishi* dance first performed by Nakamura Utaemon III in 1811. It was the custom in January every year for a certain type of acrobatic dancer to come up to the big cities like Tokyo and Osaka, from Echigo Province, and perform a dance in the streets, which was very popular on account of its gaiety and animation. The dancers wore a colourful costume, with a bizarre lion mask over their head and brandished a peony branch, while beating a small drum attached to their chest. They were known as *kakubei jishi*. The lion mask was of wood, surmounted by a bunch of black feathers and fastened on top of a crimson silk canopy worn over the head to hang down the back, the face of the dancer being visible. On the stage, the mask is made of papier mâché to facilitate dancing, but the costume is more or less faithful to the original. The *Echigo Jishi* dance of the Kabuki is divided into three parts. The first portrays a dancer on his way to the big cities, wearing the mask, beating his drum and carrying a peony branch. The second part gives variations on the gay movements of the *Echigo* dancer who has by this time discarded mask and drum. The third part does not actually concern the lion dancer, but depicts a village maiden washing clothes in a stream, thus bringing into play a dance accessory known as *sarashi*, a strip of white cloth more than three yards long and a foot wide, mounted on a grip which is held in the hand. It is manipulated to form figures while dancing and finds a parallel in the 'scarf' dance of the Chinese theatre.

A dance form peculiar to the Kabuki is the *michiyuki*, literally 'travelling on the way'. The stock theme is that of two lovers on their way to commit suicide. The *hanamichi* is essential in this, for the lovers always make their entry by it and wander sadly along together, recalling their past, or grieving for their misfortunes, and, arriving on the stage, they dance and posture in melancholy fashion. A normal sequel was for a peddler or travelling merchant of some description to arrive at this point and advise them against death.

The *michiyuki* was a regular feature in the main *Soga* dramas. In Chapter IX it is said that it was customary to change a part of the main performance in a theatre in March and add a *sewamono* play. If the latter had a tragic sequel, it had to conclude with a *michiyuki*. Later the *michiyuki* was developed independently, but it continued as a necessary item in any performance until the last years of the Tokugawa era and the dawn of the Meiji era in 1868.

The word *michiyuki* is used in a broader sense to describe a dance theme, which portrays a character or characters who are making a journey or travelling, not necessarily the two lovers who are the victims of fate, although some romantic implication is attached to the journey. There is, for instance, the famous *michiyuki* in the eighth act of *Chushingura*, in which the maiden Konami is being escorted by her mother to the home of her lover Rikiya, who appears to have deserted her. The mother wishes to arrange a formal betrothal and this *michiyuki* scene describes a long journey on foot from Kamakura to Yamashina. On the way Konami is distressed because fortune has been unkind to her, but although her fate may be compared to a white cloud disappearing from Mount Fuji, she prays that her unhappiness will disappear when the bonfire is lighted at her wedding. Eventually, they see the bridal train of a *daimyo's* daughter passing through an avenue of pines and Konami is filled with envy. Her mother trys to cheer her up, but on crossing a river, she is reminded that a man's heart and the current of a stream are alike fickle. She fears that her lover's affections may wilt under misfortune, and so her mother tries to dispel her daughter's doubts as they travel on their way. All this time, the two principal characters are posing and gesturing to *joruri* accompaniment, while the bridal procession of the *daimyo* gives an added diversion on the stage.

Another famous *michiyuki* is the fourth scene of the long play *Yoshitsune Sembon Zakura*, which is always given as an independent dance play today. Shizuka, the beautiful mistress of the feudal warrior Yoshitsune, is travelling to seek her lover in hiding. She arrives at Mount Yoshino, which is covered with cherry blossoms, playing a hand drum, *kotsuzumi*, which belongs to Yoshitsume and has been left in her charge. There she is met by Tadanobu, a faithful retainer, who is really the spirit of a fox in disguise, and who, fascinated by the notes of the drum, the skin of which was once his father's, eventually saves Shizuka from capture by enemies of Yoshitsume. This little piece is a complete fantasy but contains some delightful dancing by both Shizuka and Tadanobu, the latter performing what is known as *kitsune roppo*, vigorous dancing which represents a fox spirit. The play, whose independent title is *Michiyuki Hatsune no Tabi*, is notable also for its stirring musical accompaniment, this being an occasion when the orchestra contains many more than two players and the dance music of *gidayu* is heard at its best. The *michiyuki* originally developed from the doll theatre and the play described above is also performed by the doll theatre today, although with many interesting variations on the Kabuki version. The Kabuki adapted many of the *michiyuki* numbers it took from *gidayu* to *tokiwazu* or *kiyomoto* settings, turning them into independent dance numbers.

A landmark in the history of dance plays was the performance of *Kanjincho* by Ichikawa Danjuro in 1840, for it foreshadowed developments which were to play a great part in shaping the character of the Kabuki theatre during the period following the Meiji Restoration in 1868. *Kanjincho* is described in more detail in the chapter on Kabuki plays; all that need be said here is that, in its day, it was a completely new type of dance based on the technique of the Nō drama. An independent *shosagoto*, imitating the Nō play, was a revelation to ordinary people of the time, who previously had not been able to see this older style of theatre.

It is true that both the Nō drama and *kyogen*, the comic plays inserted between the main items in a Nō programme, had influenced the Kabuki from the earliest days in numerous ways, but, during the nineteenth century, it was the first time that imitation of Nō and *kyogen* had been direct. The Kabuki passed through a period of decadence in the early years of the century and, in a feverish desire for novelty, there were many abnormal developments in dance plays, nothing was considered too sacred to travesty for cheap effect. The advent of plays like *Kanjincho*

and many others of its kind which succeeded it, did much to re-
store the dignity of the Kabuki theatre and introduce a new and
higher level of achievement.

The Meiji Restoration brought a new type of audience to the
Kabuki theatre who had previously known little about it. Plays
based directly on Nō and *kyogen* technique appealed to the intellect of these playgoers, and although the diehards frowned
upon them at first, such plays quickly became popular and have
remained as the most representative in spirit of the Meiji
theatre.

Two great actors played a leading part in the development of
the Kabuki of this time, they were Ichikawa Danjuro IX and
Onoe Kikugoro V, who were responsible for staging most of the
new dramas which came into the category described above. The
two men worked in friendly rivalry, and as one produced a new
item which received acclaim, the other would follow with his
fresh contribution and, in this way, they left behind them dancing plays which remain among the best of their kind and are still
favourites.

Kanjincho had been a unique experiment in its time, and, as
it was one of the famous eighteen best plays which belonged exclusively to the Ichikawa family, it was naturally one of the
notable pieces in the repertoire of Danjuro IX. In 1881, Onoe
Kikugoro V staged a new play *Tsuchigumo*, 'the Ground Spider',
which was to be the first of its kind, based on a Nō drama of the
same title. The legend by which a monstrous spider can assume
human shape is a very old one in Japan, and the theme had been
used as a dance long before Kikugoro's new version taken direct
from a Nō play, but with Kabuki forms added, the main dance
being more complex than in the Nō.

The story concerns Raiko, a nobleman who is sick with a
mysterious illness, and the priests of all the Buddhist temples
have been asked to pray for his recovery. A high priest comes to
visit the sick man in his chamber at midnight, he is really the
spider in disguise, and tries to kill Raiko with his sorcery. Raiko
attacks him with his sword and the false priest disappears leaving
a trail of blood behind him. Retainers arrive on the scene and
four of them follow the blood tracks and trace the spider to its
lair, and, after a struggle in which it tries to ensnare its opponents
in its web, represented on the stage by long streamers of paper

Figure from a dance play: Mashiba in 'Ibaragi'

which are hurled out as the spider dances, the monster is killed.
Dancing plays of this nature, i.e. with a demon or fiend as a
central character, follow a consistent pattern in the Kabuki. First
the monster appears in disguise in order to deceive its opponents,
and, in the second half of the play is seen in its true colours as a
demon which calls for a terrifying painted face make-up. The
two parts of a play like this are bridged by a comic dancing number, generally featuring retainers or servants. It adds a touch of
lightness to the horror, but it also serves the very practical purpose of allowing the principal actor to make the transformation
in costume and make-up, which is necessary in such an instance.

Onoe Kikugoro followed up *Tsuchigumo* with another play in
Nō style in 1883. This was *Ibaragi* written for him by Kawatake
Mokuami (1816–93). Its construction is based on the principles
outlined above. The story concerns Watanabe no Tsuna, who has
previously cut off the arm of a fiend, which has been terrifying
the capital. A soothsayer has ordered him to confine himself to
his mansion for a seven-day fast and to admit no one to his presence. In this way the attempts of the fiend to return can be
thwarted. The arm of the fiend is being kept under close guard
in a wooden chest and Tsuna is preserving an extra vigilance on
the seventh day. His old aunt, Mashiba, arrives from a long dis-

tance to see him; after at first stoutly refusing to see her, he eventually succumbs to her tearful pleas. Once inside, she persuades
him to let her see the arm on the pretext that she is an old
woman who will soon be dead and therefore never have such an
opportunity to satisfy her curiosity again. When shown the limb
she suddenly becomes transformed and seizing it, appears in her
true guise as the fiend and after a furious struggle with Tsuna
escapes bearing away the prize.

As a rival performance to Kikugoro's successes in this type of
dancing play, Danjuro IX staged *Funabenkei* in 1885. Like
Tsuchigumo, it is based on a Nō drama of the same name. The
story concerns the celebrated Yoshitsune, his mistress Shizuka
and his faithful retainer, the warrior priest Benkei. The three
are at sea fleeing from the capital where Yoshitsune has fallen
out of favour with the Shogun, Yoritomo, his brother. Suddenly,
before their ship, the spirit of Tomomori, general of the defeated
Heike clan, rises from the water to attack them, but Benkei
succeeds in exorcising the spirit by calling upon his gods to bind
it with a rope. The Kabuki version has an independent value of
its own, the graceful dancing of Shizuka in the first half and the
dance of Tomomori's spirit in the second half are connected by
an interlude in which the boatmen dance. The play as a whole
typifies the strong individuality of the Meiji theatre.

In addition to dance plays, which imitated the Nō theatre
closely, there were those which took their theme from the Nō,
but retained no trace of its technique, being completely Kabuki
in style. Such a play was *Momijigari*, staged by Danjuro IX in
1886. The plot described how Taira no Koremochi is out on the
mountains, enjoying the red tinted foliage of autumn. A beautiful maiden, Sarashi Hime, appears and offers him wine; after
drinking he sleeps. In his sleep the God of the Mountain comes
to him and tells him that he is in danger. Awaking, he finds the
maiden has gone and in her place stalks a demon, who attacks
him, and whom he finally destroys with the aid of his trusty
sword. *Momijigari* is distinguished by the fact that it combines
gidayu, *tokiwazu* and *kiyomoto* alternately as musical accompaniments, it is the only dance to contain such a feature.

The close of the Meiji era heralded a new age of experimenta-
tion and novel ideas in the stage dance. New technical forms were
introduced into old styles and new musical accompaniments de-

vised which ignored tradition; on the other hand, old musical styles like *gidayu* were adapted to new dances. The advent of an independent movement in the dance saw a new phase in its relations with the Kabuki. Previously the dance was born in the theatre, now it was often created outside the theatre. It is with the former type only that this chapter is concerned. The plots outlined here are those which have made a significant contribution to the general characteristics of the dance play over a period of time, other important ones are described in the main chapter on plays. They in no way give a complete history of the dance drama, but they do provide a key to the appreciation of one of the most interesting aspects of the Kabuki theatre.

CHAPTER VII

THE ACTOR'S TECHNIQUE

⚜

THE Japanese use a word *kata*, literally form, when speaking of the actor's speech and movements on the stage. The term is extended to cover stage properties, costume, wigs and make-up, for in the Kabuki these are not just decorative background accessories but are also necessary aids to the technique of the actor. In view of what has been said in the chapter on dancing it would be logical to list the special gestures and poses of the Kabuki actor there, but as all aspects of *kata* are being described here no such division has been made.

MIE

The *aragoto* technique of Ichikawa Danjuro I (1660–1704) has already been mentioned previously. From *aragoto* developed a form known as *mie*, which singularly typifies the art of the Kabuki actor. It is so familiar to all Japanese that it has passed into their everyday vocabulary in the characteristic phrase, *o mie wo kiru*, literally 'to cut *o mie*', meaning to seek a dramatic effect, or 'playing to the gallery'. It has been immortalized in the prints and drawings of the artist Sharaku, that strange genius. Time and time again, his prints depict the moment when the actor has reached the climax in his acting and poses rigidly for a moment to impress his emotion and fiery ardour on the audience. That is the art of the *mie* and Sharaku's brush captured it with superb skill.

There are different kinds of *mie*, but they all have a common aim, the actor must impose himself upon his audience with the maximum power of his resources. Facial expression is important and what is called *nirami*, literally glare, is a characteristic of the technique. The actor draws himself up into a pose and gestures, often with the palms outwards and fingers outstretched, at the same time he performs what is called *senkai*. In this he moves his head several times with a circular motion, the body and shoulders remaining rigid, and finally ceases the action either full face or full profile to the audience. By this time his eyes are dilated as though about to leap from their sockets and the pupils slowly turn inwards. This is *nirami*.

The *mie* has a motionless quality about it; it is the climax to all preceding movement. It may be likened to the curve of a shooting star through the sky, there is a bright flash but the flash is the apex in an arc of light, which to the eye rises and fades with even speed. This is the quality which is so important in a *mie*, it must merge in the action which precedes and follows without any apparent effort. It is unquestionably a difficult art to acquire and one which was practised far more in former times than it is today. According to many Japanese critics the real art of the *mie* has been lost and modern actors fail to get the quality of continuity in their action. Whether this is so or not, it remains a dramatic technique which appeals with its naïvety of exaggeration.

A *mie* is always performed to *tsuke*, i.e. the beating of wooden clappers in rapid tempo upon a wooden board at the right of the stage. It may be performed either standing or seated, though generally speaking a standing posture is more customary. A property known as an *aibiki* is used on the Kabuki stage, it is a kind of stool held by a stage attendant behind the actor, who supports himself against it. This gives him the effect of being seated in a way which emphasizes his dignity or power and a *mie* is often performed in such a position, usually if there is a discussion or heated words between two characters.

An action frequently used in a *mie* is one called *hadanugi*; in this the hands are pulled inwards through the sleeves of the actor's *kimono* and the upper part of the garment forced down, or the actor sometimes seizes the hem of his *kimono* and pulls it sharply back to expose his leg. A standing position is required for the most powerful type of *mie* and in this the heels may sometimes be together or sometimes apart; at other times the actor supports his body with one leg bent.

A play often concludes with all the characters posed in one big tableau, the *mie* being prominent. It creates the effect of a pictorial composition and for this reason is known as a pictorial *mie*. In such a finale, there are sometimes two leading figures performing a different style of *mie* and while there is a harmony of line in their composition, at the same time there is the feeling of straining against each other and an atmosphere of tension. It is called *hippari no mie*, literally pulling *mie*, and represents a conflict in will power.

The *mie* is a technique used by both good and evil characters who emphasize their feelings and emotions accordingly with it. It is also used by women characters on the stage more particularly when they are distraught, representing a supernatural character or someone of bold nature. There are some differences in the feminine *mie*, however, *senkai* or circling the head is on a more modified scale whilst *nirami*, staring, is never performed.

A type of *mie* which is now confined to use in one play only must be mentioned, the *Genroku mie* seen in the play *Shibaraku*. It survives from the roaring, rampaging theatre of Ichikawa Danjuro I, and to witness a performance today makes it possible to hear the ghostly shouts of appreciation of the citizens of old Yedo, as their idol, the great Danjuro, stalked the stage. In this play the hero, Kagemasa Gongoro, attired in the most bizarre and colourful costume and make-up, which gives him the appearance of a gigantic insect, and holding a monstrous sword over his shoulder, makes his exit from the stage down the *hanamichi*. As Kagemasa Gongoro leaves the stage the rest of the actors are calling out '*Arrya, korrya*' in a tempo which gradually diminishes in speed. The words are used as an exclamation rather than to give any literal meaning. The hero wears a style of theatrical costume known as *suo*, a feature of which is a long baggy trouser-like garment, that completely encases the legs and feet and trails away for several feet on the ground behind the actor. In this case the whole effect is grossly exaggerated to create a more fantastic appearance. The actor makes a vigorous exit by thrusting the left leg forward with the right leg bent, one hand holds the sword on his right shoulder, while the free arm with clenched fist is swung right back behind him and then forward again with open palm as the position of the legs is changed. With every lunge forward of his lowered body, the actor shouts aloud in time with his movements, '*Yattoku toccha, untoka na!*' The words have no meaning except as a cry of exultation which symbolizes the lusty power of the whole thing, emphasizing the concluding movement of the Genroku *mie*. It commences on the stage where the hero swaggers, struts, poses and slices off half a dozen heads, stage dummies, of course, with one sweep of his mighty sword. As he goes down the *hanamichi* in this fashion, his tempo of move-

ment gradually increases and the other actors on the stage cry
'*Dekke!* . . . How big he is!' It is a relic of the cries of admiration
used by audiences of long ago. It sums up just that quality which
the *mie* attains.

ROPPO

A spirited movement associated with the *mie* and also descended
from *aragoto* is called *roppo*. There are different kinds which are
used by the actor during his entry or exit by the *hanamichi*.
Roppo is a dancing technique which was originally based on the
exaggerated manners and behaviour of the *samurai* class in
public at the end of the seventeenth century. There is a type
known as *tanzen roppo*, which is used in several plays, another
kind called *tobi roppo*, which features in one particular drama,
and a third called *kitsune roppo*, which represents a fox spirit in
dance plays. All of them are characterized by vigorous and violent
movement.

Tanzen roppo is said by Japanese authorities to have developed
in the following fashion. During the Tenwa era (1681–3) there
were some celebrated public baths in front of the mansion of
Tango no Kami Matsudaira in Yedo. The baths were noted for
the physical attractions of the girls in attendance and were in
consequence largely patronized by the men about town. They
became named Tanzen Buro, baths in front of Tan, because of
their location. In those days, the country was at peace and the
samurai were idle. With so much leisure they passed their time
cultivating exaggerated manners of speech, walk and dress; it was
these dandies and *braggadocio* who were to be seen consorting
at the baths described. It was too good an opportunity for the
actors to miss, they soon began emulating such manners on the
stage and were received with wild acclaim by the Yedo commoners. A particular method of walking was the basis of the
technique at first, both arms being swung wide in unison, and
this is still seen in *roppo* on the stage. Many types of *roppo*
existed in the old theatre, and it became a competition among the
actors to create new forms; there were various changes through
the years but most of the earlier inventions have disappeared
now, those which remain have been incorporated and adapted to
form a general part of the actor's dancing technique.

Tobi roppo occurs in the finale of the play *Kanjincho*. Here the

Deba—Sukeroku on the hanamichi

hero, Benkei, warrior priest, goes down the *hanamichi* in boisterous manner. The actor performs a kind of hopping step which
commences slowly but increases in tempo. The right arm is
thrust out beyond the player who inclines forward on one leg
and the arm is flung back in a wide arc behind his head, as he
changes to the other foot. His left arm grasps a stave which is
held to his side and the whole action is carried out to the beating
of a drum. It symbolizes a spirit of exaltation in having escaped
from a difficult situation. *Kitsune roppo* has already been mentioned in the dancing chapter, a good example of it occurring in
the play *Michiyuki Hatsune no Tabi*. A feature of this style is
the leaping of the actor with arms bent and held high in front
of his chest, hands with fingers pointing down to the ground
rather in the posture of a begging dog. It symbolizes of course
the animal spirit which is concealed beneath a human form.

A form closely related to *tanzen roppo* is *deba*. In former days
an actor could not pass along the *hanamichi* without dancing, even
if the play did not require it. The actor's appearance was the most

important thing to the audience and *deba* assisted their admiration by emphasizing the actor's handsome presence. This practice was abandoned later but still survives in the play *Sukeroku*, in which the hero appears on the *hanamichi* with a large paper umbrella and poses and struts for the space of several minutes before he goes on to the stage itself. He represents the handsome, swaggering young idol of early Yedo; he had formerly been a *samurai* but turned commoner, and with his devil-may-care attitude feared no man. Much of his posing in this entry scene is in effect a form of *roppo*.

TATE

Another form which originally sprang from *aragoto* is *tate*. *Tate* is technique used in fighting or in more aggressive action, the term covers a wide divergence of forms under the one heading. The *mie* plays an important part in *tate*, which is sometimes devised solely for the purpose of emphasizing the *mie* to better advantage; artistically performed *mie* are considered the focus from which *tate* develops throughout a play. *Tate* emphasizes the strength of the righteous in championing the weak and the exaltation of power in overcoming the evildoer, however superior in numbers he may be. Sword fighting, called *tachimawari*, is a notable element of *tate*, the fighting is purely stylized and rhythmical in construction, although there are plays today which make it cheaply realistic. If, as often happens, the chief character in the play fights with his sword against many adversaries, who have come to seize or arrest him, there will be a lively display of acrobatics. The hero weaves in and out kicking one attacker, overturning another or seizing him by the collar, but although a rough and tumble is being staged, the aim must be for the attackers to preserve a harmony of form with the leading figure all the time and it develops into a kind of rhythmical dance.

Often what is known as a *tombo*, literally dragonfly, is performed, a high leaping somersault which requires great agility and skill. There are special actors who perform this technique. In the past it was customary for a leading actor to execute a *tombo* in the midst of a struggle to emphasize his strength and power, but the critics have it that it is a dying art today. *Tombo* is often seen performed as a diversion in the midst of the main story of the play, when a single acrobat or at most two will make an attack on the leading character. This is called *karami*.

Tate calls for special instruction, and there is always a teacher attached to every theatre whose special task is to instruct the actors in fighting technique. He is known as the *tateshi* and has invariably trained as an actor, but through his special skill and knowledge is retained as an instructor.

Pantomime or dumb show in the Kabuki is called *dammari*, and it is largely bound up with *tate*. There are different forms of *dammari*; in the more realistic type it customarily depicts the efforts of a principal character to gain supremacy over another, or wrest an object from an adversary at some lonely spot in the countryside. Another type always has an historical setting and is designed as a spectacle in which many actors take part. Sometimes a *dammari* performance is a short item inserted between other plays as an extra, but whatever form *dammari* takes, it is characterized by the use of dumb show; there is no speech of any kind to assist the actor's movements.

When *karami* takes place the leading actor is assisted by what is called a *kōken* to perform the acrobatics. The *kōken* deserves further mention. Whenever a principal actor is performing in a dancing play he will be seen sitting in dignified fashion to the rear of the stage. He is generally attired in *hakama*, traditional Japanese formal dress, or sometimes costume if the play requires it. It is his duty to help the actor with the various changes of costume on the stage, adjust it when necessary, hand him the various small properties he requires and assist him in general. It is part of the training of all young players to carry out the duties of *kōken*, which indeed is a skilled task that requires among other things a good stage presence. On special occasions even a leading actor will act as *kōken* to a colleague. Normally the pupils of actors assist their teachers in this way.

The *kōken* should not be confused with the *kyogen kata*, the people clad in a black hooded costume who dart about the stage like figures from another world. *Kyogen kata* literally means people of the play, and they perform a multitude of duties which range from prompting to wielding the *hyoshigi*, or wooden clappers, when the curtain is drawn. They always assist the actors in plays of puppet origin, and are sometimes referred to as *kurombo*, blackamoor, in view of their special costume. There is a wide difference between the *kōken* and the *kyogen kata*, for it is the task of the latter to make himself as inconspicuous as possible, whereas the former is a prominent part of the composition on the stage.

ITO NI NORU

In the plays which are of doll theatre origin, the actor frequently employs various techniques which may be listed under the one heading *ito ni noru*, keeping pace with the strings, the strings referred to being those of the *samisen*. It is the puppet's performance developed through the human actor. The rhythm expressed through the *samisen* playing and narration of *joruri* is interpreted outwardly in the movements of the actor; he matches his acting to the words of the narration and times himself by the *samisen*, to which he is subordinate, every gesture is exaggerated, but at the same time creates a harmony of pattern with the music. The simplest of movements, picking up a fan, putting down a teacup, achieve an intensity which enrich the general dramatic effect and provide a symbolic quality which is divorced from realism.

This is well exemplified in *kudoki. Kudoki*, it will be remembered, is a term used also in describing a certain musical form (see Chapter V), the implication in both cases being the same. *Kudoki* on the stage is used only to display the art of the *onnagata* or female impersonator. It depicts the innermost feelings of a woman and the love kept secret in her mind, it reveals the single-mindedness of her passion as she bewails her past and present circumstances with sighs and tears. A famous *kudoki* passage occurs in the play *Hadesugata Onna Maiginu*. In this, Osono is a faithful wife who has been deserted by her husband in favour of a courtesan. Osono's father took her away from the house of her parents-in-law, as a result, but returned her because she grieved so much. While he is discussing her affairs with her husband's parents, Osono is left alone in the room and reminisces on her unhappy fate. This is *kudoki* at its most typical. She moves about the room in time to the music carrying out all kinds of simple domestic actions, clears away the teacups, tidies the room, arranges the lamp and folds away her father-in-law's *haori*, a coat worn over the *kimono*. She gestures and weeps and moves about the room on several more errands, and finally sinks down beside the lamp in great distress. All this is pure *ito ni noru*, acting used in the case of *kudoki* to give outward expression to feminine emotions. During the scene, Osono's actions are controlled by the music and match the descriptions of the narration which is broken at intervals by her own monologue and weeping, the latter invariably forming a climax to a particular passage. This scene is regarded as one for only the most experienced artists in both the Kabuki and doll theatre. It is, for instance, one of the favourite roles of Yoshida Bungoro, the old genius of the doll theatre, and in the Kabuki it is a prerogative of the leading *onnagata* actors.

Monogatari is another characteristic form of *ito ni noru* acting. *Monogatari* is a narration of past events and happenings and often concerns the heroic deeds or tragedies of battle. By means of the *monogatari*, the actor tells a story to other people present and through them to the audience. A fan is used by the actor to perform symbolical movements while the story is being related in part by the *chobo*, and in part by himself, but every one of his movements is in harmony with the rhythm of the music, again it is pure 'keeping pace with the strings'. A very famous *monogatari* occurs in the play *Kumagai Jinya*, the camp of Kumagai. The story concerns the struggles between the Genji and Taira clans. Kumagai, a noted general of the Genji clan, has been ordered by his superior to kill Atsumori, who, though only a boy, is of Imperial blood and belongs to the Taira camp. Kumagai is in a plight, for in the past, both he and his wife owed their lives to Atsumori's mother, and yet he must do his duty to the cause he is fighting for. To satisfy his leader and his conscience, he substitutes the head of his own son for that of Atsumori, whom he has taken prisoner. This form of sacrifice is a favourite theme in many of the *jidaimono* plays. The story of the play is based on an actual historical event which is famous in Japanese literature. The substitution of the boy's head is a creation of the theatre introduced in order to give dramatic surprise and suspense. The true facts have it that Kumagai actually beheaded Atsumori in battle, but afterwards, appalled at the tragedy of the boy's fate, became a monk and retired from the world to pray for the repose of the boy's soul. In the play Kumagai also renounces his military career and becomes a monk in the final scene.

The *monogatari* takes place when Kumagai describes to his

wife and to Atsumori's mother, who has arrived to try to stab him, how the boy was slain. Everyone is unaware of Kumagai's tragic secret which is well concealed in the story he tells. It is customary when a *monogatari* is about to commence for the *chobo* narrator or *tayu* to sing: '*Monogataran to za o kamae*— he sat erect about to tell his story.' Kumagai is seated holding a large gold fan on which is a scarlet rising sun, the emblem of the Genji. With this he performs movements which represent combatants on horseback, the brandishing of swords and the pinning down of a captive; his monologue alternates with that of the *chobo* narrator in unfolding the tragic events past and his movements are co-ordinated to the rhythm of the music. Atsumori's mother is weeping bitterly as she hears of her son's noble behaviour in his last hour and a famous passage of Kumagai's narrative runs:

'. . . Those words moved me to tears. My son Kojiro may lose his life just like that young man on whom I sat astride. What cruel sufferings a warrior must undergo! With such feelings I could scarcely draw my sword when Hirayama called out behind, "Kumagai, if you spare Atsumori while sitting astride him you must be called a traitor!" Then I made up my mind, what could I do? I told him, if you have any word to leave behind I will listen and convey your message. He said with tears, "Father went down at sea, my mother is my only concern, formerly she lived in Imperial circles, but now the situation has changed and I am worried how she fares. This is the only thing I fear in going to the next world. Convey my words to her, Kumagai, please." After his words I had no choice but to behead him.' This is a typical piece of *monogatari*. The use of the fan in *monogatari* is called *shikata banashi*.

The custom of beheading a high ranking adversary in combat and presenting the head for proof, was an ancient procedure which gave rise to a special technique on the Kabuki stage known as *kubijikken*. This again is *ito ni noru*. On the stage the head is contained in a wooden cylindrical box, *kubioke*, the top of which is lifted off by the character whose duty it is to inspect the head for proof. The inspection always marks an emotional climax in a play and is conducted in an atmosphere of great suspense, the more so as the head is invariably one that has been substituted for personal reasons of sacrifice, in place of the one of the supposed victim. The movements of the actor performing such a scene are slow and deliberate and accompanied by a good deal of facial expression, but at the same time it is done in conjunction with the timing of the *chobo*. *Kubijikken* sounds rather bloody and horrifying to Western ears, but there is a certain impersonal and abstract quality about it all which marks it as a device for creating dramatic suspense rather than a desire to display gory realism.

Another favourite device of *ito ni noru* technique is what is called *teoi no jukkai*. This consists of the confessions of one who is dying and regretting past misdeeds, always in the agonies of a severe injury, more often than not due to *seppuku* or *harakiri*. If not exactly an evil character the dying person has always some repentance to make and such scenes reveal a general connection with the Buddhist tenet known as *modori*, or return, according to which man is born fundamentally good and on his death, whatever his earthly sins, he returns to his original state. *Teoi no jukkai* is naturally highly emotional in its appeal and among the feminine members of the audience at any rate, such occasions call for much surreptitious brushing away of stray tears.

Gochushin is one more form of *ito ni noru*. This technique is seen in *jidaimono* plays, when a brave young warrior returns from the field of battle to report how the fight is going to his superiors. The actor playing such a part wears a special form of costume and carries an unsheathed sword in one hand, making his entry by the *hanamichi*. On arrival on the stage, or sometimes on the *hanamichi* itself, he goes down on one knee and cries, '*Gochushin, gochushin!*', meaning 'I have come to report to you'. He then tells his story in words and gestures with his sword in time to the rhythm of the music. The actor uses a sword here in the same way that the fan is used in the *monogatari* described earlier. *Monogatari* literally means a narrated account or description and *gochushin* and *teoi no jukkai*, therefore, are really forms of *monogatari*, but the term is usually more specifically applied to stage technique when it takes the form described in the first instance.

All these forms came from the doll theatre and might be said to represent the puppet turned human. There is one technique which puts the process in reverse and turns the human actor into a puppet. It is called *ningyo ni naru*, literally becoming a doll. It

Yoten costume worn for gochushin technique

is often seen when the curtain is first drawn; the actors are all in position and remain motionless and expressionless until they suddenly spring to life at the command of the musical accompaniment. There is a good example of this in the celebrated play *Chushingura*, the figures on the stage are sitting with bent heads when the play opens and they raise them one by one according to the announcement of the *chobo*. A somewhat different version of *ningyo ni naru* is seen in the play *Kinkakuji*, or 'The Golden Pavilion'. The heroine, Yukihime, has been confined in the house of an evil nobleman who has her bound with ropes to a cherry tree in his garden. The falling blossoms of the tree turn into white rats, who gnaw through the ropes and free Yukihime. At this point two stage attendants appear dressed as *ningyo tsukai*, or doll handlers, and Yukihime proceeds to do a charming dance among the fallen blossoms at their behest, exactly as though she were a doll. It is an inconsequential interlude which emphasizes that touch of fantasy inherent in the Kabuki and adds a never failing variety to the performance.

SERIFU, THE SPEECH OF THE ACTOR

In the Kabuki the speech of the actor himself is referred to as *serifu.* Jōruri does not relieve the actor from the necessity of cultivating a good speaking voice and eloquence is as necessary an accomplishment to the Kabuki player as. it is to those on any other stage, and one old theatre maxim had it that it was the first requirement in any actor.

Serifu can be defined under two headings, monologue or *dokuhaku*, and dialogue or *taihaku*. These forms are used both individually and in conjunction with *joruri*. Some uses of monologue have already been touched upon in the descriptions of *ito ni noru* technique. In all true Kabuki *serifu* the use of rhythmical metre and conventional forms of intonation is common in some degree. Even in the more realistic plays these qualities are present in some part of the *serifu*, while the natural rhythm of the Japanese language is also used to provide a degree of euphony that it is impossible to describe in words. Much of the speech used in the older Kabuki plays is archaic in construction and not readily understood if heard for the first time, furthermore it is often distorted to make a rhythmical sound pattern rather than a straightforward literary statement. Plays such as those of the *sewamono* type use the colloquial speech of the Yedo period which is familiar today, even if many of its forms are no longer used in ordinary speech. There are, of course, modern Kabuki plays in which the *serifu* used is more or less straightforward colloquial speech. For instance, in *Saigo to Butahime* by Ikeda Daigo, who died in 1942, the dialogue of Kyoto is heard.

Some *serifu* is even meaningless and used only for special effect, as the passage in *Shibaraku* quoted at the beginning of the chapter. Playing on words and punning is a very common device in *serifu* and to break the monotony in long speeches, the same phrase is repeated with variations often with a double meaning, a device known as *nani nani zukushi*. *Serifu* sometimes contains references which may be obscure to the layman unless the sources are understood, a case in point being the use of Buddhist terminology in *Kanjincho*.

What is called *tsurane*, or relay dialogue, is used when a long line of actors all playing similar parts, e.g. a company of *tobi* or firemen of old Yedo, line up on the *hanamichi* and recite individual pieces one after another all the way down the line. Another *serifu* device often heard is *warizerifu*. In this three or more actors relate an event or happening, the speech of each

player being recited in sequence to form the complete statement. The New Year celebration play *Soga no Taimen* contains
good examples. The plot describes how the Soga brothers, Juro
and Goro, meet their bitter enemy Suketsune for the first time
since they were small children; Suketsune was responsible for the
death of their father and he now begins to realize that retribution
has come to him.

Suketsune:

Now I remember, it was around October the tenth in the
second year of Angen . . . young retainers of Izu and Sagami
provinces followed Yoritomo to the hunting. Returning from
the hunt they wished to console him. . . .

Juro:

A horseman came riding without the least knowledge of the
men in ambush on the Kashiwa Toge slopes of Mount Akazawa,
it was Sukeyasu. . . .

Suketsune:

He was clad in hunting cloth and carried a bow bound with the
young shoots of the bead tree.

Juro:

His bamboo hat was weathered by the winds. . . .

Goro:

In his path there were places difficult to ride a horse but he
avoided them. . .

Omi Kotota:

Expectantly waiting behind the trees was Omi no Kogenta, the
first to attack. . . .

Hachimansaburo:

The second was Saburo Yukiuji who shot an arrow successfully. . . .

Suketsune:

Omoidaseba o soreyo. . . . Angen ninen Kannazuki,
Toka amari no koto nari shiga,
Suke dono o nagusamento,
Izu Sagami no waka dono hara,
Okunonokari no kaerusa ni. . . .

Juro:

Akazawa yama no minami ozaki,
Kashiwa Toge no hanpuku ni,

Hito ya matsu tomo shiratsukige no,
Koma matagari Sukeyasu ga. . . .
Suketsune:
Shikamo sono hi no hidetari wa,
Akino no suttaru kariginu ni,
Sendan do no yumi tazusae,
Juro:
Takegasu satto kogarashi ni fuki so rashii,
Goro:
Zessho akusha no kire enaku,
Shizu, shinzu to o ayumasetari.
Omi Kotota:
Machimoketaru konata niwa,
Shinoki samban kotate ni tori,
Ichi no mabushi wa Omi no Kogento.
Hachimansaburo:
Nini mabushi wa Saburo Yukiuji
Kitte hanateba ayamatazu. . . .

This typifies *warizerifu*, but an English translation of such a passage cannot convey the rhythmic order of the words, for the dialogue of each actor rises and falls with an emphasis on certain endings that only the original Japanese can give. The romanized version given here is in the correct order, the speech of each actor being broken down into the separate lines which give the metre.

The citizens of Yedo were famed for their repartee and this is embodied in the actor's *serifu* by what is called *akutai*, defiant or abusive talk characteristic of the *Edokko*, or citizen of Yedo. The play *Sukeroku* makes full use of it and that spoken by Agemaki, the courtesan, is counted a model of its kind. The ability to speak it effectively is considered a true test for the actor in this role. In the first scene in the play, Agemaki is abusing Ikyu, an evil old roué who is slighting her lover, the gay, handsome, swashbuckling Sukeroku. Sukeroku typifies the idol of the town in former days, a genuine *Edokko*. Part of a well-known passage is quoted here to give the general effect, but it should be realized that translation in another language cannot convey the same nuances as the original.

Agemaki:

'Hey, Ikyu, when I compare you with Sukeroku he is a man as handsome as you look wicked and ill natured, let me talk by simile. You may be compared to the difference between snow and ink. Every *suzuri* (ink stone) has a *umi* (water container), the straits of Naruto are also called Naruto no Umi. Although the word is the same *umi*, the former is shallow while the latter is deep. My feelings towards you and Sukeroku are just like that, shallow for you who are only a patron, and deep for Sukeroku who is my lover. With no real lover the life of a courtesan is plunged into darkness but even in that darkness I would not mistake you for my dear Sukeroku, not I!'

(*Moshi Ikyu san, omae to Sukeroku san wa konarabete miru toki wa acchi wa rippana otokoburi kochi wa ijino waru so na tatoete iwaba yuki to sumi suzuri no umi mo Naruto no umi mo umi to yugi wa hitotsu demo fukai to asai wa kyaku to mabu. Sa! mabu ga nakereba joro wa yami kuragari de mitemo omae to Sukeroku san tori chigaete narumono kai na.*)

The Japanese naturally contains a sparkle and pace, lacking in the clumsiness of translation.

The actor's narration is often enlivened by an important technique known as *shichigo cho*, or seven-five syllable metre. It was commonly heard in popular songs, and is also used a great deal in the Kabuki. When it occurs in the *serifu* of the actor it is referred to as *yakuharai*. It is a favourite device in the *sewamono* plays and the dramatist Kawatake Mokuami was fond of introducing it into his work. *Yakuharai* is often heard suddenly in a play when an actor who has certain facts to relate relapses into *shichigo cho*, the general effect being as though he is reciting a poem and thus giving a dramatic emphasis to the situation. There is a classic example in the popular play *Genyadana*. In this, Yosaburo, a handsome young man who has sunk to the gutter, appears at the house of a certain lady with his rascally companion. Otomi, the lady, turns out to be Yosaburo's former lover for whom he has suffered all his misfortunes. In great disgust, he makes an impassioned speech which is a highlight of the play and is rendered in *shichigo cho*. While the actor is reciting this passage there is the low accompaniment of a single *samisen* from the *kuromisu*. The romanized Japanese version is given here, again broken down into the lines which give the rhythmical quality but it is impossible to give the inflections of the actor's voice which in this speech rises and falls, races through a sentence or pauses to draw the words out in long emphasis in such a fashion as to bring a variety of colour to the whole speech. In the first line, for instance, there is great emphasis on the two words '*Shigane koi*', which are almost hurled out, with a powerful intonation, there being a long emphasis on the word *koi*, the next three words '*no nasake ga*' follow in a slightly lower but more or less even tone. The first syllable of the word '*ada*', i.e. *a*, drops considerably, the following syllable *da* being raised to a sharp final which closes the line with a snap.

(*Shigane koi no nasake no ada,*
Inochi no tsuna no kireta no wo,
Dotoritometeka Kisarazu kara,
Meguru tsukihi mo mitose goshi,
Edo no oya nya kando uke,
Yondokoronaku Kamakura no yatsu shichi go wo kuitsumetemo,
Tsura ni uketaru kamban no,
Kizu ga mokke no sewe ni,
Kirare Yosa to imyo wo tori,
Oshigari yusuri mo narawo yori,
Nareta jide no Genjidana,
Sono shirabake ka kurobe no koshizukuri no kakoimono,
Shinda to omotta Otomi ta,
Oshaka sama demo ki ga tsuku me,
Yokumo onusha tassha de ita na. . . .)

This may be translated as follows:

Because of my chance love for you, three years ago, I was on the verge of death. Fortunately, or unfortunately, I had a narrow escape from Kisarazu. My parents in Yedo disowned me and I had nowhere to go, so I called on one acquaintance after another in Kamakura. When I could find no one else to help me, I took advantage of my scarred features, as I was nicknamed Kirare Yosa. And here in Genjidana I found a mistress living in a house with a latticed door, surrounded by a high black fence. I thought you were long since dead, Otomi. Even the great Buddha himself could not know you were living in circumstances like these. You've done very nicely, haven't you. . . .

This type of dialogue, *yakuharai*, may on occasion be employed by two actors speaking in rotation instead of just the one player, but the same rhythmical effect is achieved.

KESHŌ, THE MAKE-UP OF THE ACTOR

One of the outstanding features of the Kabuki actor's make-up, or *keshō*, is the use of painted faces known as *kumadori*. It is a characteristic shared with the Chinese theatre. There are differences in treatment in the two, Chinese *lien p'u* as they are called, being in general more complicated and brightly coloured, as well as more numerous in the number of different designs used. In the Chinese version, the face is divided into separate areas of colour, which are often based on shapes like those of the bat, butterfly or moth, and they completely hide the muscular formation of the face. Both Chinese and Japanese painted faces have a common function, however, they symbolize qualities of human nature.

The origin of the painted face in the Chinese theatre is uncertain, but it was definitely used in the theatre of the Ming Dynasty (1368–1644). Ichikawa Danjuro I (1660–1704) was the innovator of the *kumadori*, or painted face, of the Kabuki theatre, but it is more than likely that the idea first came from China and Danjuro adapted it to suit the purposes of the Kabuki drama.

The Japanese *kumadori* is simpler than its Chinese counterpart, being generally a bold linear pattern which exaggerates the muscular delineation of the face. It serves to retain a tensity in the emotional expression of the actor's face, while at the same time adding to the general colourful effect of his appearance and defining his character. The *kumadori* usually consists of bold lines of colour painted around the brows, cheeks, eyes and mouth of the actor in symmetrical curves. One edge of all the lines in a pattern is softened to give a gradation of colour and this is known as *bokashi*. It was a device first used by Ichikawa Danjuro II (1688–1758), who is said to have conceived the idea looking at the petals of a peony in his garden. It sounds very feasible, as Danjuro II was responsible for developing and completing the art of the *kumadori* initiated by his father, and it is the kind of

A kumadori make-up: suji kuma

incident that might happen to any artist casting about for new ideas for his work.

The principal colours used in *kumadori* are red and black on a white background. In making-up, the actor applies the colours with a brush, working down from the brow and the eyes. Every Kabuki actor wears what is known as a *habutae*, which is a form of skull cap made of silk that fits tightly round the forehead. It acts as a foundation for the wig and a protective covering for the actor's hair, and the *kumadori* design can be carried right up over the front of the *habutae*. After applying a foundation dressing of oil the actor covers the whole of his face, neck and the front of the *habutae* with *oshiroi*, a matt white cream which gives a smooth surface. Both the eyebrows and the lips are obliterated with *oshiroi*, the coloured design including eyebrows are then painted on this white surface.

There is a variation of *kumadori* known as *aiguma*, which is used for the faces of demons, spirits and people of evil character, and in this the predominating colour is indigo. Brown is another colour used in the faces of fiends. Many styles developed from the original designs of Danjuro II, and actors handed on to their successors their own variations. A number of the old designs have become obsolete on the stage today, but several, particularly of Danjuro II's, remain in constant use. Three important designs which came from Danjuro II are the *suji kuma*, the *mukimi* and the *ippon kuma*. The *suji kuma* represents a courageous warrior with an expression of rage and indignation; it was first used by Danjuro I but later adapted by his son, using the *bokashi* technique, in which form it has remained. In this design, the eyebrows sweep upwards in bold black curves which are offset by the broad graded lines of red, which also curve upwards from the nose and brow and round the cheeks.

Mukimi, the second of Danjuro's most notable make-ups, is used for a youthful and handsome hero. It is seen in roles such as Sukeroku and Goro in *Soga no Taimen*. In *mukimi* the greater part of the face is covered with the same dead white and painted with two spatula-shaped eyebrows, which are set in straight lines at a slight angle. Gradated red lines beneath the eyes curve up to meet the outer tips of the eyebrows. The top lip is outlined as a thin curve in red, with a touch of black at each corner, which imparts a downward twist to the line of the mouth.

Ippon kuma was adapted from the *suji kuma* of Danjuro I and also represents the expression of a young hero. It is used by Umeo Maru in the play *Kuruma Bikki* and the father lion in the dance play *Renjishi*. It is characterized by an almost vertical broad red line taken upwards from the outer corner of the eyes, while the nostrils are heavily outlined in red. Another old style of *kumadori* still in use is the *saru kuma*, invented by Nakamura Denkuro (*circa* 1622–1713). It represents a brave man of yore, but it has a humorous expression and takes its name from its resemblance to a monkey's face. It is seen in the play *Soga no Taimen*.

The original from which all designs for female devils and fiends sprang is called the *hanaya*, and was devised by Yamanaka Heikuro (1632–1724). It forms the basis for the design used by actors in the role of the spirit of the serpent in the dancing play *Musume Dojoji*, although different actors adopt variations of their own in this case. The *hanaya* is a fearsome make-up whose indigo lines are painted in a writhing pattern, the eyes and mouth being heavily outlined in black, the lips giving the impression of a snarl.

In some of the roles which use *kumadori* the arms and legs of the actor are also shown with the muscular formation emphasized to form a conventional pattern using *bokashi*. Formerly the design was actually painted on the limbs of the actor, but now it is done on what are known as *meriyasu*, close-fitting coverings of thin cloth over the legs and arms.

The make-up of the *onnagata*, or female impersonator, is in direct contrast to the *kumadori*. It portrays a symbolic ideal of a woman's beauty and facial appearance. In the case of young maidens, princesses and similar roles, the convention aimed at is that of the *urizane gao*, the oval-shaped face with a small mouth, named after its supposed resemblance to a melon seed. Such a face was the mark of feminine beauty in the eighteenth century and is seen time and time again in the prints of an artist like Utamaro (1753–1806).

Facial contour is an important factor in deciding what roles an actor may play. A broad round face, for instance, is a disadvantage to anyone wishing to play the great feminine roles of the Kabuki stage however skilful an actor he may be. The appearance of the leading characters in the various plays is characterized by conventions which must be reproduced again and again for audiences and the use of traditional make-ups assists this process. One of the secrets of Kabuki make-up is to achieve a harmony when natural features are the wrong shape by the skilful emphasis or reduction in the delineation of eyes, mouth and brows, but unless his face has the correct general proportions, the actor is under a handicap.

Actors playing the part of matrons and married women always blacken their teeth. This was actually the custom of all Japanese women who achieved marital status in former days and further-more they shaved off their eyebrows. Both customs are still per-petuated on the Kabuki stage. A substance known as *ohaguro* is used in the theatre to achieve the appearance of blackened teeth, it is made from a mixture of black sugar and the resin of pine cones. In all foundation make-up, the eyebrows of the actor are in any case obliterated under the *oshiroi*, and in the case of married women roles this is all that is necessary. In the young unmarried women or courtesan roles, the eyebrows are first pencilled in lightly in rouge or *beni*, and afterwards drawn firmly in with *sumi* or black. The effect aimed at is the most delicate line of brow and to facilitate this in their make-up, most *onnagata* keep their own brows trimmed.

The dead white of the *onnagata's* make-up with its finely shaded brows is relieved by the outer corners of the eyes being marked in with rouge and the curves of the small mouth painted in with *kuchi beni*, lip rouge. Sometimes in the case of young maidens a delicate pink tinge is given to the cheeks and around the eyes by rubbing in rouge or *ho ho beni* with the *oshiroi*.

The white face with firmly marked eyebrows and rouged eye corners is also used with a bolder emphasis in handsome young male roles. Child actors, too, use this flat white make-up, as do actors playing some of the *kataki yaku*, or villain parts, but in the last case there will be a heavy outlining of the eyes, brows and mouth with *sumi*, the lips being given a heavy downward sneer. The faces of the aged are made up with sallow complexions and deeply drawn lines in much the same way as in the Western theatre.

There are dozens of variations within the styles of make-up named here, but they all adhere to the general principles out-lined.

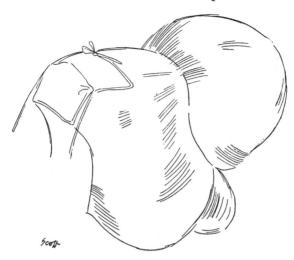

Katsuyama mage: a theatrical wig

KATSURA, THE WIGS OF THE ACTOR

The *katsura*, or wig, is a vital accessory in the costume and make-up of the Kabuki actor. There are scores of varieties based on the hairdressing fashions of men and women in the past, each of them has symbolical as well as decorative significance and a knowledge of them will enable the spectator to deduct the character, status, age or nature of occupation of the wearers. The *katsura* of the Kabuki retain a special significance in themselves as visible reminders of their drama for Japanese theatre-goers.

The wigs are made from real hair, which in the past was largely imported from China, and they are the creations of master craftsmen who devote their lives to their art. In addition to the wig makers there are the wig dressers, *tokoyama*. They are indispensable members of the theatre staff, for their job is to dress and repair the wigs for each day's performance, complicated processes which require long hours of painstaking and accurate workmanship. Backstage of any Kabuki theatre will be found the wig room; here sit the *tokoyama*, highly skilled craftsmen who spend as long as ten years in apprenticeship before they are fitted to take up their task. Each *tokoyama* is responsible for several wigs during the monthly performance and he must be on the alert to go to the dressing rooms with a wig in perfect order for fitting before an actor's call comes, the wig being returned to his charge after the performance. The *tokoyama* work in small groups of four or five under the direction of a master craftsman. One of these in the Kabuki za, Tokyo, known to his colleagues as *Tora Chan*, the tiger, has with his assistants given long hours of most valuable help to the writer. These types of craftsmen are remarkable men; day in day out they work steadily at their appointed tasks, their lives are bound up in the theatre, they eat, talk and sleep theatre. They have little recreation and if it comes to that little recompense, their task in life is to see a job of craftsmanship well done. Endowed with a sense of humour, their philosophy of life is bounded by the standards of workmanship, not gain; they do not understand those who think otherwise. These characteristics are not peculiar to the *tokoyama* only, but to all that body of craftsmen who by their unsparing efforts keep the theatre alive, the small property men and many others too numerous to mention at this stage.

Wig making, like all crafts in Japan, is a family tradition which is carried on from generation to generation. When the plays for a performance have been decided, about ten days beforehand preparations are set in hand for making the wigs. The measurements of an actor's head have been taken and those of all the principal actors are known to the craftsman. It is possible, for instance, for anyone familiar with the actors to know their individual wigs just by looking at them, for each actor imparts his own characteristics to a particular wig, although the same style is used time and time again by different people. From the measurements a thin copper framework, *daigane*, is prepared. This is the foundation of the wig which is fitted over an actor's head for adjustments, a process known as *awase*. The hair is attached to silk known as *habutae* fitted over the metal foundation and after this, the wig is ready to be made up by the *tokoyama*.

The most complicated and elaborate wigs are naturally those of the *onnagata* and they can be divided into several classes; *hime*, young ladies of high birth; *musume*, maidens and young girls of the ordinary classes; *nyobo*, middle class married women; *gegi*, *geisha* and *keisei*, courtesans. Within the main divisions there are many different styles, each of which has its own particular name among the *tokoyama*, some of them containing technical references which are lost upon the layman.

A geisha showing the taka shimada hair style

During the Tokugawa era, it became customary for women to wear their hair done up in a knot, or *mage*, instead of hanging loose which had been characteristic of former times. After the Genroku era the introduction of a dressing known as *kyara abura* enabled new styles to be created by allowing the locks to be held firmly in place. Many fashions were devised to suit people of different ages and status and for different occasions and these became more and more complex as time went on. As the styles themselves became more complicated, so too did the many hair ornaments used, made of a variety of materials such as silver, tortoiseshell, lacquered wood and so on. There were bars around which the hair was knotted known as *kogai*, long pins for fastening known as *kotoji*, combs of different shapes, *kushi*, ornamental pins and decorations called *kanzashi* and *bira*, while strips of crepe silk known as *tegara* and gold and silver threads were also used as hair decoration. The styles of this period and the various ornaments used are embodied in a large proportion of the wigs worn by the *onnagata* on the Kabuki stage.

The main parts of any wig, male or female, may be listed as *mae gami*, the hair above the forehead or front hair, the *bin*, the sweep of hair at either side of the face, the *tabo*, the coil of hair in the nape of the neck, and the *mage*, or knot, on the top. These are dressed with special pomades which allow the hair to be set in firm and glossy shapes. The many styles of knot used in the case of women have given rise to a great variety of fashions, but two basic forms are important on the stage, they are the *shimada* and the *marumage*. The first is used by young unmarried women and the second by married women. Until before the war versions of these two styles, which had remained unchanged in essentials since the Yedo period, were the accepted traditional hair styles for Japanese women. They still survive, but the *marumage* is rarely seen worn except by some old-fashioned type of woman from remoter districts; the *shimada* is worn by the *geisha* and young people on festive occasions, while the bride in a traditional Japanese wedding customarily wears it, but in wig form, since the proportion of women who wear their hair naturally long and dressed in the old styles is negligible today.

The *marumage* is seen a great deal in the *sewamono* plays, while in the *jidaimono* a wig is often worn in married women roles called the *katsuyama*. This was in fact the original style which later gave rise to the *marumage*. When the actor wears a *katsuyama* wig, a little patch of purple silk is attached by a tape on the front of it directly over the forehead. This is known as the *boshi tsuki no katsura*, literally head covering attached to the wig; the *tokoyama* refers to it as the *murasaki boshi*, or purple head covering. It is sometimes seen in grey on the wig of an elderly woman role, in which case it is referred to as *baba boshi* by the wig dressers, i.e. grandmother head covering. The *boshi tsuki* is one of those curious traditions so common in the Kabuki which have a significance now lost in the past. When the Wakashu Kabuki was prohibited by the authorities in 1652, the actors of the time were ordered to keep their hair shaved on the front of the head to prevent their appearing too attractive, with the result that they took to wearing pieces of various coloured silks to cover the offending spots. Later this became the distinguishing mark of the *onnagata*, or female impersonator, who always wore the

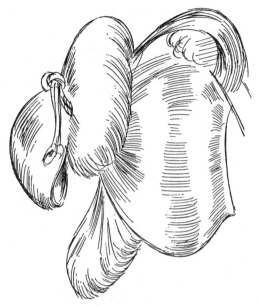

Tsubushi shimada: a theatrical wig

boshi tsuki both on the stage and off. It is always worn with the *katsuyama* on the stage and with other hair styles on occasion. The *shimada*, a name which refers to the *mage* or knot of this particular hair style, has many variations. There are two different opinions as to the origin of the name as a hairdressing mode, one being that it was a style favoured by the courtesans of Shimada, a town on the Tokaido highway and another that it was originated by a Kabuki actor called Shimada Mankichi in the Kanei era (1624–43). Clay figures found buried in ancient tombs show a similar hair fashion, however, so it would seem to have very early origins indeed. Whatever the true origin, during the Yedo or Tokugawa era, it was adopted as the hair style of the young unmarried women of town and country and first became popular about 1659. Around 1685 it was taken up by the courtesans of Shimada and so received its name. During the Genroku era certain refinements were adapted to this coiffure.

The *taka shimada* is one of the representative versions, in this the *bin* or side pieces of the hair are made as ample as possible and the *mage* or knot is elevated above the crown of the head. It is very often seen worn by palace maids and attendants in

Kabuki plays; a formal style worn only by young and unmarried women, it later gave rise to another form known as the *tsubushi shimada*, literally flattened down *shimada*. This is also an important theatrical wig. It was first created in the Tempo era (1830–43), and in some cases replaced the *taka shimada* as a style. It became very popular with the *geisha* and was also adopted by the courtesans of Yoshiwara although they wore it in slightly different fashion, being a little higher at the back. Because of its connections with the gay quarters the *tsubushi shimada* fell into disfavour with many women and eventually it became the prerogative of the *geisha* who still use it, although only in wig form. In the Kabuki, two styles are used; it is often seen in courtesan roles, but on occasion it is worn by actors playing a different kind of part. The *uiwata* is another type of *shimada mage* which was worn by the daughters of townspeople in the later Yedo period, it is commonly used in the *sewamono* plays.

Actors who play the parts of a princess or young unmarried lady of high family always wear a wig known as the *fukiwa* which is characterized by a high broad *mage* and elaborate hair ornaments.

One more wig worn by the *onnagata* must be mentioned, the highly ornate coiffure of the *oiran*, or courtesan. This is characterized by what is called the *hyōgo mage*, an exaggerated semicircular arrangement of the hair at the back, which by means of false hair is made to stand up stiffly from the head. The whole coiffure is ornamented still further by the use of large *kanzashi*, *kotoji* and *kushi*. A large knot of gold thread is worn on the back of the *hyōgo mage*. It is a replica of the actual hair style formerly used by the courtesans in the gay quarters and can be seen portrayed again and again in the *ukiyoe* prints of Utamaro (1753–1806). The wearing of this wig is no small feat on the part of the actor, as it is exceedingly heavy and, worn in conjunction with the elaborate costume that is used in the courtesan's role, provides a test of endurance which would daunt any but the most skilled player.

A special technique used in certain plays by the *onnagata* actors, called *kami o sabuku*, requires what might be termed a trick wig. For this, the actor must suddenly let down the hair to present a dishevelled appearance. It signifies a state of mind when a woman loses her feminine character, i.e. turns into an evil spirit or becomes mad with jealousy or aggressive. The wig is constructed so that, by a quick pull of threads, an elaborate coiffure can suddenly be released and allowed to hang down as loose hair.

The most elaborate wigs worn in the male roles are those used in *aragoto* plays; in these hair styles are exaggerated in grotesque fashion with no attempt at reality. One example is the fantastic *bin* or sidepiece of the wig known as *kuruma bin*. The projecting portions are waxed and polished and the making of it is considered one of the more difficult tasks for the wig maker and the *toko-yama*. The illustration will give some idea of its appearance. It is symbolical of supernatural strength and the courage of a hero. A style of wig commonly worn in *kataki yaku* or villain roles is the *oji*, a bushy mane which hangs loose down the back bound into a single tail. It symbolizes a man of high birth or position who is engaged in some scheme or plot to usurp power.

Apart from the more fantastic wigs which exaggerate particular features for symbolical purposes, those of the male role actors adhere realistically to the hair styles in use in old Japan. The principal features of the male and female wigs are exactly the same, i.e. *mae gami*, *bin*, *mage* and *tabo*. The *mae gami* or forelock in a male wig signifies a boy or youth, for it was the practice of all adult men to shave the front part of their head. The size of the area shaved and the style of *mage* or top knot varied through the years and defined the various styles of men's hairdressing, which indicated rank and status by certain differences. It was considered essential to keep the hair oiled and dressed daily as well as the front part of the head cleanly shaven. The shaven part of the crown is represented by a thin blue plate fitted on the top of a theatrical wig, around which the hair is built up. Sometimes a stage character is seen to have the shaven part of his head covered with a thick, bristly growth which shows someone of unkempt appearance, who may be a bad character, a gaol bird, or a sick man or, alternatively, one who is living in hiding away from the amenities of civilization. There were two main methods of wearing the top knot in the early Yedo period, and both these are seen in various forms on the Kabuki stage. The first was called *chasengami*, because of the resemblance to a whisk used in the tea ceremony. The lower part of the knot was coiled tightly with string, so that the top half

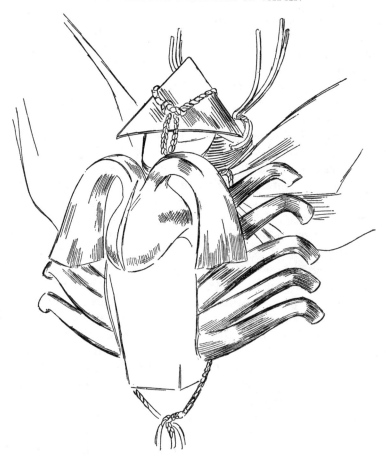

Kuruma bin: a theatrical wig

stood out from the head in a large tuft. In the second method, the knot was stiffened with wax in a cylindrical shape and bent forward over the crown in various lengths, this was called the *mitu ori* style.

Later in the Yedo period, the shaven part of the head became smaller in area and the sidelocks more elaborate, while a knot called the *chō mage* became the vogue, worn flat along the centre of the crown almost as far as the forehead. This style is seen a great deal in the *sewamono* plays and was the hair fashion that remained in vogue until the Meiji Restoration of 1868 when all men commenced to crop their hair and the *mage* was abolished.

Wigs for child actors playing boys' parts in the Yedo era show the *mae gami* or forelock left intact, the head being shaved between the forelock and the *mage* as was the custom. Priests on the Kabuki stage wear what is called a *marubozu*. It could hardly be termed a wig, for it is made of very thin metal and fits closely to the head giving the ecclesiastical appearance of the Buddhist priest whose head is completely shaved. To name all the wigs used in the Kabuki is an impossible task here, it would require a book in itself. What has been described therefore represents some of the basic styles only.

ISHŌ, THE COSTUMES OF THE ACTOR

The character of a personality depicted in a Kabuki role is symbolically represented by outward appearance. The costume in conjunction with the make-up is largely responsible for this. Every traditional role had its costume strictly defined down to the last detail and woe betide any actor or costume man who ran counter to this in the past. There is a little latitude today and leading actors may adopt their own preferences in colours and patterns, but on the whole there has been no change in the main styles of the dress worn in the most famous roles during two hundred years.

Just as in the case of the wigs, there is a special room in every theatre where the costume experts or *ishō kata* work. Here the costumes are stored folded up flat on shelves and are kept ironed and pressed and ready for each performance. Like the wig dressers, the costume men are all skilled technicians, who work under the direction of an expert whose family have carried on the same work for generations. Once a new performance has been decided, he must see that all the correct costumes are available; it is an intricate task especially in the case of some of the female costumes, which all have their special *obi*, undergarments and accessories. If new costumes have to be made, the head of the *ishō kata's* room must consult the many different types of craftsmen required to produce the finished garments. There are the dyers, the embroiderers and the dressmakers themselves. Sketches are prepared and the finished costume finally has to be fitted personally in the case of a leading actor.

The *ishō kata* are responsible for garments and the accessories that go with them. Hats, headdresses and footwear are the responsibility of the small property men, as is also all armour used in military scenes.

The layman is apt to think of costume in the Kabuki as being historically accurate and representing the true costume of former days. This is only half a truth. Of course Kabuki costume is based on the dress worn in the past, but it is often exaggerated or changed to suit dramatic purposes; stage effect is considered before anything else. Besides this, many of the older plays make no attempt at consistency and the costumes and hair styles of Yedo times are indiscriminately mixed with those of earlier periods.

In the *sewamono* plays, which deal with the lives of the commoners in the latter part of the Yedo period, costume in all the roles is consistently authentic and these can be more or less called genuine period pieces. There are modern types of plays which pay great attention to accuracy of historical costume, but it must be confessed they are apt to be very dull. One of the delightful qualities of the genuine Kabuki is the use of costume as fantasy rather than realism, this apart from the *sewamono* plays, whose realistic costumes have a quietly dramatic effect of their own.

As with the wigs of the actor, the costumes all bear technical terms which are used by the men who look after them. There are so many varieties that again it would be impossible to list them in detail. Certain basic styles occur throughout the drama, together with techniques of the actor which depend on the wearing of special costumes. These things are described and illustrated here to provide a general understanding.

The word *kimono* used in speaking of Japanese costume is a generic name which literally means a thing to wear. It is applied to both men's and women's dress. It might be described as a loose, full-sleeved garment which covers the whole of the body and is bound round the waist with an *obi* or sash. A *kimono* may be made of silk or cotton, plain or patterned and lined or unlined. The cut of the *eri*, or collar, length of the *sode*, or sleeve, and the *suso*, or hem, are the main features which in the past have been varied to define the character of different wearers; particularly in the case of women, the basic form of the *kimono* has remained unchanged for hundreds of years.

The *obi* is a characteristic accessory to the *kimono*. In the case of men it has been relatively simple and severe but for women it became a highly ornamental feature of their costume. Made of heavy brocade or damask silk, the modern *obi* is about two feet wide and eleven feet long and is wound round the waist and fastened in an elaborate knot at the back. It is further secured with a silk braided cord, known as the *obi domi*, knotted around its centre. The methods of tying the *obi* are relatively few in number today, but formerly women vied with each other in the elaborate styles used, many of which are still seen on the Kabuki stage, and in the eighteenth century, actors themselves were very often responsible for devising new *obi* fashions which were taken up by the ladies of the town.

Symbolism in colour has always played a part in the costume of everyday life in Japan. A housewife would never wear the bright patterns of a courtesan or *geisha*, for instance, whilst certain colours and patterns were only used at certain ages, becoming progressively more sober the older one grew. This aspect of real life costume is naturally observed in theatrical dress in addition to its own unique symbolism. Towards the end of the eighteenth century the Government brought in many regulations against luxury. These had their own effect on costume. Forbidden outward displays of prosperity, the *chonin* began to concentrate on the quality of the material of their clothing. The exteriors became simple, gaudy showy dress was regarded as in the worst of taste. Traditional weaves and patterns and the richness of texture were the basis of all that was best in clothing. A result of this trend was the wide use of the *kōshi*, or check pattern, and the *shima*, or stripe, which is such a marked characteristic of Japanese dress. The love of subdued colour and pattern, which was at the same time refined and of exquisite quality, has always remained a feature of traditional dress since those days and particularly in the case of all people connected with the theatre.

In the early days of the Kabuki, the actors had to provide their own stage costumes, another factor which was responsible for creating a certain simplicity in elegance. The stage dress of those times was based on that of the common civilians rather than the higher classes and nobles and this called for a good deal of improvization, not to say ingenuity, in costume design. During the later years of the Meiji era a tendency for the use of the elaborate and the gaudy in theatrical dress arose, and this is still reflected in some of the actor's costume today. A certain simplicity has disappeared. A Japanese critic, scolding the modern theatre for its ostentatiousness, pointed out that the great Danjuro IX was so skilful in his art that it was an easy matter for him to pretend that cotton was velvet, and the critic goes on to adjure modern actors to remember the virtues of their predecessors. There is probably something to be said for his point of view, too often in these days the picturesque is over-emphasized at the expense of inner feeling in the classical arts of the Orient and Western influence is sometimes to blame in this.

The modern Kabuki actor no longer has to provide his own costumes, they are all the property of the company which in these days means the Shochiku Company. It would be quite impossible for the actor to be responsible; the making of these costumes is a more costly business than it ever was, a single garment often being valued at hundreds of pounds.

Naturally the *kimono* of the stage wardrobe has a multitude of different styles and patterns for both male and female roles. In *jidaimono* plays, the actor who takes the part of a princess or young lady of high birth and is the heroine of the piece, always wears a richly embroidered *kimono* of scarlet silk with a long flowing *suso* or hem. It is called *akahime* and worn regardless of time, season or place, it is in fact a standard symbol of this particular type of role. *Aka* means red and *hime* means young lady of high birth, hence the name. The *hime* roles are regarded as the high water mark of acting for the *onnagata*. The character parts of Yukihime in the play *Kinkakuji*, Tokihime in *Sandaiki* and Yaigakihime in *Honjo Nijushiko* form the three supreme tests for the skill of the female impersonator; once he can play these parts successfully he may be said to have arrived. A *kimono* style of a different kind is also used in *jidaimono* plays. This is the dress known as *kokumochi*, worn only by those playing the roles of *samurai*'s wives. The name literally means 'rice payment holder', referring to the *samurai*'s means of income. The *kokumochi* is always in a plain colour with no other ornamentation than the white *mon* or family crest on the sleeves, breast and back of the garment. The wearing of *mon* on the clothing is an ancient Japanese custom still preserved, particularly important in the theatre, for all actors have their own theatrical *mon*, designs which have been famous for centuries and symbolize the very spirit of the theatre.

The *kokumochi* is worn with a plain black *obi* and has a black

Right: Uchikake costume
Left: Akahime style costume with fukiwa wig

eri or collar. A colour most often used for this costume is *kuriume*, a dark maroon; two other colours are *asagi*, a pale blue, and *moege*, a light greenish tone. A *katsuyama mage* is the correct wig to go with the *kokumochi*, which symbolizes the old rule of etiquette that a *samurai's* wife must dress in quiet good taste with no ostentatious display.

As opposed to this, the finery of the courtesans of Yedo and Kyoto has been preserved in the Kabuki and provides some of the most elaborate and ornamental dress on the stage. A feature of their costume was that several long trailing skirts were worn one over the other and at the lower ends the silk lining was turned outwards, being several inches thick. The skirts were then visible one above the other like so many thick hoops around the bottom of the dress. The Yedo *oiran* wore an *obi* which was tied high above the waist and hung down in front in a broad, stiff length.

It was richly embroidered in gold and silver thread and is known in the theatre as the *manaita obi*. When walking in the streets, a cloak called *kake* was worn over the *kimono* and this too was heavily embroidered with gold and silver threads and fillets. On such an occasion, the courtesan gathered her trailing skirts high around her and was elevated on lacquered wooden clogs more than a foot high, while an attendant supported her on one side. The annual procession of courtesans in all their splendour of dress was one of the spectacles of old Yedo and Kyoto.

There were slight variations in the costume of the Kyoto and Osaka *oiran*, for the latter wore an *obi* knotted in the form of a large bow at the front and stiffened with paper; the different styles are seen on the stage. The gay quarters in Kyoto and Osaka were known as Shimabara and Shinmachi respectively and frequent references to these places occur in plays.

In the *jidaimono* plays, ladies of high rank wear an outer garment over their *kimono* known as the *uchikake*. It is a roomy cloak which gives a characteristic 'humped' appearance to the wearer where it fits over the protruding knot of the *obi* at the rear. Later an outer garment called *haori* was worn by both men and women over their *kimono* and this is seen a great deal in the *sewamono* style plays. The *haori* is still worn today.

The costumes of the Nō theatre were adapted to certain types of Kabuki plays and a heavy embroidered robe with flowing sleeves used in the Nō is seen in a slightly different style in the Kabuki. It is called the *karaori*. In costume as in everything else, the Nō has made its individual contribution to the younger drama, more particularly in the dancing plays.

Two very individual forms of dress are seen in the male roles of the Kabuki, they are called *suo* and *kamishimo*. The *suo* is a formal dress worn by *samurai* and *daimyo* which originally came from a Nō costume called *hitatare*, ceremonial wear of ancient times. The costume is in two parts, the upper being a voluminous, wide-sleeved garment worn with the lower half, which is called *bakama* and is girdled round the waist above the upper costume. The *bakama* is a kind of divided skirt and when worn with *suo*, the garment completely encases the legs and feet and trails away on the ground behind the wearer. It imparts a characteristically slow and measured pace to the gait of the actor, who must give a quick twist to the trailing lengths when he turns

Some Kabuki costumes
Left to right: ryujin maki, suo with eboshi, kamiko

and seats himself. The *bakama* is also seen as a shorter garment in which the feet are visible and in this form it is still the ceremonial dress for men today.

The *kamishimo* was the standard formal dress of the *samurai*. *Bakama* are worn as a part of it, and *kataginu*, wide shoulder pieces which stand out stiffly and squarely on the wearer. This style of costume, it will be remembered, is also worn by the theatre musicians; the illustrations will give a clearer idea of these forms of dress.

The *mon* or family crest is worn on both *kamishimo* and *suo*, but in the case of the last the design of the crest is always greatly enlarged and is called *daimon*. The long trailing *bakama* or *suo* are called *naga bakama*, or long *bakama*.

In male roles, costumes which are completely unrealistic in any kind of period sense are sometimes worn on special occasions. Such a one is *yoten*, worn by the actors playing the roles of young warriors who arrive from the battlefield to report progress and cry: 'Gochushin!' before they commence their story. A noticeable feature of their costume is a silk fringed, apron-like garment. A type of *yoten* is also worn by the *torite*, the officials who in old plays always appear to arrest someone or take them away. In *sewamono* plays of the late Edo period, *torite* however do not wear *yoten*, but dress which was common to the 'Bow Street Runners' of the times.

A unique costume is *ryujin maki*, worn by the lieutenant of a high ranking official. It is almost Elizabethan in cut with a kind of doublet, and a large square silk panel patterned with a *daimon* fixed to the left shoulder.

A curious old tradition lingers on in the Kabuki costume called *kamiko*, literally paper clothes. It is customarily worn by an actor playing the part of a handsome young lover who has come down in the world. In olden times in Japan, poor people used to paste together many layers of used writing paper and varnish it with the juice of unripe persimmon and it was then used as a form of 'cloth'. This was the origin of the actor's *kamiko*, which is black, with large irregular patches of deep lilac colour, patterned all over with Japanese written script.

Certain techniques dependent on a special type of costume are used a great deal in dancing plays. Two important ones are *hikinuki* and *bukkaeri* already briefly described. In *hikinuki* an outer garment is taken off on the stage to reveal an under garment of different colour and pattern. These are attached together by special threads which can be pulled out quickly and skilfully, causing the garment to fall apart without the audience noticing it. The process is called *tamo o nuko* and the diagram accompanying shows the order in which the threads are released. A *koken* always assists the actor in this operation which requires skill and swift fingers. One of the main purposes of *hikinuki* is to emphasize changes of mood in dancing by the appearance of the actor as well.

In *bukkaeri* the actor takes his arms out of his sleeves from inside and pushes down the upper portion of the garment to hang around his waist revealing a completely different patterned *kimono* beneath. *Bukkaeri* is used to convey the idea that the actor has now assumed a character and personality which has formerly been concealed. Depicting a change in a person's character by an outward variation in costume is a common way of inducing a different atmosphere on the stage, and these sym-

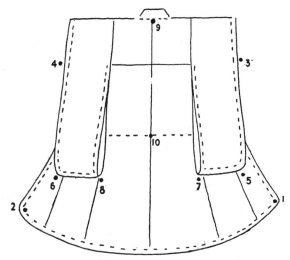

Hikinuki costume diagram showing order of process

bolic actions are responsible for immediate reaction to mood by the audience. When a character is badly hurt, for instance, he or she very often lowers both sleeves, or to emphasize a state of excitement or emotion, one only may be lowered. In fighting or showing an aggressive spirit the sleeves are lowered again. The sleeve lowering technique is called *hadanugi*, already mentioned in the section on *mie*.

In general the function of costume is to produce symbolism rather than realism in its outward effect, but even when realism is taken into account, costume by its colour and general qualities of decoration must contribute to that picture-like character which is so typical of the Kabuki stage.

KODŌGU, SMALL STAGE PROPERTIES

Kodōgu, the small properties of the Kabuki stage, are unique, a study of them fascinates by its intricacies, and gives an insight into the heart of that fairyland which is the Kabuki theatre.

Kodōgu are of two kinds, *dedōgu* and *mochidōgu*. The first means all articles which are left on the stage during a performance, such as interior furnishings like a screen or a small table, while *mochidōgu* indicates articles such as swords, fans, helmets or headdresses, anything in fact which the actor carries about with him. Both kinds of *kodōgu* are generally classed as properties which are movable on the stage, in comparison with *odōgu*, the large properties, which include all the main features of a stage setting such as a house, palace interior, bridge and so forth. Some niceties of distinction occur at times. In a play *Eihon Taikoki*, for example, the warrior Mitsuhide plucks a stake from a bamboo thicket and sharpens it as a weapon. The thicket is made by the *odōgu*, or large property men, but the stake is a small property and belongs to the *kodōgu* department.

There is a special room in each theatre where the *kodōgu* are kept and the men in charge, the *heya mono kata*, must look after the properties required throughout a performance and see that each article is available when required. The properties themselves are made outside the theatre by a special department known as the *kosakubu*. The men of the *kosakubu* make every single type of article required as small property and these are rented to theatres for a performance and returned to the warehouses of the makers at the end of a run.

This work has been carried on by the family of Fujinami for several generations. In early days, the *kodōgu* were made in the theatre itself, but in 1872 Fujinami Yohei I broke away from the tradition and made his craft independent and this has been the position ever since. Once a new performance is decided upon, the head of the *kodōgu* department is told what is required in the way of small properties, designs are drawn up for new ones and craftsmen set to work on them, whilst imperishable articles, such as swords and armour already in stock, are taken from the store rooms. Everything has to be ready for the day before the opening of the performance; it will mean long hours of feverish activity and labour and the men of the *kodōgu* will get little sleep until the curtain goes up on the first day. Every conceivable kind of craftsman is necessary for the manufacture of *kodōgu*, carpenters, carvers, sculptors, metal workers, armourers, lacquer workers, painters and many more who must be prepared to make anything from a suit of armour to a plate of pastries, both of which must be correct in period detail, but whilst the pastries will be of papier-mâché and for effect only, the armour must be an accurate reproduction of ancient military wear in all its artistry of craftsmanship to be worn by the actor. Some idea of the attention paid to detail may be gathered from the fact that in the Fujinami storehouses in Tokyo, there is a collection of over

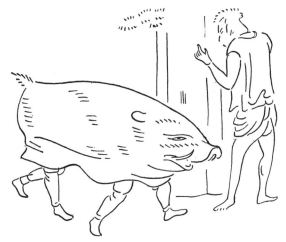

*Kodogu—the wild boar in 'Chushingura' after an illustration in
'Gekijo Kummo Zue'*

two thousand swords for stage use. Each one is designed correctly according to its period and no detail is lacking except, of course, the blades are not real cutting edges. In addition to correct reproduction of historical forms and designs, the *kodōgu* craftsman must also be prepared to soar into the realms of fantasy and imagination and create ghosts, monsters and all kinds of creatures both four legged and feathered. There is in fact no limits to the calls which may be made on his skill and ingenuity.

An unusual small property is the *kirikubi*. The name literally means a human head severed from the body but on the stage refers to those artificial heads used as properties by the actors in *jidaimono* plays. The *kodōgu* men distinguish three different kinds. *Dakubi*, or low class head, is one stuffed with wood shavings and covered with Japanese paper pasted over. *Hariko no kubi*, or papier-mâché head, is made of wood with paper pasted over, and finally *jokubi*, or high class head, is one carved directly in paulownia wood. In the past the latter type were made by master carvers who created them in the likenesses of the great actors of their time. Some of these are still preserved in the Fujinami warehouse; they are unique testimonials to the exquisite craftsmanship of the old carvers as well as uncannily life-like death masks, if such a contradiction in terms may be used, of great actors gone from their earthly stage long years ago.

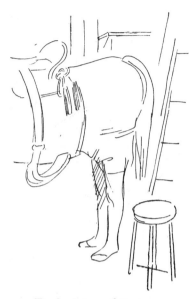

The back legs of the horse

Perhaps one of the most famous of all stage properties is the Kabuki horse. This consists of an elaborate framework constructed of wood and velvet representing a real horse complete with flowing mane, long tail, bridle, stirrups and saddle. Two actors take the part of front and back legs respectively, their own lower limbs being clad in velvet tights. Astride this steed sits the equestrian actor in professional style. The Kabuki horse is a tradition which has remained unchanged through the centuries and is still accepted today, albeit with a certain amount of amusement, by the modern Japanese playgoer. There is more often than not a ripple of laughter from some part of the house whenever the theatrical steed makes its appearance now. It is in a way indicative of the general change in audience reaction. In former days the playgoer accepted the convention seriously as a necessary part of stage technique; his successor is sometimes moved to levity by the less sophisticated aspects of the Kabuki. To foreigners, there is at first sight something incredibly comical about the Kabuki horse, it brings back memories of the pantomime of childhood days, and they are attracted by the particular rather than the general, especially the very human legs. Longer acquaintance with it may produce a different reaction; like other things in this old theatre it falls into place as part of the general scheme of things and the eye learns to accept it. Impressionism rather than realism would be an apter description for the Kabuki horse and as such it is intended. No one pretends that it is true to life; a convention has been devised which, in conjunction with a certain amount of outward trapping, creates the impression of a mounted figure in the minds of the audience. The convention says here is a rider on a horse and the audience has already accepted it as a necessary technical preliminary to the action of the play. It is the actor on the horse who is the focus of attention, his mount merely serves to isolate him and emphasize his presence in the circumstances demanded.

In times past the term *uma no ashi*, legs of the horse, was commonly applied to actors of indifferent merit. The custom seems to have fallen into disuse today, although a cynic has remarked that modern audiences would not appreciate the differences anyway. It is a fact that the men who constitute the horse's legs are generally people who have failed to merit a more conspicuous position on the boards. Nevertheless theirs is a task which requires its particular skill and considerable physical stamina and who shall say they are not artists in their own particular sphere. In addition to the velvet tights in colours to match those of the horse, these invisible specialists wear padded shoulder jackets to take the strain. A veiled aperture is situated in the front of the neck of the horse to enable front legs to see what he is about. It is not recorded what is said within the dark interior when some actor of more than usual weight sits heavily upon the saddle.

The horse is one of the stock items in the *kodōgu* warehouse from which they are led forth whenever required. There are fewer of them today for several perished during the war and are unlikely to be replaced. Other creatures which appear from the 'menagerie' of the *kodōgu* department are tigers, elephants, foxes, monkeys, dogs, cats, bears, hawks, snakes, rats and toads. A formidable list, some of them are quite realistic and others require the same powers of imagination in the audience as does the horse.

The craftsmen of the *kodōgu* department are experts in their own particular fields, and all of them have inherited their skill from their fathers and grandfathers before them. The older hands have worked under the direction of the head of the house of Fujinami since their youth, and it was a grievous loss to them all when their beloved master Fujinami Yohei III, grandson of the original Fujinami, committed suicide at the end of 1952. Fujinami Yohei III was born in 1891; a remarkable man, he was a strange genius of the theatre whose like will not easily occur again. His death in its own way was more significant for Japan than many people realized, for it symbolized with startling clarity the passing of an era.

Master craftsman and perfectionist, the third Fujinami was mourned by actors, artists, writers and scholars, for he had friends in every walk of life and his house was always a lively centre of discussion and exchanges of views on every topic connected with the arts and the world in general. A scholar himself as well as artist, he was widely read in the cultural history of his country and throughout his life carried out exhaustive researches in various branches of the arts and crafts related to his profession. He wrote and published many articles on his work and experiences in the theatre, one of which is quoted in this chapter. His sons have in their possession letters that he wrote them in their childhood, wonderful letters full of drawings, sketches and explanations concerning all the fascinating secrets of his craft. In this fashion he prepared his children with knowledge they would later be able to use.

Fujinami Yohei III was highly skilled in a number of crafts, but was particularly noted for his genius in reconstructing the armour of ancient times for use on the stage. In whatever he turned his hand to he achieved perfection and never rested until he had completely mastered his subject. He was an architect and designed houses, among them that of the head of Shochiku Company. A connoisseur of food, he was himself a skilled chef and confectioner and invented a brand of Japanese pastry of his own. Ever ready to give his advice and help to those who asked for it, he was loved for his generous nature. What made such a man take his own life?

There were two things that he did not understand, indifferent workmanship under any pretext and the love of financial gain. These things appeared to him to dominate a new world and so he took his life. He suffered heavily during the war, for he lost a great part of his valuable collection of properties through bombing. The war ended, he found it difficult to get craftsmen who could work to his standards; he became more and more uneasy at the trend of affairs and when people told him that he had better produce inferior work and so save expenses, he was both shocked and angry. The ideals which had been the guiding force of his life and that of his forefathers it seemed, were to disappear beneath the ruthless materialism of people who no longer understood the integrity of the artist. He left a message to his family which concluded with the simple words, 'I can do no more so I go.' They contained a tragic intensity, for the life of Fujinami Yohei III symbolized more than any other the true spirit of the old theatre and the artistic honesty of the past.

His son, Fujinami Yohei IV, a young man not yet thirty, with his mother and brother, continues his father's work; sincere in heart and conscious of the great weight of his responsibilities. Those that are left of the old craftsmen still carry on the family tradition with him; one of them, Matsuo Kajiro, a vigorous old man of seventy, is typical of all that is best in the old Japanese craftsmen and artists. A sculptor, carver and mask-maker, he is bound by the same integrity of spirit as that of the master he served. His life, he will tell his friends, has been one long series of disasters; fires, earthquakes, wars and poverty. These he can ignore, but the disaster he dreads most of all is to be seriously interrupted in the middle of his work. He used to tell new apprentices on their first day under him that they were not allowed to talk although they might hum!

The following story, related by the late Fujinami, will serve as a fitting conclusion to this section on the art of the small property men. Not only does it reveal something of the character of a great actor, but it also gives an insight into the spirit of the master of the kodōgu himself and the qualities which endeared him to those who worked under him. In March 1893, a new dance play was staged by Danjuro IX called Kagamijishi, which eventually became one of the most popular dramas of its kind in the Kabuki theatre. It tells the story of a palace maid-in-waiting who is commanded to dance with a ceremonial lion's mask at the New Year. She does so and eventually the spirit of the lion enters into her and she disappears to leave only a lion sporting with two butterflies among the peonies. The lion's

Kodōgu—Shishi gashira: wooden lion's mask used by Danjuro IX

mask carried by the dancer in this play is an important small
property and this is the story that Fujinami III tells about it.
'The lion's head used in this play was made of paulownia wood
carved, Nara doll fashion, so as to show on it bold traces of the
chisel and finished with special care, so that the natural texture
of the wood might not be hidden beneath the varnish. For its
eyes a pair of jade balls were put into the sockets and the lower
part of the teeth was gilded with gold dust. *Shikoro*, the covering
cloth attached to the back of the mask, was of crepe-de-chine
dyed in bright yellow colour. The lower jaw could be moved
freely up and down by the operation of a thumb thrust into it,
and altogether it was a work of art in every way. The maker of
this lion's head I cannot at this date identify with certainty, but
if I may hazard a guess, I would say it was the work of Yasumoto
Kamhachi I, who knew Danjuro intimately. Danjuro wore it
when he performed in *Kagamijishi*.

'In 1879 or thereabouts Fujinami Yohei II, the writer's father,
was called to the house of Danjuro at Tsukiji, when the great
actor produced from his warehouse the above mentioned lion's
head and asked him to repair the mask. Yohei examined it

closely, but not a single spot could he detect in it that seemed in need of repair. Puzzled, he asked Danjuro what was wrong about it, to which the actor merely replied, "Don't argue, Yohei. Just take it along with you and see how you can mend it for me." Though still sceptical, Yohei could not but obey Danjuro's command. So he came home with his precious charge, but when he entered his workshop, he had to cudgel his brains to solve the riddle set him by the ninth Danjuro. Gradually he recollected that he had previously received similar orders from Danjuro about the three swords of *Shibaraku* and the breastplate of Ebimaru. By putting two and two together he now understood, or at least he thought he understood, the hidden meaning of the great actor.

'Thereupon Yohei summoned Kobayashi Masakichi, who was a master craftsman in his employ, and ordered him to make a mould of the lion's head. For this purpose Kobayashi used a modelling apparatus such as dentists use for the making of tooth moulds, and obtained a concave mould of the original. Next he poured plaster into it and produced an exact model of Danjuro's treasure. With this plaster model by his side, Kobayashi set to work on a block of Nambu paulownia wood and finally perfected a lion's head which in every detail reproduced the characteristics of its prototype. When all was over, Yohei took back the original lion's head to Danjuro's residence and said to him, "It's in good order again, sir." "Well done, Yohei!" replied he, looking satisfied with the whole transaction. So I am told.

'After this Yohei had two replicas made by Masakichi and I remember that when Kikugoro IV played *Kagamijishi*, he used one of our lion's heads. Moreover, hearing what had passed between Danjuro and Yohei, he also desired a replica for himself. He said to me, "Yotchan, as you have a model of my Tsukiji uncle's lion's head, why not let me have a reproduction too?" So Masakichi produced another replica. This was after the earthquake of 1923, and I imagine it is still carefully preserved in the house of Kikugoro VI.

'Speaking of the earthquake, it is sad to recall that the warehouse of Danjuro's Tsukiji residence having been destroyed, all the precious properties for well-known Kabuki plays were reduced to ashes. But as luck would have it, the Fujinami warehouse survived the earthquake, so that the lions' heads, together with their plaster model and other stage properties for Kabuki masterpieces which were all housed therein, remained safe and in good condition. In the recent war, too, they were successfully protected against its ravages, as they, including of course the lion's heads and the three swords, found refuge in the Chichibu Hills.

'It is a well known fact that Kabuki and Japanese dancing have always set great store by those traditional formulae and patterns, upon which is made to depend so much of what is essential to these arts. A natural consequence of this was an attitude of determined secretiveness, which jealously concealed from the public the intricacies of such formulae and patterns, not excluding those connected with stage properties, thereby seriously hampering the popularization of theatrical art.

'All honour, therefore, must go to the memory of Danjuro IX, whose greatness of soul rose so far above the narrowmindedness of his age as to allow him to put his family treasure into the hands of Fujinami Yohei without the slightest sign of reserve or secretiveness. And the most charming part of it all was the human and humorous way in which he took my father into his confidence. By so doing he put into his debt not the Fujinamis alone, but the whole world of Kabuki and Japanese dancing. The episode only deepens our admiration for the great actor, when we consider how much thought he gave even to matters of the minutest detail for the future of the Japanese theatre, in defiance of the shackles of deep rooted feudalism which beset the Kabuki world. Danjuro's noble example, I should say, is a challenge to all of us today who have taken it upon ourselves to preserve and hand on to the next generation the traditional art of this country and I myself have found it a guiding principle in my work.'

ŌDŌGU

Odōgu, the stage settings of the Kabuki, like the *kodōgu*, have been the prerogative of one family, the Hasegawas, for generations. *Odōgu* are constructed in the theatre both behind and on the stage; before a performance opens the men of the *ōdōgu* will be working all night to have the last set in position in time. Not all the large properties are newly built, there are standard sections which can be stored for use again. The head of the *ōdōgu* department works in conjunction with the stage manager and has to draw up a plan first, if a new play is being staged or new effects introduced into an old play.

The chief materials used in the construction of *ōdōgu* are wood and paper, and a process known as *harimono*, the pasting of paper on wooden backgrounds and frameworks, is one of the special techniques of the *ōdōgu* craftsmen. Two kinds of workers are employed in this process, *harikata*, the men who do the pasting, and *nurikata*, the men who paint them. The latter class deals only with roofs, fences and perspective views of large halls called *senjo jiki*. There are special scene painters for landscapes and trees on flats. The carpenter, naturally, is a prominent member of the *ōdōgu* and one of his tasks is to construct the platforms or *dai* which form such an important part of Kabuki stage sets.

An important convention in a Kabuki setting is the reproduction on the stage of a Japanese style building, it may be a palace, a poor cottage or a tea house. Sometimes the whole structure is built flat on the stage, *hira butai*, but very often it is elevated on a platform called *niju butai*. In the latter case a flight of three wooden steps, the *sandan*, connects the front centre of the platform with the stage. Whatever type it is, the building is always made as though the façade has been removed so that the audience sees things as it were with the lid off. A general plan of such a set is as follows. The centre portion of the set consists of a main room, either *hira butai* or *niju butai*, if the latter, it is connected to the stage by the *sandan*, but in both cases sliding doors or an entry at the rear of the room allows the actor to enter from behind. The centre portion of the set connects at the right, i.e. audience's right, with a smaller room, the *tsugi no ima*, that presents a façade consisting of a closed, latticed, paper-covered window to the audience. The left of the stage always represents the main outer entrance to a building, a necessity because the *hanamichi* is built at the left side of the theatre. A wooden gate called a *kido* is placed on the stage, to divide the main part of the set from the outside world, represented by the extreme left portion of the stage and the *hanamichi*. There are various kinds of *kido*, but the three main types are *sewa kido*, representing a city residence, *yama kido*, representing a rustic background, and *shiyorido*, a very low gate which is sometimes placed on the *hanamichi* itself and is often seen in dancing plays. The *kido* is a dramatic device that is telling in effect. It allows

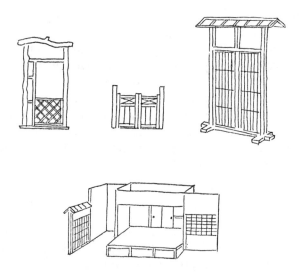

Top row: Odōgu
L. to R.: yama kido, shiyorido, sewa kido
Bottom: General plan of typical Kabuki stage set

the audience to watch the actions of different people and even the workings of their minds simultaneously. It overcomes time and dimension and enables the onlooker to see through walls; many powerful scenes in Kabuki plays are staged using this particular arrangement of *ōdōgu*. There may be variations on the form described here, but the general principles remain the same in all traditional plays which have any kind of building as a stage setting.

An interesting convention is seen in some of the *jidaimono* plays when the set represents a palace or mansion. At a certain emotional climax in the drama, the sliding doors at the rear of the set will be removed to reveal a painted perspective of large rooms, each with their sliding doors wide open so that the eye travels on and on into the distance. It gives pictorial emphasis to a situation, adding breadth to the feelings expressed by the actors. Palace interiors are always represented with black painted woodwork and in some of the famous *goten* or palace scenes, the set will be a glittering structure with what are called *kinbusuma*, the panels and sliding doors of the interior painted a rich gold texture. If a shrine is represented on the stage there will always be a red painted fence and in the rear a *tori*, the sacred arch which is a feature of Japanese temples.

There are many other conventions which have to be observed in the making of *ōdōgu*. Highways are always shown with pine trees on either side, but the depths of the mountains are symbolized by cryptomeria trees and bamboo thickets, and, at the rear of the set, is hung a black curtain called the *kuromaku*, which indicates dim light or nightfall. There are several curtains used in Kabuki plays other than those which are used at the opening and close of a performance, and these are the responsibility of the *ōdōgu* specialists. There is the *asagi maku*, a turquoise blue curtain which is suspended to conceal the actors when the main curtain is drawn. The *asagi maku* is ripped away by cords to reveal some striking pose, and this introduces an element of surprise to the audience. Another is the *namimaku* on which waves are painted and which is used for sea coast scenes.

Tsuri eda is a decorative feature peculiar to the Kabuki stage, it consists of sprays of cherry or plum blossom suspended above the stage along the top of the proscenium opening. These artificial blossoms are the work of the *ōdōgu* as is also the snow, which is used to such effect in making decorative winter landscapes on the stage, reminiscent of many of the old woodblock prints. The snowflakes are small, triangular-shaped pieces of paper which are contained in openwork bamboo slings suspended high above the stage. These are rocked at increasing speed causing the flakes to fall.

It is the *ōdōgu* men who look after the *seriage* and *serisage*, trapdoor devices by means of which actors appear and disappear through the stage. A whole set representing a palace can be made to sink into the earth by these means. Two complete stage sets are built on the revolving stage by the *ōdōgukata* at the same time; the exterior of a building may be represented before the audience, for instance, and the stage revolves to show an inner room with the characters in place, or as if entering from outside, or completely different characters may have been introduced. There is no end to the ingenuity of the *ōdōgu* men in constructing stage settings and the various effects that go with them, at the same time they perform a number of functions. Before a dancing play is performed the stage and *hanamichi* are covered with raised platforms made of cypress wood, they are called *shosa butai* and *shosa dai* and are laid down in sections. Sometimes the *hana-michi* is covered with matting, *goza*, and sometimes the stage is laid with strips of matting called *usuberi*, the dragging away of which indicates a change from indoors to out of doors. Boats and ships are realistically constructed to sail across the stage and all these come under the jurisdiction of the *ōdōgu* department, together with *tsuke uchi*, i.e. the beating of wooden clappers on a board at the side of the stage, described at the beginning of the chapter.

Although like other forms described here, *ōdōgu* is supplementary to the acting, being largely concerned with the construction of stage settings, it is so important at times that it is inextricable from the actor's technique. A good example may be given in a play whose most dramatic moment occurs when the heroine pulls open a skylight in the roof of a country dwelling and poses, holding the long cord used to operate the window. This drama long ago became called *Hiki Mado*, 'Pulling open the Skylight', by the Japanese in lieu of the full name of the play and *Hiki Mado* it has remained. It is an instance which amplifies what was said at the beginning of the chapter, namely that the properties of the Kabuki theatre are a vital aid to the art of the actor in a way which marks them apart from those of other theatres.

CHAPTER VIII

THE ACTOR

THE Kabuki theatre is a harsh task master, enforcing the most rigid discipline upon the actor who can expect hard work, hard criticism and hard living in the pursuit of his career. If at the end of long years of initial training, he attains a mastery of his craft and is accepted by the hierarchy of the profession, he must then stand trial before his audience in a way that no other actors do, except those of the Chinese theatre.

The profession of the Kabuki actor is a hereditary one, hereditary in a double sense. With very few exceptions, Kabuki players are connected by blood ties to the theatre in some form or another, however humble they sometimes be. A large proportion of actors are descended either directly or by marriage from the acting families of former times. Once an actor has achieved professional standing he is known to the public by a stage name in itself hereditary, which has been passed on from generation to generation, and it is this which condemns him to a test peculiar in its severity before he can hope to attain the minimum of appreciation. There is no chance for the young Kabuki actor to make his name overnight in a new play as a Western actor might do. He has to contend with an audience that knows the rules thoroughly, and is not so much interested in the play as the technique of the actor and his interpretation, and that all the time applies a mental criticism to his performance in the light of the masters who have held the name before him. The new actor has to recreate a stage character in a traditional form, but yet have a subtle enough personality to give it life and spirit and not make it mere flat repetition.

It is a human and excusable trait to consider yesterday as far superior to today. The Kabuki theatre by the nature of its professional ethics to a certain extent encourages such a philosophy, and audiences have always been reluctant to admit that the actors of the present can ever hope to compete with the heroes of the past. In listening to criticisms of modern actors it is always necessary to apply a sense of perspective. However there is undoubtedly some logic in a part of the criticism.

To preserve a living continuity through the years, the Kabuki has one major prerequisite, a sufficient body of youthful talent to take over and carry on the traditions of the older actors when death or retirement takes them from the stage. The last war dealt a severe blow to the Kabuki theatre, for the careers and training of younger actors were retarded. The position was made more difficult in that some of the greatest actors died during or just after the war, at a time when they were most necessary to inspire and assist the younger people who had so many difficulties to overcome. Nakamura Utaemon V died in 1940, Onoe Kikugoro VI and Ichimura Uzaemon XV in 1945, and Matsumoto Koshiro VII in 1949. Within the short space of a few years, four of the most distinguished names covering the principal types of Kabuki acting had disappeared from the rolls of the theatre, and there were others besides.

The younger actors of post-war Japan were faced with a bleak prospect. Deprived of some of their most cherished leaders on the one hand, on the other they faced economic and social conditions which were anything but favourable to a resuscitation of the Kabuki drama. It is all the more remarkable that the Kabuki has achieved the position it holds again and gathered together such a talented body of actors as it still possesses.

The burning problem for Kabuki actors now is an economic one. Although they are never made public, it is generally known that the salaries are not high under modern living conditions and there is no form of protection among the actors, no benefit societies, no union. In common with most artists they are not noted for financial acumen. The mad struggle for existence in contemporary Japan poses a serious problem for the survival of the genuine Kabuki actor. The older actors in their efforts to live are overworked and at the same time younger players are not given sufficient opportunities to test their mettle and develop their talents. It is a vicious circle. Many of the younger people, unable to exist by Kabuki, lend their talents to the cinema to ease economic difficulties. Nothing could be more disastrous for the technique of the Kabuki actor. Such conditions can only lead to frustration among the younger people and have an adverse effect on the theatre in general.

Stage names in the Kabuki theatre are a key towards an understanding of the actor's profession. An actor's name will be seen to consist of three parts, for example Nakamura Utaemon VI. The first name is the theatrical family to which the actor belongs and to which he generally owes his training and professional debut, although sometimes an actor has been adopted into another theatrical family, whose name he assumes, later in his career. The second name, Utaemon, indicates personal status as an actor. Such a title can only be assumed after the death of a previous holder, under a succession system which jealously guards the reputation of actors' titles. The Roman numeral at the end of the name shows the generation, so that the present Nakamura Utaemon is the sixth actor to bear the title since it was initiated. The naming system can be better understood by giving an example in detail.

Nakamura Utaemon first made his stage debut in 1922, under the title of Nakamura Kotaro; in 1933 he became Nakamura Fukusuke, in 1941 he assumed the title Nakamura Shikan and finally succeeded to his present title, Nakamura Utaemon, in 1951. These names are the prerogative of the Nakamura family to which Utaemon belongs and can only be taken by members of that family. They indicate rising stages of professional achievement, the latest one being the most famous and in the case of Utaemon, the highest name the actor can achieve in the Nakamura family. No other actor can take this name during the present holder's lifetime therefore. If there are several members of an acting family they obviously all cannot achieve the highest name, and it is the eldest son, if he is considered worthy, who is in the direct line of succession. The present Utaemon is in fact the second son of Utaemon V, who died in 1940. The first son died while still holding the title of Nakamura Fukusuke, leaving direct succession to the family names open to his younger brother, who eventually became the present Utaemon VI. Had the elder brother not died and finally succeeded to the supreme title, the present Utaemon would have remained Nakamura Shikan, the next highest title. He would then probably have brought fresh lustre to this name. If an actor through force of circumstances fails to attain the highest name, it is not necessarily a reflection on his professional attainments, and he may well make the secondary name even more famous than before.

There is a further complication in actors' names, for there are often different branches of the same family. For instance, on the Tokyo stage at present there are three famous actors bearing the name Nakamura; Nakamura Utaemon, Nakamura Kichiemon and Nakamura Kanzaburo, but each one belongs to an entirely different branch of the Nakamura family. In Osaka again there are two different acting branches of the Nakamuras. Every actor besides his professional name bears what is known as a *yago*, or shop name. Members of the same theatrical branch of a family bear the same shop name, but different branches use different shop names. In the case of the Nakamura family just quoted, the *yago* of Nakamura Utaemon is Narikomaya, that of Nakamura Kichiemon is Harimaya, whilst Nakamura Kanzaburo is called Nakamuraya. An Osaka branch of the Nakamuras, on the other hand, bears the shop name Tennojiya. In contrast to this the shop name of Nakamura Kichiemon, just mentioned, and that of the Tokyo actor Nakamura Tokizo is identical, i.e. Harimaya, as they both belong to the same branch of the Nakamura family.

These names are connected with the personal backgrounds of the famous acting families. In some cases they may be corruptions of birthplace titles, or contain a reference to the occupation of the family of the founder of a line. Often the original source may be obscure or lost in the past. Whatever the explanation the *yago* are hallowed by long tradition and have been used as familiar references by generations of playgoers through the centuries. They are shouted out aloud in the theatre by the fans who wish to greet the arrival of their favourite on the stage, or to express appreciation of a particularly skilful piece of acting or approval of the way he speaks his lines. To the newcomer, there is at first something a little disconcerting in the cries which burst like pistol shots in a quietened auditorium as some veteran acknowledges the great ones on the boards. Besides the shop names the seasoned theatregoers express themselves with many other pithy phrases. *Makemashita*, 'I am defeated', and *yakemasune*, 'I am jealous', are two common ones. Again, at the conclusion of some well-known passage, *matte imashita*, 'I was waiting for that', makes the rafters ring. There are always the humorists of course who see fit to hurl some quip or jest from far up in the *tachimi*, or gallery, at a particular moment. A regular visitor to the theatre soon learns to accept this tradition, which indeed is symbolical of the very essence of the old play-

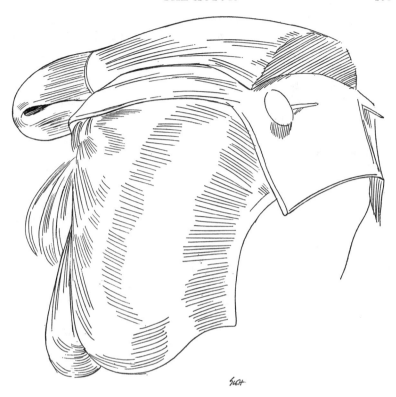

The wig worn by onnagata actors on ceremonial occasions

house. There is a menace who has arisen in modern times and who, in his ignorance, tries to show off by giving vent to vocal expression often at the most inappropriate moments. He is on a par with the foreign visitors who leap up and down during a performance taking flashlight photographs of the actors. Apart from this, it can be said that once the shop names and the old expressions cease to be called out by the veterans, the Kabuki theatre will have passed into the limbo.

When an actor succeeds to a title, a special ceremony called *shumei hiro* is held in the theatre. Leading actors present their newly-named colleagues to the audience, each making a speech in turn. Ceremonial costume, i.e. *kamishimo*, is worn with the colours and crests of the families to which the actors belong. Special wigs are also worn, those in the case of *onnagata* actors being a female style wig known as *kōjō no katsura*. The name *kōjō* is often used instead of *shumei hiro* to describe a name-taking ceremony. In this event, the actors face the audience in a row, placed according to rank with their protégé in the centre. Each remains prostrated in a deep bow throughout the ceremony, only raising his head when it is his turn to speak. At the conclusion they all sit upright together as the curtain is drawn before the admiring audience. It is a custom which has great dignity and dates back to very early days in the Kabuki.

Before he dies a famous actor may indicate whom he considers best qualified to succeed to his title, but the succession is finally decided by a number of people, the hierarchy of the acting profession and the world of the theatre including the relatives of the deceased actor. It is customary for a space of many years to elapse even so, before such a privilege is granted. Kabuki actors in general do not reach maturity until middle age and the judges are stern and do not readily assent to the continuance of a great title. One of the most famous titles in the history of the Kabuki, Ichikawa Danjuro, lapsed with the death of the ninth Danjuro in 1903 and has never been revived. Danjuro IX, one of the most renowned actors in the history of the Kabuki, was the last of a long line which had continued in unbroken succession since the end of the seventeenth century. His ancestors were responsible for some of the major developments in the theatre and a knowledge of their names is important in any survey of the Kabuki. Their dates and particulars are given below. Ichikawa Danjuro IX died without leaving any male heirs and so far no actor has arisen who has been considered worthy of carrying on this great name. The titular head of the Ichikawa family at present is Ichikawa Sansho, who was not connected with the theatre at all but was a banker until he married the daughter of Danjuro IX. He was then trained in actor's technique but has remained only as a figurehead to administer the affairs of the Ichikawa family. He appears on the stage on special occasions and has made a point of reviving old plays which have ceased to be acted, but he is not and has never been regarded as a true actor and has no natural talent. He is respected for his historical researches into the theatre in its relations with the Ichikawa family and for his administrative position rather than as an artist.

THE ICHIKAWA DANJURO LINE

Ichikawa Danjuro I
Born in May, the third year of Manji, 1660. Died in February, the first year of Hoei, 1704.

He was born the son of a *samurai* family, but took to the theatre and was the powerful moving force in the development of the Yedo Kabuki. He was the advocate of romantic bravado and was the inventor of the technique called *aragoto*. He was a playwright as well as an actor, and was responsible for some of the famous *juhachiban* creations. He did a great deal to develop theatrical technique, and exerted a profound influence on generations of actors who followed him. He first wore stage costume patterned with the bold design which has since become the celebrated crest of the Ichikawa family, the three white squares fitting one inside the other on a persimmon coloured background, said to have been based on three rice measures.

His career ended tragically, for he was murdered in the theatre by a jealous fellow actor.

Ichikawa Danjuro II
Born in October, the first year of Genroku, 1688. Died in September, the eighth year of Horeki, 1758.

He was the first son of Danjuro I and assumed his father's title soon after his tragic death. He improved his father's plays and technique and did much to develop stage costume and design. He was skilled in all branches of the actor's art and was said to have had great powers of eloquence on the stage. The story is told of him that he once played in Osaka where the audiences were hostile to Yedo actors. The house on this occasion was particularly difficult and recited his speech before Danjuro had even commenced; with great presence of mind he immediately repeated the whole thing backwards and so saved his reputation.

Ichikawa Danjuro III
Born in the sixth year of Kyoho, 1721. Died in February in the second year of Kampo, 1742.

He was the real son of Sanshoya Sukejuro, but became the adopted son of Danjuro II and succeeded to the title in 1735, on the retirement of the second Danjuro.

Ichikawa Danjuro IV

Born in the first year of Shotoku, 1711. Died in February, the seventh year of Anei, 1778.

He is said to have been a real son of Danjuro II, but in 1713 he became the adopted son of the actor Matsumoto Koshiro, to whose title he succeeded in 1735, and did not take the title of Danjuro until 1754. He was not reckoned as the greatest of the Danjuros and had a somewhat chequered career.

Ichikawa Danjuro V

Born in August, the first year of Kampo, 1741. Died in October, the third year of Bunka, 1806.

An outstanding actor, he added fresh lustre to the family name. He was the real son of Danjuro IV and became Matsumoto Koshiro III in 1754. He succeeded to the Danjuro title in 1770.

Ichikawa Danjuro VI

Born in the seventh year of Anei, 1778. Died in May, the eleventh year of Kansei, 1799.

He died at the early age of twenty-one. He was the illegitimate son of Danjuro V and succeeded to the title at the age of fourteen.

Ichikawa Danjuro VII

Born in April, the third year of Kansei, 1791. Died in March, the sixth year of Ansei, 1859.

His name is remembered as one of the great Yedo actors and he was a public idol in his time. He lived in great style and in middle age was exiled by the Governor of Yedo for his extravagance. He was responsible for the revision and selection of the famous *juhachiban*, or eighteen best plays.

Ichikawa Danjuro VIII

Born in October, the sixth year of Bunsei, 1823. Died in August, the first year of Ansei, 1854.

He was a brilliant young actor but his father's troubles weighed upon his mind and he committed suicide at Osaka at the age of thirty-two.

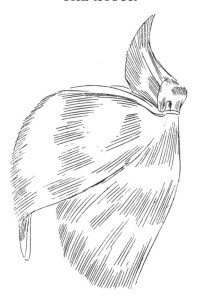

The theatrical wig worn by Ichikawa family actors on ceremonial occasions

Ichikawa Danjuro IX

Born in October, the ninth year of Tempo, 1838. Died in September, the thirty-sixth year of Meiji, 1903.

The ninth Danjuro, because of his extraordinary skill and dramatic talent, ranks as one of the greatest actors Japan has produced. He was the fifth son of Danjuro VII and became the adopted son of Kawarazaki Gonnosuke VI, but later returned to the Ichikawa family to become Danjuro in 1874.

A family tree like this gives a good idea of the continuity that has been preserved in the acting profession. A stage name in the Kabuki has a deep significance; it is a sacred trust to the actor, a criterion of standards which he is bound to honour and again pass on. It defies the grave and makes him one with the past yet keeps the flame burning for the future. It is a symbol of the immortality of the spirit.

Like his brother in the Chinese theatre, the Kabuki actor must conform to a strict code of etiquette in his training. He is disciplined by the most rigorous conventions and must pass through long years of study in following his career. His theatrical life begins in childhood and he may make his first appearance on the stage at the age of six or seven. The plays of the Kabuki contain many children's roles and it is in these that the actor of the future first tests his mettle. He becomes accustomed to the atmosphere of the theatre and acquires stage poise. It is quite common for father and son to appear on the stage simultaneously.

The system of adoption is a very marked feature of Japanese life and is found a great deal in theatrical circles. The relationship of father and son in the Kabuki does not necessarily mean the same as in the West. An actor may adopt a son into his family who is the child of another actor, or it may be of a non-acting family if the child shows promise. Sometimes an actor of quite mature years may become the adopted son of a celebrated actor. Naturally, adopted sons qualify for succession to an actor's name, in fact, that is one of the prime reasons for adoption. On the other hand, actors' real sons are just as much in evidence on the stage, but the position may appear somewhat complicated by the fact that an actor can have sons by different wives or a mistress and factors like these make the family trees of acting families quite involved.

The child actor today receives a normal education at the same time that he is finding his theatrical legs, and leads a busy life. Dancing lessons take up a great part of his training; almost as soon as he can walk the embryo actor commences to learn the art of the classical dance, and must continue to practice for the rest of his days. There are no theatrical schools as such; the young player will have a dancing master and receive individual instruction from various other people, but it is under his father or the actor whose family he is attached to that he acquires his knowledge and in the theatre itself. The day that he makes his first appearance on the stage in a play marks his theatrical christening; he assumes a name which is the junior title of the family he belongs to, after that he acquires his next name on the succession principle, marking his climb up the rungs of achievement. The grace and self possession of these tiny players of the Kabuki theatre are a never failing source of wonderment to all who see them.

The life of the Kabuki actor, like his brothers' in other theatres, is surrounded with a good deal of glamour in the eyes of the layman. To the actor himself there can be little glamour about it. He knows that perfection in any form of art is only arrived at through the hardest of work, even drudgery. There is no respite in his lifetime, a beginning but no end. Everything must be subordinated to a single aim. The physical strain is enormous, the mental discipline required can only be appreciated by those who undergo it. The day in the life of the average Kabuki actor makes a call upon physical and nervous energy which would appal the ordinary person with its severity; it requires a devotion to his task unequalled in other walks of life.

A Kabuki actor must possess great versatility in a number of technical ways; the importance of dancing has already been emphasized. Another necessary qualification for a good actor is a suitable voice, not for singing but for the measured diction and special intonation required in Kabuki dialogue. It must be clear and resonant, and have a pitch suitable for expressing varying emotions, often in accompaniment to the most vigorous action.

The art of wearing stage costume is an essential part of the Kabuki actor's technique. The *kimonos* worn in the women's roles, for example, are often exceedingly elaborate and lengthy garments, which sweep away for yards on the stage. The *onnagata* actor, who always walks with short steps and toes turned in, must bring manipulation of costumes such as these to a fine art, not only when he is in movement but in repose too. His stance, the way he sits and the manner in which his costume assists correct posing are all important factors in the keen eyes of the theatre *habitués*. The same thing applies in its own way to the actors in all types of roles.

A modern Japanese playwright recently remarked to the writer, that one of the reasons he considered new Kabuki actors inferior to those of former days was the fact that they had lost the art of wearing stage costume. This he attributed to the fact that actors now wear *yofuku* or foreign style dress off stage and so are becoming unaccustomed to the feel of the *kimono*. One can see his point. Japanese traditional costume has a uniform simplicity and formality and actors in the past have always been noted for their elegance. It was, for instance, *de rigueur* for every actor to turn up for rehearsal wearing formal *kimono*, *obi* and *haori*. Now at a rehearsal it is quite common for people to appear in the nondescript garments from the West, which seem to have a fatal attraction for the East in modern times, the sweater and the windbreaker, the abominable necktie and the even more abominable 'Hawaii' shirt, which appear irrevocably bequeathed to us as sartorial symbols of a new age. There are still those actors who adhere to tradition in matters of dress, but they are in an increasing minority. The criticism of the playwright emphasizes very sharply some of the intangible qualities in the actor's performance which are vital in the opinion of the Japanese playgoer, and which are less easily appreciated by the foreigner to whom perhaps the mere decorative appearance of the costume might appear the ultimate criterion.

Another demand made on the actor is that he have a physical appearance which fits him to play the various character types dictated by Kabuki roles. The heroes, heroines and villains of the stage have outward appearances which are hallowed by convention and long tradition and are never varied, and although skilful make-up and the genius of the actor can mitigate physical disadvantages to some degree, it will be found that most actors who are successful in a particular field have faces and forms which are eminently suitable to the conventions demanded of the roles they play. Usually an actor is noted for his skill in playing certain types of parts and only those. In the past, for instance, *onnagata* actors or female impersonators never played any other kind of role, and this applies in general to the most important *onnagata* actors today, but it is possible to find actors who play a variety of roles, including both men and women, and this interchangeability is quite a marked feature of the Kabuki stage. The late Onoe Kikugoro VI (1885–1945) acted in both male and female roles with equal distinction and his performances in either are still remembered as classics.

The main types of roles are listed under certain titles. *Tateyaku* denotes all the important male roles and the characters represented are loyal, good or courageous. In opposition to these are the *katakiyaku*, the bad characters. *Wakashu kata* denotes the parts of young men while *nimaime* is applied to parts which represent young men of a milder disposition. Sometimes they are lovers, at any rate their acting is not bold and forceful but restrained, at times almost effeminate. The female impersonators are often cast for *nimaime* roles. The term *nimaime wagoto* is often used to describe acting in such parts meaning in direct contrast to the *aragoto* style of bold acting. *Doke kata* are the comic roles, and include the humorous villain as well as the pure *farceur*. *Koyaku* signifies children's parts. The actors who play the parts of women are called *onnagata* or *oyama*. The main female parts are called *tachioyama* roles.

The senior actor and leader of the troupe is always known as the *zagashira* in a Kabuki company. Once an actor succeeds to a name which enables him to play significant roles and not just walking on parts he is called *nadai*.

The art of the female impersonator is one which both the theatres of China and Japan have made peculiarly their own. In both countries the development was due to the same cause, the refusal of authorities to allow women to appear on the stage at all. As any schoolboy knows, female impersonation was at one time common in the theatre of the West, but it has long since ceased to have any part in Occidental tradition, and it necessitates an adjustment of values for those brought up against the background of the modern Western theatre. No one will pretend that the *onnagata* has any place in modern drama and in these times when the Kabuki is encroached upon by much that it is only a superficial projection of the old tradition, the convention at times becomes meaningless. In the real Kabuki the technique of the *onnagata* is an inextricable part of the drama, it is in this art paradoxically enough that the strength of the Kabuki lies.

The Kabuki is artificial, it makes no pretence at being otherwise. Everything is exaggerated, conventionalized and emphasized to make a pattern for the eye and ear. The *onnagata* is a major unit of this pattern and by his creation of a subtle convention for femininity provides the degree of formality which sets the standard for the whole. It is not simply a question of being effeminate, the good *onnagata* must symbolize feminine qualities in a way that no actress can do. He must idealize and emphasize where the actress can only fall back upon easier and more natural qualities with a loss of the power of expression dictated by a drama such as the Kabuki.

The layman tends to think of the *onnagata* as playing the parts of the young and beautiful only, but there are many other roles to be filled, the matron or the elderly woman, characterizations that require a depth of technique and a power which, in relation to the general formal standard of the Kabuki, it would be difficult for an actress to attain. Some plays require the *onnagata* actor to take two consecutive parts of a very different nature.

Nakamura Utaemon VI as a courtesan

This is well exemplified in the famous dancing play, *Kaga-mijishi*. In the first part the actor must play a shy young maiden who, while dancing, is transformed in to the spirit of a lion, in which role he dances in the second half. It requires a vigorous technical metamorphosis and considerable physical strength. It has been common in recent years for women dancers, particularly the *geisha*, to give dances like this one in public. While they perform with great charm and grace, they never attain the power and vigour of the male actor. For those with the prejudices of the West, this is undoubtedly a difficult argument to follow, and indeed the implications of it can only be appreciated by seeing the Kabuki drama for oneself, attempting to appreciate it as a dramatic form whose background is quite different from that of any other. The fact remains that so long as the genuine Kabuki drama exists, the *onnagata* actor must remain a part of it.

The greatest *onnagata* actor in the Kabuki today is Nakamura

Utaemon VI, who was born in 1917. He is the son of Utaemon V who died in 1940 and was himself the most distinguished player of feminine roles in his time. The present Utaemon is an actor in the great classical tradition. Still young by acting standards, he bids fair to be a Japanese Mei Lan Fang, that great Chinese actor still talked of with respect and admiration by Japanese theatre people, who have never forgotten the visit he made to their country thirty years ago.

The acting of Utaemon delights the eye with its delicacy and grace of movement, and his exquisite dancing once seen is never forgotten. At the same time there is strength and virility underlying the finer qualities. His control of gesture is unsurpassed and displays the supreme achievement of the great artist, unity. He has the power to co-ordinate everything in a single pattern of line. His popularity is such that the strain upon his physical powers is enormous; between 11 a.m. and 9 p.m. on seven days a week he will have to appear in several plays, each role a leading one demanding the utmost from him. It is difficult for the layman to appreciate what the life of such an actor entails; there is no relaxation from one end of the year to the other. Anyone who imagines that a leading *onnagata* lives a soft life is labouring under an illusion.

The art of Nakamura Utaemon VI is the best possible proof that female roles in the Kabuki drama are essentially the creation of the male actor; even if women did play such parts it provides the curious position of women imitating men imitating women, and the probable result would be a degenerate and confused technique.

The *onnagata* actor today lives a normal life for such little time as he passes outside the theatre; in the past, however, he sacrificed his whole personality in order to achieve perfection in his acting. His daily life was conducted solely for the purpose of achieving the essence of perfection in his technique, and offstage he both dressed as a woman, wore his hair long in feminine coiffures and copied the movements and gestures of the ladies in every possible detail. There are many amusing stories related of actors of other days in this connection. A typical one describes the opening of the old Shintomiza theatre in June 1879, and concerns Iwai Hanshiro VIII, a famous *onnagata* of the period, who preserved a feminine appearance in everyday life. The occasion was an unprecedented one; foreign diplomatic officials had been invited, there were military bands and to add to the novelty of things all the celebrated actors and playwrights appeared on the platform wearing the new-fashioned frock coat which had recently been introduced from the West. The great Danjuro IX was so attired, along with many other famous stage personalities, all sitting stiffly on chairs instead of on the traditional *tatami*. The greatest rounds of applause, however, were reserved for Iwai Hanshiro, who arrived on the stage in frock coat, but with his hair done up in the usual woman's coiffure worn by *onnagata* actors off stage.

Yoshizawa Ayame (1673–1729) is generally regarded as the father, or should it be mother, of *onnagata* actors. He was an accomplished actor who did much to develop techniques which became the basis for all who came after him. His sayings and ideas were written down by the playwright Fukuoka Yagoshiro under the title *Ayamegusa*. It became the text-book of the *onnagata* actor. A summary of some of its main points follow; it is of interest in giving an idea of the principles which the old actors worked on. It must be remembered that at the time of their publication, these sayings were regarded as absolute revelations to be jealously guarded by actors, and were not for the public to read.

AYAMEGUSA
Related by Fukuoka Yagoshiro

Yoshizawa San is the most skilful *onnagata* of the age, and I have here set down things he has told me from time to time, and answers to questions I have asked him. I have arranged these under thirty articles entitled *Ayamegusa*. They will serve as a guide for those engaged in the profession, but must be kept secret and not told to the public, for they contain the mysteries of his art.

1. Yoshizawa San was asked by another *onnagata* actor what was the most important qualification for a female impersonator. He answered: 'The most important thing for an *onnagata* is to be able to act the part of *oiran* (courtesan). If an *onnagata* becomes skilled in that part he will be good in any part. The reason is this, as he is a man, he has a naturally strong character,

but if he wants to display the character of a courtesan, he cannot let a day of his life pass without studying her more subtle feminine qualities.'

(The meaning of this may appear obscure to the reader. In former times the courtesan was expected to have a strong character, she was not easy to approach by any would-be admirer. She had a strict code of etiquette while at the same time she was expected to be generous in spirit, quick witted and not to be imposed upon by anyone, this in addition to her more gentle qualities of womanly charm. Yoshizawa Ayame's point was that as an *onnagata* was really a man, he already possessed the more masculine qualities as a basis for the feminine characteristics he must simulate on the stage. The courtesan's nature, therefore, combined qualities which were best fitted to serve as a model for the male actor creating a convention of femininity on the stage.)

2. When an *onnagata* asked Ayame about correct acting he replied: 'When you play the role of a wife of a daimyo's retainer and you defeat the villain, you are likely to handle a sword skilfully, conscious all the time that you are a warrior's wife. But a woman does not wear a sword even though she is the wife of a daimyo's retainer, therefore you are a poor *onnagata* if you handle a sword skilfully. The only thing to do is to show are you not afraid of the sword. You cannot go further than that.'

3. One of the important things for an *onnagata* is attitude of mind. Even though you are good-looking by nature, it appears overdone if you are too conscious of looking pretty. On the other hand, it looks disagreeable if you appear too indifferent to feminine appeal. You cannot be a good *onnagata* unless you are like a woman in your daily life. The more you become conscious on the stage of playing a woman's part the more unsuccessful will you be. You must be exact in your daily life.

Yoshizawa repeatedly advised his pupils in this way.

4. I heard Ayame tell Jujiro: 'No matter how cheerfully the audience applauds you must not try to make them laugh. It is a good thing if you lead them into laughter by your actions without intentionally trying to do so. It is against a woman's nature deliberately to make them laugh.'

5. If an *onnagata* happens to hear others about him say: 'He would do well in *tachiyaku* roles (brave men)', he should be

ashamed of himself. No actor can be skilful in both *onnagata* and *tachiyaku* roles.

6. When you play with an unskilful actor you must endeavour to make that actor look skilful. Always bear this in mind.

7. At a meeting at Nizaemon's house someone advised Ayame, 'You had better visit Shinmachi (Osaka gay quarters). During the last five years manners have changed, you are acting in the style of courtesans of five years ago. The audience notices the difference.' Ayame said: 'I appreciated his kindness, but I thought if five years had brought such a great change in manners, there must be an even greater one between the present courtesan and the one of twenty years ago. In my opinion, a courtesan should remain old-fashioned, only a tea house girl or bath house attendant being up to date.'

8. An *onnagata* should never forget he is an *onnagata*, even in the greenroom. When he takes lunch he should turn his back to other persons present in the room. If he eats heartily in company with the *tachiyaku*, and then has to play a love scene with them on the stage he will be unsuccessful, for it will be difficult for him to portray tender feelings.

9. If an *onnagata* is a married man he must be careful not to show it in public. If someone says to him 'Your wife Mrs so and so', he must appear so embarrassed as to blush. No matter how many children he may have, he must not lose his innocence of mind.

10. Ayame said: 'The other day I went to see a flower show at Tennoji. Plum blossom was at its best, but people paid little attention, saying there was nothing new about it. They admired other flowers. However, I am deeply impressed by plum blossom, just because there is nothing new about it. The same thing may be said about the *onnagata*. All he has to do is to express the sentiments of an ordinary woman. If he tries to show something novel he fails. People tire of novelty. An *onnagata* must be careful not to step beyond the bounds of the ordinary woman.'

11. 'An *onnagata* is called young even if he is over forty years of age. The one word "young" keeps his mind flexible, it is very important to an *onnagata*,' Ayame used to tell his disciples.

12. *Shosagoto* (dancing) is a flower that blooms on the tree of the ordinary act. If you try to make a hit by *shosagoto* alone, you will not succeed. There are other things which may be compared

to fruits, flowers bloom only to produce the fruit, remember this.

13. Once in Kyoto there were three Kabuki companies. Two were equally matched in the abilities of their actors, the third was a little inferior. Sakata Tojuro told me: 'Those two companies will waste their time in competition with each other, while the third will strive alone unaffected by the competition of the other two, and eventually lead in popularity.' Sakata Tojuro was right in his anticipations.

This forms the gist of some of the more important sayings of a document which surely must be unique in the annals of theatrical history.

The Kabuki actor in other days was regarded as a social outcast by the authorities who governed a feudal Japan. He was confined in closed areas in the cities and treated with no token of respect. It was during the Meiji era (1868–1912), and largely through the efforts of a great man like Ichikawa Danjuro IX, that public prejudice against the members of his profession was broken down and the actor began to take a more normal position in the life of the community.

In spite of this, the Kabuki actor in old Yedo was a figure unrivalled in popularity among the ordinary folk, his professional skill was closely studied by the fans, his dress styles and the different articles he used marked him apart as a leader of fashion. People aped his mannerisms and avidly followed the details of his personal life. Once a year the *Yakusha hyobanki*, or 'Remarks on the Actors', was published and eagerly read by the theatre lovers. In it, the actors were graded according to their achievements during the year and admirers rejoiced accordingly when their favourites attained high places. In addition, stories about the more intimate side of an actor's life were published to satisfy that particular brand of human curiosity which is universal.

There is a survival of the tradition, for magazines are still published which give photographs and sketches of the careers of all the principal actors, the biographies inevitably finishing with a description as to how much wine an actor drinks, his tastes in food, his hobbies and sometimes his opinion on the modern girl!

The Kabuki actor of Yedo was a public idol who impressed his personality on the populace in countless ways. If he was famous, he often lived in great style and the fate of Ichikawa Danjuro

VII, who was exiled from Yedo by the authorities for his sumptuous ways of living, is a notable case in point. The importance of the Ichikawa Danjuros in the history of the Kabuki theatre has already been described, but there were many others besides and most of the great names of the modern Kabuki stage were held by men whose genius remained a legend after them, as well as some of their more personal characteristics, the last giving rise to many amusing anecdotes which have been handed down. Not every actor was handsome: Matsumoto Koshiro V (1768–1838) had an ugly face with small eyes and a tremendous aquiline nose, but he made his features famous in the roles of villain, and his acting technique was regarded as impeccable. He was particularly skilful in the performance of *mie*, using his bold profile to great advantage on these occasions. The story has it that his nose was so large he created a wind when breathing! He was in direct contrast to Segawa Kikunojo II, who died in 1773, aged 33, but who in his time was an *onnagata* actor lauded for the beauty of his make-up, which enabled him to play the parts of young girls to perfection. His dress and all the accessories of his apparel were the envy of the ladies of the town and he became the leader of fashion, his styles and patterns being widely copied.

Something has already been said about the great acting genius of the Meiji era, Ichikawa Danjuro IX, but a few more details will not be amiss here. Danjuro was largely responsible for shaping the future of the Kabuki theatre during a unique period of transition in Japan, and without his influence the position of the actor would not have improved to the great extent that it did. In 1887 he was asked to play before the Emperor; it was an unprecedented event in the history of the Kabuki and marked the esteem in which Danjuro was held and the new level of respect to which he raised his profession. Danjuro was a hero in Yedo, but he also achieved great popularity in Osaka where, until then, Yedo actors had always been received in hostile fashion, as the many stories about his ancestors show. When he died the whole country mourned him, for it was realized a great force had gone from the theatre and that Japan had lost one of her greatest sons.

Coming down to the present century, four of the most popular actors of the modern Kabuki theatre, who all died within a few years of each other, were Nakamura Utaemon V (1865–1940), Matsumoto Koshiro VII (1879–1949), Ichimura Uzaemon (1874–

1945) and Onoe Kikugoro VI (1855–1945). These actors are still talked about by playgoers, their memories are fresh and their interpretations and technical achievements serve as lodestones for all younger actors today. Their names spring readily to the lips of the old theatre *habitués*, for whom these actors can never be replaced. They were representative of an age now gone. Utaemon was a great *onnagata* and was particularly famous for playing the women's roles in the *jidaimono* plays. A man of striking physiognomy, which on no account could be described as handsome from a feminine point of view, he yet had a vivid personality which transformed every role he played and a command of technique which made his symbolism some of the most powerful on the stage. Koshiro VII was an adept at the more robust roles incorporating *aragoto*. He was a dancer of great accomplishment and the head of the Fujima school. It was said that he should have been the legitimate successor to Ichikawa Danjuro IX, whose pupil he was, but that in some way he offended Danjuro seriously. Whether this is true or not, in the eyes of the theatregoing public, Koshiro VII was the actor best fitted to have carried on Danjuro's title. The three sons of Koshiro have become well-known Kabuki actors, and one of them, Ichikawa Ebizo IX, has been hinted at in theatrical circles as a possible successor to the great name of Danjuro should it ever be revived, so Koshiro's son may yet achieve the honour for the family. Kikugoro VI was the son of the great Meiji actor Kikugoro V, and a most versatile actor who excelled in every type of role he played, which included both male and female parts. He was a superb dancer and equally skilled in *shosagoto*, *jidaimono* or *sewamono* plays, and one of the most universally popular actors. Uzaemon XV was another idol of Kabuki audiences, particularly the ladies, for whom he was the epitome of charm and good looks in his interpretations of the handsome young hero roles. He was a brilliant and talented actor with a magnetic stage personality, which endeared him to the playgoers. His diction was regarded as perfect, and one Japanese critic has recorded that when Uzaemon stepped upon the stage, to hear him sounded like music from heaven. His son and successor never achieved his father's greatness and died of cancer in 1952. With his death the great name of Uzaemon remains only a memory in the theatre, there being no successors.

Kichiemon

The doyen of the Kabuki today is Nakamura Kichiemon, a man of seventy, in poor health, but still appearing regularly on the stage. He is the leader of the Kichiemon Troupe, one of the two main acting companies in Tokyo. Kichiemon has been decorated by the Emperor for his services to the theatre, official recognition of a long and distinguished career. He is one of the few actors with little ancestral prestige and made his first stage appearance in 1900. His special talent lies in playing the loyal male roles of the *jidaimono* plays, the *samurai* of high principles or the faithful retainer of a noble house are his particular forte. Such parts require a skilled command of the formal, but at the same time emotional, technique used to express the psychological contents of these dramas. Kichiemon is one of the last of the old prewar school of actors and so a good deal of nostalgic respect attaches to his position on the stage. Many modern critics consider that Kichiemon should have retired and that, by remaining active in spite of his poor health, he is damaging his own reputation. Whether this is so or not it seems inevitable that his theatre days are numbered; when he goes Tokyo will lose a last remaining link with an older school of acting.

Kichiemon, having only a daughter, has adopted her son

The actor Mitsugoro
at a Noh play Nov 28/53

Mannosuke as his theatrical heir. The father of Mannosuke is the actor, Matsumoto Koshiro VIII, the second son of the late Koshiro VII. The boy actor often appears on the stage with his father and 'theatrical father'. In addition, Kichiemon has two brothers on the Kabuki stage, Nakamura Tokizo III and Nakamura Kanzaburo XVII. Tokizo himself has three sons who are Kabuki actors, a fact which further helps to demonstrate the complexities of relationships between acting families.

Another veteran player of a different calibre is Bando Mitsugoro VII, who was born in 1882 and is still prominent on the Tokyo stage. A wiry little man with an impish face, he is the son of Morita Kanya, a famous theatre manager, who died in 1897, and who introduced many innovations into theatrical construction and procedure. Mitsugoro is not particularly distinguished for his acting, but is regarded as one of the greatest dancers on the stage and nearly all his appearances are in pure dance numbers. He is the leader of the Bando school of dancing, as noted in Chapter VI. An old man who is well liked by everybody, he spends a great part of his leisure in watching Nō drama. The critics have from time to time hinted that Mitsugoro too should retire, but he has remained indifferent to their suggestions. Nakamura Tokizo, born in 1895, is the senior *onnagata* or female impersonator of the Tokyo Kabuki, and plays the *tachioyama* roles, i.e. the main female parts in the plays of the old repertoire. He is particularly skilled in the plays of doll theatre origin but has acted in a considerable number of new dramas which have been written specially for him and the actor Ichikawa Enno-suke II.

Ennosuke, who was born in 1889, astonishes by his vigour and energy, for he probably plays more senior male roles than any other actor on the stage today. A short thickset man, in his younger days he travelled in Europe, and was afterwards associated with many new developments in the Kabuki and attempts to improve it with Western influences. The truth of the matter is that Ennosuke is not a classical Kabuki actor at all. His real achievement lies in comedy, particularly comic dancing, and his talents would have more scope in a Western style theatre. By the vagaries of fate he now occupies a position as one of the senior classical Kabuki actors, although his performances in traditional style acting receive little praise from the critics, this being reserved for the occasions when his particular accomplishments find an outlet in modern dances and plays. Ennosuke is generally admired by many foreign playgoers, for whom his lack of Japanese subtlety but extraordinary command of technical tricks, acrobatic dancing and virility, provides great entertainment. He leads his own acting troupe which often combines forces with the Kichie-mon and Kikugoro troupes, the two main Kabuki companies.

A Tokyo actor who rivals Nakamura Utaemon VI in popularity as an *onnagata* player is Onoe Baiko VII. Born in 1915, he was the son of the famous Kikugoro VI and made his first stage appearance in 1922. Today he is the leader of the Kikugoro troupe, of which he took control after the death of his father. He is an extremely popular actor, brilliant dancer and an adept at portraying the women characters of the *sewamono* plays, wives of merchants and shopkeepers, in which perhaps he shows his greatest talent. Offstage he is a small man inclined to be a little stout, who looks anything but an actor. He plays golf and baseball and is a modern type whose daily life is divorced from the stage as much as it is possible to be. His small son Ushinosuke, a mischievous-faced little boy, has already made his stage debut and appears regularly in Kabuki plays.

Ichikawa Ebizo IX, born in 1909, is the leading player of the

*Ebizo in
Kumadori make up
'Mukimi'*

young heroes and handsome rakes of the Kabuki. He is supreme of his kind today and has come to assume the mantle of the late Ichimura Uzaemon XV, whose style he has studied closely, and to whom, when in costume and make-up, he bears a certain resemblance. He is an actor in the best classical tradition, with a good voice and a commanding stage presence, an artist who symbolizes the spirit of the old theatre in his particular field of acting. A humble and modest man off stage, he has a small son Natsuo, who made his first stage appearance with his father on October 1, 1953, the occasion being a ceremonial performance to commemorate the fiftieth anniversary of the death of Danjuro IX, an event not without significance if rumours about Ebizo's future prove correct.

An actor of different talents is Nakamura Kanzaburo, born in 1909, who shows great versatility in a number of ways. An accomplished dancer, he excels in roles which require a sense of wit and humour. He is particularly good at representing the members of the lower strata of old Japanese society, from a bibulous ragpicker to a tea house maid and is a comic actor with a balanced sense of restraint and subtlety of feeling.

These are some of the bigger names in the modern Kabuki theatre, there are many more, the men who play the leading roles and are foremost in the public eye. There are others, however, who hold a more modest status and never achieve the glory of stardom, whose task it is to interpret the numerous minor roles which occur in Kabuki plays. It may be a shopkeeper, a city clerk, an old retainer or a *samurai* of lower rank; whatever the character these parts well acted contribute that touch of humanity which is the pre-requisite of all drama. Such an actor is Ichikawa Arajiro II born in 1889. Whatever role he plays or however short his time upon the stage, he brings distinction to his interpretation, brief though it may be, in a way which delights the eye and ear of the connoisseur. Among his other qualities, Arajiro possesses a diction which in its clarity is second to none. Unfitted by nature to play handsome parts, his colleagues nickname him 'Peanut', because of his long face; nevertheless, he has his own talents and actors of his kind are as vital to the theatre as are the men of more dazzling reputation.

As in the Chinese theatre, there are, on the Kabuki stage, many actors who never have speaking parts. They may be court attendants, soldiers, waiting maids, townspeople and so on. Sometimes they may have to perform acrobatics while acting as adversary to a bold hero, or give a group dance in a palace scene. Mostly they are drawn from the ranks of young actors being given their first chances to stand upon the stage, or else they are older men, whose talents do not allow them to achieve more ambitious heights. Actors' careers vary; there are some who after a brilliant youth never consummate their earlier talent and disappear into the obscurity of minor roles, there are others who after long and difficult years in which they receive little recognition, suddenly appear as mature actors and proceed to go from strength to strength. One thing is certain, in the Kabuki it is never wise to make conclusive statements about a young actor, however distinguished his connections; it is not until the age of forty or so that it can be judged whether he will stay the course as a leading artist.

Nevertheless, from *zagashira* down to the 'legs of the horse', actors have one thing in common, a loyalty to the theatre; it is their whole life and outside it they have no existence that matters. The position of the Kabuki actor is not an easy one today. In the eyes of some, nothing he does can ever equal past achievements, to others yet again he is an anachronism in a new age. He has to contend with a background which is still to some extent feudalistic and which works to his disadvantage in the press of modern times. In spite of it all he enjoys a universal popularity, but it is a popularity which is hard won and demands that he works harder than any actor has worked before for the minimum remuneration. If he is not given sufficient parts he has to be prepared for lean times and to many of the rank and file of the profession they are lean times indeed. Taking all the difficulties of a modern civilization into account, the Kabuki actors are a body of artists who deserve respect for their industry and achievements.

The following is a biographical list of some of the more important living Kabuki actors. The stage name comes first, their shop name following. Besides his theatrical titles, every actor has a real name of course, but these are not given here as being irrelevant. The actors listed are those who are playing at the time this book is being written.

NAKAMURA KICHIEMON I * HARIMAYA
Born March 1886.

The second son of Nakamura Karoku, his mother was the daughter of Manga Kichiemon who kept a tea house in the old Ichimura za. He took the name Nakamura Kichiemon I in his childhood and made his first stage appearance in 1900. He became a *nadai* or fully-fledged actor in 1905. He became distinguished for his technique in the chief roles of the *jidaimono* plays, in this sense he is a limited actor for he does not dance at all. He is famed for roles like those of Moritsuna in *Moritsuna Jinya*. Kichiemon is the senior actor in the Kabuki today, a position he assumed after the death of Kikugoro VI in 1945. He is the leader of the Kichiemon Troupe and a member of the Geijutsuin, or Japanese Art Academy. His only daughter married the actor Matsumoto Koshiro, whose son Mannosuke is also the adopted son of Kichiemon. He is a writer of *haiku*, Japanese seven-syllable poetry, and has published a book of his verse.

BANDO MITSUGORO VII * YAMATOYA
Born December 1882.

The first son of Morita Kanya, the famous theatre manager of the Meiji era. He made his first stage appearance in 1889 as Bando Yaosuke. In 1906 he became a *nadai* actor and took the name Bando Mitsugoro. His talent lies in dancing, of which he is the most distinguished exponent in the theatre and he is the *iemoto*, or leader, of the Bando school. He is a member of the Japanese Art Academy and a keen follower of the Nō drama. An old man with classical tastes, he is liked for his genial disposition. He has a son Minnosuke, who is an actor in the Osaka Kabuki.

ICHIKAWA ENNOSUKE II * OMODAKAYA
Born May 1888.

The first son of the late Ichikawa Danshiro II, he made his first stage appearance in 1892 as Ichikawa Danshi. In 1910 he succeeded to the title Ennosuke. During the Taisho era (1912–26), he was known as a progressive actor and travelled in Europe studying Western drama. He has performed in many new dance plays and the more modern types of Kabuki drama. His real forte lies in comedy. In the traditional sense he is not a true Kabuki actor at all, although today he appears in most of the important classical plays. A small, stocky man, he possesses tremendous vigour for his age and leads his own troupe.

NAKAMURA TOKIZO III * HARIMAYA
Born June 1895.

He is a brother of Nakamura Kichiemon and made his first stage appearance in 1901 as Nakamura Yonekichi. He is noted for his acting of the female roles in the *jidaimono* plays, and for many years played opposite his brother. Since the war he has played a great deal with Ennosuke, a number of new plays having been written for them. He is the senior *onnagata* actor of the Tokyo stage. He has a large family and four of his sons are Kabuki actors.

ICHIKAWA SADANJI III * TAKINOYA
Born August 1898.

He is the son of Ichikawa Monnosuke and became a pupil of Danjuro IX at the age of five. He made his first stage appearance in 1902 as Otoro. He later became the pupil of Kikugoro VI and succeeded to the title of Ichikawa Omezo VI in 1917. He succeeded to the title of Sadanji in June 1952. He plays both male and female parts but has been noted for his acting in *nimaime* roles, i.e. young heroes and lovers of mild and unaggressive character; versatility rather than specialization in any one type characterizes his acting in general. With Onoe Baiko VII he controls the Kikugoro Troupe.

ICHIKAWA SANSHO * NARITAYA
Born 1882.

His real name is Harikosi Hukuzaburo. He is a member of a banking family, and he himself was engaged in this profession. He married the daughter of Ichikawa Danjuro IX and was ordered to undergo training as an actor. He made his first stage appearance under his own name in 1903, succeeding to the title Sansho in 1917. An actor who owes his position simply to his marriage connections, he is something of an exception to orthodox Kabuki tradition. He is the titular head of the Ichikawa family and it is in the administration duties attaching to this and in the researches into the Danjuro family history which he has undertaken, that his theatrical position is justified. The rare occasions when he appears on the stage are regarded as courtesy acting only by the profession as a whole.

NAKAMURA KANZABURO XVII * NAKAMURAYA
Born 1909.

He is the fourth son of Nakamura Karoku and is therefore brother to Kichiemon and Tokizo. He made his first stage appearance as Nakamura Yonekichi in 1917. In 1929 he became a *nadai* actor and succeeded to the title Nakamura Masho; he became Nakamura Kanzaburo in 1940. He was distinguished for his playing in various classical roles, both male and female. He left the Kabuki to follow new style drama for a time, but he did not add to his laurels. After the war he began to make a steadily increasing reputation in the Kabuki and is now one of the leading actors of the Kichiemon Troupe. He is married to the daughter of the late Kikugoro VI, an actor whom he emulates to some extent, particularly in dancing and *sewamono* plays. He is a skilful character actor and a dancer with a whimsical humour of his own.

NAKAMURA UTAEMON VI * NARIKOMAYA
Born January 1917.

He is the second son of the great actor Nakamura Utaemon V. He made his first stage appearance as Nakamura Kotaro in 1922. In November 1933, after his brother's death, he succeeded to the title of Nakamura Fukusuke, Nakamura Shikan VI in 1941 and finally Nakamura Utaemon in 1950. He has never played any other than *onnagata* roles and early mastered the great parts of the *jidaimono* plays such as *san hime*, the three princesses. His career has been a series of progressions from strength to strength, except for some time when the war interrupted his development. A superb dancer, his technique is in the purest classical tradition and he is the most polished *onnagata* actor on the stage. He is a skilled musician and plays *samisen*, *koto* and *kokyu* with equal facility. A man of strong will and determined character, in spite of the nature of his acting, he is universally accepted by the critics as carrying on the great traditions of his ancestors. He has no children.

ICHIKAWA EBIZO IX * NARITAYA

Born January 1909.

He is the first son of Matsumoto Koshiro VII and made his first stage appearance as Matsumoto Kintaro in 1915. In 1929 he became Ichikawa Komazo, but later became seriously ill and retired from the stage. He returned to the Kabuki, however, and in 1939 he became a member of the Ichikawa family and the adopted son of Ichikawa Sansho. In 1940 he became Ichikawa Ebizo IX. After this his reputation gradually increased until now he holds supreme place as an actor of the handsome young men roles of the Kabuki. He is one of the most popular actors on the stage and in his particular field remains unequalled today. He preserves a classical style in his acting and has an excellent stage presence. He first rose to prominence after the war in the role of Sukeroku. His son Natsuo made his first stage appearance with his father in October 1953, at the memorial performance for Danjuro IX at the Kabuki za, Tokyo.

ONOE BAIKO VII * OTOWAYA

Born August 1915.

He is the eldest son of Onoe Kikugoro VI and made his first stage appearance in 1922. In accordance with his father's wishes he received a university education and took no important parts as a young actor. In 1935 he took the name of Kikunosuke II and began to make a name as a new *onnagata* actor who rivalled the present Utaemon. In 1947 he succeeded to the title Baiko, and on the death of his father in 1949 he took control of the Kikugoro Troupe. An extremely popular actor, he has distinguished himself in most of the principal *onnagata* roles and has had considerable success in the *sewamono* plays. Off stage he appears like a successful young businessman and plays golf and baseball. His son, Ushinosuke, has already made his stage debut and has often appeared with his father.

MATSUMOTO KOSHIRO VIII * KORAIYA

Born July 1910.

He is the second son of the late Koshiro and made his first stage appearance as Nakamura Junzo in 1915 and in 1931 became Ichikawa Somegoro V. He was brought up in the family of Nakamura Kichiemon, whose daughter he married. He made his real successes after the war and succeeded to the title Koshiro in 1949. He specializes in male roles of *jidaimono* and *shosagoto* plays. His son Mannosuke has already appeared on the stage many times with his father.

ONOE SHOROKU II * OTOWAYA
Born March 1913.

He is the third son of Matsumoto Koshiro VII and is brother of Ebizo and the present Koshiro. His first stage appearance was as Matsumoto Yutaka in 1918. He was put under the charge of Kikugoro VI in whose school he studied. A skilled dancer, he became head of the Fujima school in succession to his father. He has been successful in recent years in *katakiyaku*, villain roles in *jidaimono*, as well as in some of the more evil characters of the *sewamono* plays. A jovial man full of pranks, he gives his hobby as sleeping in the greenroom.

SAWAMURA SOJURO VII * KINOKUNIYA
Born January 1888.

He is the third son of Sawamura Sojuro VI. He made his first stage appearance as Sawamura Gempei in 1913, and in 1926 succeeded to the title Sawamura Tossho V. In September 1953 he became Sojuro, at the same time that his son Gempei VI succeeded to his father's title of Tossho VI. He is noted for his *onnagata* roles, particularly those of the evil women of the *jidaimono* plays.

MORITA KANYA XV * KINOJIYA
Born March 1910.

He is a nephew of the actor Morita Kanya XIV, but later became his adopted son. He made his first stage appearance in 1914 as Bando Tamasaburo, and took the name Bando Shuka in the same year. In 1942 in conjunction with an Osaka actor, Kataoka Gato, he founded a company known as the Seinen Kabuki, in which he played the lead in the handsome young men roles and became exceedingly popular. He succeeded to the name Morita Kanya in 1935. His theatrical star has waned somewhat today.

ICHIKAWA DANSHIRO III * OMODAKAYA
Born October 1909.

The eldest son of Ichikawa Ennosuke II. He made his first stage appearance in 1913 as Ichikawa Danshi and became Danshiro in 1930. He has travelled abroad a great deal and at one time showed leanings towards the modern stage. He plays male roles and acts in modern style Kabuki drama with his father; his small son Danshi has already made his stage debut.

NAKAMURA MATAGORO II * HARIMAYA
Born June 1914.

He is the eldest son of the actor Matagoro I and made his first stage appearance in 1922 as Matagoro. He was noted for his skill in playing the *koyaku*, or child roles of the traditional repertoire. He became a *nadai* actor in 1944 and now specializes in the *nimaime* roles.

BANDO HIKOSABURO VII * OTOWAYA
Born June 1916.

Eldest son of Hikosaburo VI, he made his first stage appearance in 1921 as Kamesaburo. He succeeded to the title of Hikosaburo in 1942. He assists Onoe Baiko in the control of the Kikugoro Troupe. He specializes in male roles and plays some of the important secondary characters in both *jidaimono* and *sewamono* plays. His small son is already on the stage as Kamesaburo.

NAKAMURA FUKUSUKE VII * NARIKOMAYA
Born March 1928.

He was the first son of Nakamura Fukusuke V, elder brother of the present Utaemon. He made his first appearance as Kotaro in 1933. He succeeded to the title of Fukusuke after the death of his grandfather, Utaemon V, in 1940. He has specialized in female roles in accordance with the traditions of his family and of recent years has received liberal praise from the critics for his acting in the traditional *onnagata* parts.

NAKAMURA KICHINOJO * HARIMAYA
Born November 1886.

He was not born of a theatrical family but was chosen as a child actor for a special show organized in the provinces in 1892, by

Nakamura Karoku, the father of Kichiemon, Tokizo and Kanza-buro. He afterwards took the name Harinosuke and made his first Tokyo appearance in 1894. He became a *nadai* actor in 1918 and took the title Kichinojo. He holds an administrative position in the Kichiemon Troupe but appears in many of the minor roles to which he brings distinction.

ICHIKAWA ARAJIRO II * DAIKOKUYA
Born October 1889.

He is the son of Ichikawa Arajiro I and made his first stage appearance as Kuranosuke in 1894. He succeeded to the title of Arajiro in 1910. Arajiro acts only the minor roles in Kabuki plays, but to these he brings a skill and quality of technique which mark him as an accomplished and conscientious actor in his own sphere. He visited Russia with the troupe of the late Ichikawa Sadanji II who went there on invitation in 1928.

ICHIKAWA YAOZO IX * TACHIBANAYA
Born July 1906.

In 1913 he became the pupil of Koshiro VII and in 1929 became a *nadai* actor as Matsumoto Komaguro I. He succeeded to the title Yaozo in September 1953. He is an important partner to Arajiro.

ICHIKAWA CHUSA IX * TACHIBANAYA
Born November 1896.

The second son of the late Danshiro, he is the brother of Ennosuke and made his first stage appearance as Ichikawa Matsuo in 1913. In 1918 he became the adopted son of the late Ichikawa Chusa VIII, succeeding to the name of Yaozo in the same year. He acted with his brother's troupe for many years, but left the stage at one time for story telling, at which traditional art he is an expert. He returned to Kabuki, however, and is now an important actor of male roles and assists his brother in running the Ennosuke Troupe. He succeeded to the title of Chusa in September 1953.

NAKAMURA SHIKAKU III * SHINKOMAYA
Born April 1900.

He is the son of Nakamura Denkuro, a famous theatre manager, and made his first stage appearance as Yoshimaru in 1905. He took the name of Utanosuke in 1911 and in 1919 became a *nadai* actor taking the name Shikaku. He became a most promising *onnagata* who vied with the late Fukusuke V for popularity. Now he is an independent actor who specializes in the roles of elderly women and matrons in *sewamono* plays. Often these are not major roles, but he brings to them a skill and understanding of characterization which mark his parts as minor masterpieces.

KATAOKA ROEN V * MATSUSHIMAYA
Born July 1910.

He was the oldest son of Kataoka Nizaemon XII, and made his first stage appearance in 1916 as Hajime. He took the title of Roen in 1934, when he was taking a prominent part as an *onnagata* actor in the Seinen Kabuki of Morita Kanya. He then acted with his father until the latter's murder, after this he became independent but remained in obscurity for some time. Within recent years he has had a particular success with roles such as maidservants, *geisha* and courtesans, into which he introduces a depth of feeling that is peculiarly his own.

ICHIKAWA SHOCHO IV * WAKAMATSUYA
Born September 1928.

He is the adopted son of the late Shocho III and made his first stage appearance in 1933 as Ichikawa Takashi. He grew up as a pupil of the late Uzaemon XV and was a very skilful child actor. After the death of his teacher, he joined the Ennosuke Troupe and succeeded to the name Shocho in August 1946. He is a popular actor and one of the most promising of the younger *onnagata* in the Kabuki today, and appears well qualified to play the great female roles such as *san hime*. He has appeared in a number of more modern style Kabuki plays and has had a success in acting with Ennosuke and Tokizo in their special productions. A young man of happy temperament, he is typical of the newer school of actors in the best sense of the word.

KAWARAZAKI GONZABURO IV * YAMAZAKIYA
Born February 1918.

He is the first son of the actor Kawarazaki Gonjuro and made his first stage appearance in 1935 as Kaoru; he became a *nadai* actor in 1946 and succeeded to the name Gonzaburo. He is skilled in playing the *nimaime* roles and has a good stage presence which makes him a valuable actor in supporting roles.

KATAOKA ICHIZO V * MATSUSHIMAYA
Born February 1916.

He is the son of the late Ichizo IV and made his first stage appearance in 1923, and succeeded to the title Ichizo in 1934. His career was interrupted by military service and he joined the Kikugoro Troupe after the war. He has had good criticisms in many of the supporting male roles and he is a useful all round actor.

KAWARAZAKI GONJURO II * YAMAZAKIYA
Born August 1881.

He is the son of a theatre tea house proprietor and was brought up in the atmosphere of the theatre of other days. He made his first stage appearance in the winter of 1885 as Ichikawa Kaoru. He became a *nadai* actor in 1900 and succeeded to the title Ichikawa Gonjuro and finally became Kawarazaki Gonjuro in April 1919. An old time actor who has a fund of reminiscences of the great names and traditions of the past, he is still active on the stage and plays regularly in supporting male roles.

ONOE KAISABURO III * NANBUYA
Born December 1897.

He is the son of the actor Nakamura Gansuke and made his first stage appearance in 1913 as Onoe Kutosaburo. He became a *nadai* actor in May 1920, and succeeded to the name Kaisaburo. He acted in many of the new plays of Kikugoro VI and today is on the general staff of the Kikugoro Troupe.

BANDO SHUCHO IV * YAMATAYA
Born March 1910.

He became the adopted son of the late Shucho III at the age of four and made his first stage appearance in 1917 as Bando Katsumi, and in 1940 succeeded to the title Shucho. He has played both male and female roles, and acted in the Ennosuke Troupe.

PLATE III

Ichikawa Ebizo IX

A mie. Matsumoto Koshiro VIII in 'Ibaragi'

Nakamura Utaemon VI

Nakamura Kichiemon

PLATE IV

Kitsune Roppo. Ichikawa Ennosuke

Onoe Baiko VII

Actor on the hanamichi. Nakamura Utaemon VI

ONOE BAICHO IV * OTOWAYA

He was a pupil of Kikugoro VI and made his first stage appearance in 1903 as Onoe Kanejiro and became a *nadai* actor, succeeding to the name Baicho in 1929. He plays *onnagata* roles, and is a valued teacher for younger actors in the forms of this type of acting.

NAKAMURA TAKESABURO I * NARIKOMAYA
Born September 1882.

He is the son of a professional story teller and became a pupil of Utaemon V. In 1890 he made his first stage appearance as Nakamura Fukuyaku. Ten years later he took the name Shikazo and finally became a *nadai* actor in 1909, taking the name Takesaburo. He was an independent actor for many years as an *onnagata*. He is an important supporting actor and a useful instructor for young players.

ICHIKAWA TERUZO II * TAKINAYA
Born January 1886.

He made his first stage appearance in 1894 as Ichikawa Takinoko. He later took the name Hyozaburo and finally became Teruzo and a *nadai* actor in 1912. He has played a good deal in *sewamono* plays as a useful supporting actor.

SUKETAKAYA KODENJI * SUKETAKAYA
Born January 1909.

He is a son of the actor, the late Tosshi VII, and made his first stage appearance in 1913 as Sawamura Chamemasu, he became Horonosuke in 1925 and took the title Kodenji as a *nadai* actor in 1927. He plays *onnagata* roles and is a member of the Kikugoro Troupe.

ICHIKAWA DANJO VIII * MIYOSHIYA
Born May 1882.

He is the eldest son of the great Meiji actor Ichikawa Danjo VII and made his first stage appearance in 1885 as Ginzo. In 1905 he took the name Momotaro, and in 1908 became Kuzo. He acted in small companies for many years and then became a member of the Kichiemon Troupe. He succeeded to the name Danjo in 1943. He has made a speciality of old men roles.

SAWAMURA TOSSHI VIII * KINOKUNIYA
Born November 1887.

He is the adopted son of the late Tosshi VII and made his first
stage appearance in 1897 as Sawamura Daisuke and took the
name Denjiro in the same year. He became a *nadai* actor in 1911.
He played in small companies for many years, acting in most of
the leading male roles. He took the name Tosshi in 1927, and
is now an independent actor.

ONOE TAGANOJO III * OTOWAYA
Born September 1887.

He made his first stage appearance in 1891 as Ichikawa Kiza-
buro. On becoming a *nadai* actor he took the name Ichikawa
Onimaru and succeeded to the name Taganojo in 1927. He is an
onnagata actor who today makes a speciality of playing the old
woman roles in the traditional plays, in which parts he shows a
particular skill.

SAWAMURA GENNOSUKE V * KINOKUNIYA
Born January 1907.

He is the son of a composer and made his first stage appearance
in 1913 as Kataoka Chiyomaru. He became a *nadai* actor in 1922,
and succeeded to the title Gennosuke. He plays *onnagata* roles
and is a member of the Ennosuke Troupe. His wife is the
daughter of Gennosuke IV.

SAWAMURA TOSSHO VI * KINOKUNIYA
Born March 1933.

He is the eldest son of Sawamura Sojuro and made his first
stage appearance in 1940 as Gempei. He plays *onnagata* roles
and appears regularly with his father in the Kichiemon Troupe.
Absent from the stage for some time owing to illness, he succeeded to his father's title Tossho in September 1953.

NAKAMURA SHIBAJAKU VI * HARIMAYA
Born December 1927.

He is the second son of Nakamura Tokizo and made his first
stage appearance as Baishi in 1936. He did not play as a child
actor, however, and received a normal school education, return-

ing to the stage on completion of his studies. He is an *onnagata* actor who shows much promise and he succeeded to the title Shibajaku in April 1953.

NAKAMURA KAISHO II * HARIMAYA
Born July 1925.

He is the eldest son of Tokizo and made his first stage appearance with his brother Shibajaku in 1936. He took the title Kaisho in April 1953 in a joint ceremony with his brother; previously he was named Tanetaro II. He plays male roles.

NAKAMURA KINNOSUKE I * HARIMAYA
Born November 1932.

He is the fourth son of Tokizo and made his first stage appearance in 1936 with his brothers. He plays *onnagata* roles and *wakashigata*, young men. So far he has acted chiefly with his father.

ONOE KIKUZO VI * OTOWAYA
Born June 1923.

He is the son of Onoe Taganojo and made his first stage appearance in 1938. In 1946 he took the name Kikuzo and so far has only played minor roles, but shows skill and talent.

BANDO KEIZO I * YAMATOYA
Born November 1925.

He is the second son of the late Bando Shucho and made his first stage appearance in 1928. He was a skilful child actor and is now one of the younger members of the Kichiemon Troupe. He plays *onnagata* roles but also acts in male parts.

BANDO MITSUNOBU I * YAMATOYA
Born May 1929.

He is the third son of the late Bando Shucho and made his first stage appearance in 1932 as Mitsunobu. After his father's death, he was placed under the care of the late Kikugoro VI and is now a member of the Kikugoro Troupe. A skilful dancer, he plays *tateyaku* or male roles.

OKAWA HASHIZO II * OTOWAYA

Born April 1929.

A pupil of Sadanji III and the adopted son of the wife of the late Kikugoro VI, he took the name Ichikawa Omemaru on his first appearance and became Hashizo in 1945. He is a skilful dancer who shows talent and plays *onnagata* roles, though he also acts in male parts. He is a member of the Kikugoro Troupe.

KATAOKA DAISUKE I * MATSUSHIMAYA

Born November 1926.

He is the third son of the late Kataoka Nizaemon XII and made his first stage appearance under his own name in 1935. After his father's death he and his brother Kataoka Roen were in an unhappy position for some time. Now Daisuke is a member of the Kikugoro Troupe where he has played subordinate roles so far.

IWAI HANSHIRO X * OMEDAKAYA

Born August 1927.

He is the son of a dancer and composer and received a university education, rare for an actor. He made his first stage appearance in 1933, in later years he joined the Ennosuke Troupe and succeeded to the title Shoen in 1940, becoming a *nadai* actor. In 1951 he succeeded to the title Iwai Hanshiro. He plays both male and female roles, and is a young actor of promise who, however, is greatly in demand for film work.

SUKETAKAYA TAKASUKE * SUKETAKAYA

Born March 1900.

He is the eldest son of the late Sawamura Sojuro V and made his first stage appearance in 1905 as Takamaru. In 1920 he became a *nadai* actor and took the name Takasuke. He plays male roles and acted in comic dance parts with his father. He is an extremely able *samisen* player and often gives private recitals to his colleagues.

SAWAMURA TANOSUKE V * KINOKUNIYA

Born October 1902.

He is the second son of Sawamura Sojuro VI, his eldest brother being Takasuke and his younger brother Sojuro VII. He made

his first stage appearance in 1908 as Yoshiziro. He became *nadai*
actor in 1920, succeeding to the title Tanosuke. He has had a
varied acting career but is now independent. He plays *onnagata*
or *nimaime* roles.

ICHIMURA KAKITSU XVI * TACHIBANAYA
Born January 1918.

He is the second son of the late Kataoka Nizaemon and was the
adopted son of the late Ichimura Uzaemon XV. His first stage
appearance was in 1922 as Kataoka Yoshinao. In 1941 he took
the name Ichimura Matasaburo and succeeded to the title
Kakitsu in 1947. He specializes in *nimaime wagoto*, the romantic
young men of the Kabuki stage. He is a skilful photographer
and has published a book of his theatrical photographs.

ICHIKAWA JUKAI III * NARITAYA
Born 1886.

He made his first stage appearance in 1894 as Takamuru, took
the name Komanosuke in 1903 and Tossho in 1905, when he
became the adopted son of Ichikawa Sumizo. In 1922 he succeeded to the title Sumizo VI and became Jukai in 1950. He was
awarded the *Mainichi* newspaper drama prize for his acting in
nimaime roles. He was a member of the late Ichiwaka Sadanji's
Troupe and after the death of this actor tried to found his own
troupe. It was not very successful and his popularity waned for
some time until he joined the Osaka group of actors. He made a
successful comeback in Tokyo, however, and is now often seen on
the stage of the capital. He is the same age as Nakamura Kichiemon but looks half his years, is an agile dancer and still skilful
in the young men roles.

All the actors named here belong to Tokyo with the exception
of Jukai, who ranks as an Osaka actor. Originally he came from
Tokyo and had all his early success there; he comes up regularly
to act with the players of the capital. He is therefore regarded
as a Tokyo actor. With the exception of the last named, everyone
belongs to the Kichiemon, Kikugoro or Ennosuke Troupes, unless
they are independent actors, in which case they may act with all
three groups. Besides performing in Tokyo these companies are
regularly seen in Osaka, Nagoya and Kyoto. The Kansai Kabuki

actors, whose headquarters are in Osaka, are a body of players quite apart from the Tokyo actors and number several distinguished artists among their ranks. The fact that they are not listed here is in no way to belittle their talents; it is due to the fact that this book is concerned primarily with Tokyo as being the centre of the Kabuki theatre today.

CHAPTER IX

PLAYS AND PLAYWRIGHTS

❧

THE Kabuki play has always laid great emphasis on visual appeal and pictorial effect. In a sense all drama aims at visual appeal, but whereas in the Occident, at any rate in more orthodox play-writing, any visual effect is merely a support to the all important spoken word, the reverse is true of the Kabuki. Here the dialogue is only a part of the general stage pattern, it supplements and assists but does not supersede movement and gesture on the stage. The aim of the Kabuki playwright, as previously noted, was to draw a picture, not a Chinese character, in short to start with pictorial not literary effect. This characteristic is predominant throughout all Kabuki plays and even when more complicated psychological elements were introduced through the stage characters, and the realism of the *sewamono* plays became so popular, this principle still held. It was inevitable that a people to whom dancing was a very part of themselves and who had an unerring sense of design seen in no other nation, should develop their drama along such lines.

Dancing had been the foundation of all entertainments in Japan, both religious and secular, from the earliest times and when O Kuni first appeared, the basis of her new entertainment was essentially dancing. For fifty years after her debut, the chief contents of the newborn Kabuki were dance forms with short farces and other diversions interspersed. Scripts and scenarios were not used in these entertainments which were probably largely impromptu. After the suppression of the *wakashu* Kabuki in 1652, some attention began to be paid to the development of the play form, the idea of making a formal scenario being taken from the Nō drama. At first, it simply amounted to the actors making a plan before going on and their performance still included a good deal of improvization. As the performances became more complicated, it became increasingly difficult for the actors to memorize the whole and so stage directions were partly written down. This was the beginning of the true scenario.

The years 1664–1680 marked many developments. The *maku*

or stage curtain was first used in this period, a factor which led to dividing plays into a series of acts. In spite of this there were still no independent playwrights; the writing of plays was done by theatre owners or the actors. It was during this same period, too, that Kawarazaki Gonnosuke, a theatre owner, prepared a dramatized version of the revenge story of the Soga brothers in a three-act series. It was the embryo of a dramatic form which was to exert a profound influence on Kabuki play construction for hundreds of years to come. Two important names connected with playwriting developments at this time were Fukui Yagozaemon of Kansai, an actor, and Miyako Dennai of Yedo, a theatre owner. The first independent playwright appeared in 1680; he was named Tominaga Heibe. Although his dates are uncertain it is known he worked mostly in Osaka. Regarded as of little importance at first, his work inspired others to follow his example and the calling of the independent playwright became recognized. The glorious period of Genroku was at hand, when there emerged two distinct influences in play writing, both of them calculated to have far reaching effects on the Kabuki stage. In Osaka, Chikamatsu Monzaemon (1653–1724) graced the theatrical scene; his was a name which was to become famous in the dramatic literature of Japan. In Yedo the great actor Ichikawa Danjuro I (1660–1704), whose pen name was Mimasuyu Hyogo, was the parallel influence. Different tendencies were seen in the two cities; in Osaka the emphasis was on courtesan plays known as *keiseigoto* and *oiemono*, dramas dealing with the struggles of *daimyo* families. There was a more realistic tendency in these dramas than those of Yedo, where Danjuro developed the *aragoto* technique, and the interest was in robust swagger and romantic symbolism and fantasy. The developments in both cities were to prove vital factors in the later construction of the drama. Geographical factors played an important part in the evolution of Kabuki plays, for between the three large theatre cities of Yedo, Kyoto and Osaka there were wide regional differences of temperament and background, and playwrights had to take into account the atmosphere of each city.

The work of different individuals finally led to the play writer becoming an accepted member of the staff of every theatre. He was known as the *kyogen sakusha*, and during the Horeki era

(1751–63), his work became defined and regulated under a set pattern. Each theatre would have a leading *kyogen sakusha* with several assistants working under him, and it became the practice when a new play was being devised to share the writing of it among them.

The piecemeal writing of a play may not sound to Western ears in the best interests of literary art, but it must be remembered that the *kyogen sakusha* were not concerned with literary masterpieces in any case. They were practical men of the theatre, devising an entertainment for the public, a public who sat in the theatre from dawn until evening. Their job was to create good stage appeal, they were craftsmen who had to take into account all kinds of traditions, seasonable customs, stage practices and techniques and adapt their work in popular form to fit these many factors. Like other members of the theatre, they were concerned with one thing only, having a good job ready for the public when the curtain was pulled aside. They were apprenticed to the theatre at an early age and had to know it in all its practical aspects before they reached the top of the profession.

A play writers' room, the *sakusha beya*, was incorporated in the greenrooms of every theatre, and here a group of writers ranging between five and fifteen in number were to be found. At the head of the group was *tatezukuri*, chief playwright, adviser to the theatre and planner of dramas. After him came the *kyakubun*, equal in status but a guest writer. Next came *nimaime* and *sanmaime*, who wrote according to the plans of their chief. They were followed by the *kyogen kata*, who had a variety of duties to perform; they still exist in name in the theatre today and carry out many of their original tasks. The *kyogen kata* watched the performance in all its aspects, acted as prompter, manipulated the *hyoshigi*, hard wooden clappers, and assisted the actors in various ways upon the stage. Below them came the *minarai*, who performed different menial tasks, fetching and carrying, delivering messages and a dozen other jobs. All these people made up the staff of the *sakusha beya* and worked under the direct control of *tatezukuri*. An apprentice had to spend many years graduating through the various stages before he was allowed to write.

There was a clearly defined formula for the performance of plays and staging was decided according to the seasons of the lunar calendar; that is to say, certain types of plays were considered suitable only for certain times of the year. It went further than that, however, for within the play itself fixed rules of construction were demanded, accepted situations had to be introduced and dance forms utilized at prescribed intervals. In the first chapter, it was explained that plays were broadly divided into three classes, namely, *jidaimono*, *shosagoto* and *sewamono*, and it was essential that the elements of these three kinds be incorporated in a day's performance.

Jidaimono, broadly classed as historical, were subdivided into *odai*, *jidai* and *oiemono*. The *odai* were plays dealing with the Heian era (781–1185), the *jidai* with the period from then until the beginning of the Tokugawa regime in the seventeenth century, and the *oiemono* with the struggles of the *daimyo* families during that regime. Strictly speaking, however, these plays differed little from one another in content, and the title *jidaimono* may be taken as an embracing one for all three. The *sewamono* dealt with the domestic life of civilians and a branch of this type of play known as *kizewamono* dealt with thieves, gamblers and the denizens of the Yedo underworld. In speaking of play types the word *mono*, literally translated as 'thing', is often replaced by *kyogen*, a generic term for play or drama.

The *sewamono* plays had their beginnings in the Genroku period with the *keiseigoto* or courtesan plays of Osaka, *yatsushigoto*, plays dealing with the loves of unhappy young men and their sweethearts, and *shinjumono*, which had the double suicides of lovers as themes. In the beginning, *sewamono* themes were considered as only a part of the main *jidaimono* plays and were not regarded as separate items in the programme. The playwright Namiki Gohei (1747–1808) was a pioneer in developing the *sewamono* as an independent form.

The third main division *shosagoto* is usually translated by the clumsy term 'posture dance' plays. The *shosagoto* is primarily a dance drama, although the word dance has a more subtle meaning than in its Western application, gesture and posing being just as important as more vigorous movement. In the barest sense, *shosagoto* means a dance performance to the rhythm and melody of vocal and *samisen* music, but it is almost impossible to give any short description of it. It is a wide term which covers many complicated types that have grown out of the developments of the various musical forms of the theatre. These range from complicated dance dramas with a complete story, to short items which were introduced into a programme for mere technical effect, and which may seem obscure without some knowledge of the theme and background of the play in which they were used. The developments of these forms have already been described in some detail in the chapter on dancing, suffice to say that when speaking of the old *kyogen sakusha* being compelled to use *shosagoto* as an element in play writing, it meant the use of dance techniques.

When co-operating in a play, the *kyogen sakusha* were allotted certain parts according to their rank. In Yedo, it was a rule in *jidaimono* plays that the first act be divided into two parts, the first part being written by *kyogen kata* and the second by *sanmaime*; the second act would again be divided into two, using different technical constructions, the first part being written by *nimaime* and the second by *sanmaime*. The third act would be a *shosagoto* piece written by *tatezukuri* or the chief writer, while the last act again would be written by *nimaime* and *sanmaime*. These customs varied in Yedo, Osaka and Kyoto, but in all three cities the same basic principles were observed in play writing. There were six theatrical performances during a year, January (New Year), March (Spring), May, July (Bon Festival), September (Autumn) and November (*kaomise*, or theatrical new year), these were all according to the lunar calendar. The continuation of each of these performances was in accordance to public response. It was customary to produce new plays in January, the New Year and in November, the *kaomise* or opening of the new theatrical year; both these were important dramatic occasions. In the Yedo New Year performance it was mandatory to produce a play with a theme based on the story of the Soga brothers. *Soga no sekai*, literally the Soga world, was a feature of the old Kabuki which had so many repercussions in play forms, that it is as well to describe it in further detail.

The story of the Soga brothers is one which has remained firmly rooted in the imaginations of the Japanese people, and was incorporated as a permanent feature of the Kabuki stage from the early years of the eighteenth century. In 1177, the father of Soga Juro Sukenari and Soga Goro Tokimune, aged five and three, was assassinated for political reasons by Kudo Saemon

Suketsune. Fearing they might one day take revenge, Suketsune enlisted the support of the Shogun Yoritomo to have the children killed. Yoritomo had himself been responsible for the death of their grandfather. Other counsel prevailed, and the lives of the two children were saved by the intervention of various influential people. Suketsune's worst fears were realized for in 1193 the two brothers killed him, attacking him at night in the Shogun's hunting camp. Juro was killed during the raid and Goro was captured and executed at the insistence of Suketsune's son, in spite of the fact that the Shogun wished to pardon him on account of his youth and filial piety.

The period in which the Soga brothers lived, and the preceding years, provided subject matter for many of the old literary epics and poetical writings which were drawn upon by the Nō drama and, in its turn, the Kabuki, for subject matter for their plots. Such an inspiration was the *Heike Monogatari*, one of the masterpieces of Japanese literature, whose influence on the drama has been boundless. The *Heike Monogatari* was intended for recitation to a *biwa*, a stringed instrument belonging to the lute family, which came to Japan from China. There were several different schools of *biwa* playing, so that there came to be many different versions of this classic, each with its own variations and in some cases additions. The authorship and dates of the *Heike Monogatari* have been the subject of a great deal of discussion among Japanese scholars; it is believed to have originally been composed in three volumes and afterwards increased to many more. It tells of the great struggle for the mastery of Japan by the Taira, or Heike clan, with the Genji, or Minamoto clan; of the fall of the Heike from its position of supremacy under Taira no Kiyomori to almost complete destruction by the Genji. The first part of the *Monogatari* relates the prosperity of the Heike with Taira no Kiyomori as the central figure, next it tells of the wanderings of the Heike and finally their destruction, the chief figure in this case being the redoubtable Kuro Hangwan Yoshitsune of the Genji. The two central figures in the accounts of the Heike were Kiyomori and his son Shigemori, the first a man of original ideas but headstrong and turbulent, the latter wise, considerate and less violent. The principal figures of the Genji were, first, the veteran Yorimasu, whose revolt and gallant death are famed in Japanese history; he was followed by Kiso Yoshinake, a brilliant leader, who eventually fell a victim to the jealousy of Yoritomo; and finally Yoshitsune, who was responsible for the destruction of the Heike. Yoshitsune, youthful, handsome and skilled as a warrior, was an ideal type whose legend has been enshrined in Japanese literature and on the stage. Some later versions of the *Monogatari* have an extra book in which the story is told how Yoshitsune, finally estranged from his brother Yoritomo, went to the shrine of Hakone Gongen to offer his treasured sword in entreating the Deity to bring about a reconciliation. He did not succeed, and after his death it goes on to relate how the Soga brothers Goro and Juro received a sword from an official of the shrine in order to avenge the death of their father. It was the weapon that Yoshitsune had deposited there and by its virtues they accomplished their aim.

Although the *Heike Monogatari* is a chronicle of battle, it is more concerned with the motives beneath, the tragedy, pathos and humour of situations than the clash of arms. Kabuki plays are impregnated with the spirit of it and its characters constantly figure on the stage in name and allusion.

The two Soga brothers early became heroes of the Kabuki; the presentation of their story was an unbroken rule in the New Year performance of the Yedo theatre until the Meiji era, and the Soga legend was employed as the central theme around which the whole of the main play developed. In one Soga drama several plays would often be contained, each independent of the other, but individually related to some aspect of the Soga story. This practice took many forms which of course departed a long way from the original legend. It was a custom, for instance, after January to change a part of the main programme and as the Soga revenge was a *jidaimono* theme, a *sewamono* was added to make a suitable contrast, but even this had to bear some outward connection with the Soga story and so the device arose whereby such and such a character would be named as being in reality Soga no Goro or Soga no Juro. The last scene of the first act of the Soga play was always Soga no Taimen, the interview with the Soga brothers, a *shosagoto* which is still staged today, generally in the New Year, although this is not an unbroken rule. Most of the old Soga themes have disappeared from the modern theatre, but there are still plays which contain seemingly meaningless references to the Soga brothers by name substitution. All kinds of styles and techniques were used to enhance the fantasy and appeal of the main Soga theme; the brothers became a theatrical symbol far removed in complexity from the original starting point.

When plays were produced for staging during other seasons, certain facts had to be considered and strict conventions observed in the same way. The March performance, for example, was regarded as light and spectacular; this was springtime, the season of cherry blossoms, and the theatres were filled with young women, the maids and attendants of the great houses, who were released to visit their homes at this time of the year. Plays with swashbuckling young heroes like Sukeroku, were therefore considered suitable for such an occasion. In May, revenge stories were in vogue, whilst September was a suitable time for *gidayu* plays, i.e. those of doll theatre origin. In July, the chief actors rested and the younger men were given a chance. This was the time for ghost plays, or *kaidan mono*, and in the play writers' room *nimaime* and *sanmaime* were allowed to give full rein to their talents at these performances. November was the *kaomise*, literally face showing, performance. It was the opening of the new theatrical year and the actors with their leader all appeared on the stage and thanked the audience for past and continued patronage, announced details of new programmes, and, in particular, new dances were inserted between the acts of the main play as extra attractions. It was an important occasion in the theatrical world and the memory of it is perpetuated, for November is regarded as the height of the Kabuki season and is still referred to as *kaomise*.

In addition to the conventions attaching to the seasonal performances, there was a certain amount of ritual in the daily procedure of the theatre. As long as a playhouse was open to the public, it was the custom to stage a dance called the *waki kyogen*, at the beginning of the day, before even the audience had commenced to arrive. It was performed by secondary actors and musicians and served as a practice performance in addition to its ceremonial significance. The contents varied according to the different theatres, each of which had its own style, and this custom remained in force until the Meiji era. Another ceremonial dance was the *Sambaso*, described in the chapter on dancing. It was always staged at the opening ceremony of a theatre, the New

Year, or a *kaomise* performance in Yedo.

Besides all the ceremony and custom which the play writer had to consider there was always the actor himself. Dramas had to be arranged to allow actors to display their particular talents, and even foibles, to the best advantage. The actor on the stage was more important than the play itself, which was written to meet his requirements.

The old system of writing plays piecemeal does much to explain why a scene can be extracted from a major drama and performed as a complete item in itself, a practice which is the rule rather than the exception today. Modern conditions and modern audiences make it neither practical nor possible to stage the lengthy plays of the leisurely days of old. Those presented, therefore, are the favourite and most celebrated scenes from the originals, in fact those which provide the fullest scope for the virtuoso qualities of the actor, and contain the acting climaxes which have appealed most to the imaginations of the audience.

The long line of *kyogen sakusha* produced many distinguished names, men who have left behind them the great plays of the Kabuki repertoire, and who besides had a lasting influence on various technical aspects of the drama. A list of the more important names follows later. The advent of the Meiji era saw the disappearance of the old style *kyogen sakusha*, whose duties henceforward were to be concerned only with stage procedure and the clerical work of the theatre. His going was heralded in the person of Kawatake Mokuami (1816–93), a remarkable figure whose achievements bridged an old world and a new. Born and trained in the Yedo theatre world, he worked in the *kyogen sakusha* tradition, while in his last years he was engaged in writing special plays for Danjuro IX, designed to satisfy the demands of a new age and outlook. The Meiji Restoration brought a type of audience to the theatre which gave impetus to a new trend in the drama. Around the tenth year of the era plays began to appear which were inspired by the Nō drama, whose technique and plots they imitated. These appealed to the new intellectual audiences who had previously known little about the Kabuki. This was the period of creation of so many of the Nō style plays popular in the Kabuki repertoire today.

During the Meiji era there were many experiments by the two great actors, Danjuro IX and Kikugoro V. Danjuro, during his lifetime, exerted his efforts in the creation of *katsureki geki*, correct historical drama. In the Yedo theatre, historical characters were used by name, but their thought and action were often contemporary. Danjuro tried to recreate the actual events and thoughts of the times he portrayed. Kikugoro V was an extremely skilful dancer and actor in the more realistic dramas portraying ordinary life. He attempted contemporary interpretations both in the technique and contents of his plays. It is in the work they did for the genuine Kabuki drama that the names of these two geniuses live on, however, a great deal of their experimental work is now forgotten, but their achievements in the orthodox Kabuki will always be remembered as long as it exists.

From the Meiji era until the present times, the history of Kabuki plays and playwrights has been one of many experiments, bound up with the influx of fresh ideas of literary men who were the pioneers of a new school of drama altogether, and who did not belong to the world of Kabuki. Ichikawa Sadanji (1880–1940), a distinguished actor in traditional Kabuki, was a pioneer in developing new style plays. In 1909, in partnership with Osanai Kaoru (1881–1928), he founded the Jiyu Gekijo, or free theatre. Here were staged plays in translation for the first time. Sadanji travelled in Europe and in 1928 was invited to take his company to Russia. He never abandoned Kabuki, but his work in the new drama showed its influence in several new plays he introduced in the Kabuki repertoire and which were specially written for him.

By the very nature of its position in the cultural life of the people, the old theatre was bound to predominate in the minds of the reformers and innovators, however much they tried to break away from it. If one surveys the position dispassionately, the greatness of the Kabuki during the last half century has lain in its actors rather than its playwrights. To ignore the many distinguished names and various movements connected with the new theatre in Japan is perhaps a little unjust, for they have without doubt also influenced the Kabuki, but when all is said and done they have produced nothing to replace the old repertoire that still remains as the essence of the Kabuki theatre, the rest is extraneous.

It is a pity that a significant modern theatre has still not emerged in Japan, whose social and economic background in recent decades has been disastrous for the development of dramatic art. Other factors militate against a new theatre, one is the selfishness of commercial interests. It is a sorry fact that there is no theatre available in Japan today where a worthwhile drama can be given a chance to grow. Another handicap is the lack of unity which exists among the younger generation of artists. Japan appears to be a country where cliques and separate factions in intellectual fields flourish more than most, and this seems to be so in the theatre where there is a lack of unity which is a great obstacle to its real progress.

As a result, the Kabuki continues to preserve an uneasy truce with a new drama. The old stage is still the vehicle for writers who, among other things, find it the most commercially profitable, but whose work should really be directed towards a contemporary stage, with a result that they often fall between two stools in ideas and production. The Kabuki stage with its conventions is a temptation calculated to lead new writers into melodrama and spectacle and seriously abuse the art of the Kabuki actor. There is the danger of the genuine Kabuki becoming more and more obscured, while at the same time there arises a type of play that is neither one thing nor the other, which contributes little to a new drama and nothing to the Kabuki.

From time to time collections of plays have been devised by famous actors as a standard repertoire and many, though not all of them, are performed regularly today. The most famous of these collections is the *juhachiban*, or eighteen best plays, compiled by Ichikawa Danjuro VII (1791–1859). These consisted of the most famous items in the Ichikawa repertoire since the days of Danjuro I, revised and adapted where necessary; among them are plays which are the best-loved favourites of audiences now. The performing and printing rights of the *juhachiban* are still held by the Ichikawa family. Titles of the *juhachiban* plays are as follows: *Kanjincho, Sukeroku, Shibaraku, Yanone, Gedatsu, Narukami, Fuwa, Fudo, Wuranari, Zonshiki, Oshimodoshi, Wirowuri, Kagekiyo, Kenuki, Kanwu, Nanatsumen, Jayanagi, Kamahige.* The first four are regularly performed on the modern stage, the rest seldom or never, many of them being obsolete. *Kanjincho* is perhaps one of the most popular of any Kabuki plays and possesses a quality which is timeless. *Sukeroku* and *Shibaraku* both are like no other plays, and hold a special place in the affections of the theatre-going public. *Kanjincho* is described in some detail later, brief particulars of *Sukeroku* and *Shibaraku* follow.

Sukeroku, the full title of which is *Sukeroku Yukari No Yedo Zakura*, was first staged by Ichikawa Danjuro II in 1713 and revised about the middle of the eighteenth century, from which time the present version dates. Hanakawado no Sukeroku, in reality Soga no Goro, is in search of a certain sword belonging to the Genji family. He frequents the gay quarters in his search, and here dwells the beautiful and witty courtesan, Agemaki of the Miuraya, lover of Sukeroku. Ikyu, an evil old *samurai*, pesters Agemaki with his unwelcome attentions and tries to discredit Sukeroku in her eyes. Sukeroku comes to the gay quarters intent on picking quarrels with all and sundry to make them draw their swords. He finally clashes with Ikyu, whose blade is the one for which Sukeroku is seeking. Sukeroku is the ideal, handsome, swaggering young townsman of old Yedo, admired by all. The attraction in this play is the bravado and posing, his witty dialogue and that of his beautiful admirer Agemaki; it is colourfully staged and costumed and has a celebrated opening scene, where Sukeroku runs on to the *hanamichi* with a paper umbrella held low over his head; he opens it and proceeds to pose with many a bold gesture, a good example of the *deba* mentioned in the chapter on technique. A procession of courtesans down the *hanamichi*, resplendent in all their finery, is another attraction in this play which appeals to the eye. Something of the spirit of the true *Edokku*, or native of Tokyo, the former Yedo, has been enshrined in the stage personality of Sukeroku, and this perhaps gives it that strong appeal to audiences, who never tire of seeing an actor like Ichikawa Ebizo in the title role.

Shibaraku is a piece of pure *aragoto*, a spectacle which relies solely on fantastic and exaggerated costume and make-up, bold vigorous gestures and full throated dialogue. The plot, such as it is, is merely an excuse for a piece of glorious theatrical rampage. It concerns Kamakura Kagemasa Gongoro, a heroic *samurai*, who foils the attempt of Kiyohara no Takehira, a wicked usurper, in his intention to have the loyal Lady Katsura no Mae and the Lord Kamo no Jiro Yoshitsuna taken off to execution. The scene takes place before the Hachiman Shrine in Kamakura, where Kagemasa appears before the assembled company and roars *Shibaraku*, 'wait a moment', at the top of his voice, frees the

Actor on the hanamichi in 'Shibaraku'

captives and then proceeds to lay about him with a lusty will, beheading several of his opponents with a single sweep of his huge blade. The whole thing centres round the bizarre posturings of Kagemasa, a mighty figure resplendent in voluminous costume who towers above all around him. This play was first staged by Ichikawa Danjuro I, but was much different from the version seen today, which is only a one-act spectacle that has been culled from a longer and more complicated drama that Danjuro II revised.

Yanone, first staged by Ichikawa Danjuro II in 1729, has already been described in the chapter on dancing.

Besides revising and preparing the *juhachiban* as a collection, Danjuro VII also commenced to prepare a series known as the *shin juhachiban*, or eighteen new plays. He died before he had gone very far with his project, the items he chose being *Roku-yata Monogatari*, *Biwa no Kagekiyo*, *Renjo Monogatari*, *Rendo Mondo*, *Tora no Naki* and *Ame no Hachinoki*. Ichikawa Danjuro IX took up the task where his ancestor left off, and added many more titles to the collection which considerably exceeded the figure of eighteen. They were *Kagamijishi*, *Takatoki*, *Funa Benkei*, *Momijigari*, *Koshikoejo*, *Sekai no Taiko*, *Sanada no*

Harinuke Tsutsu, Kiri no Otodo, Tsurigitsune, Yamabushi Settai, Ise no Saburo, Tako no Tametomo, Hidari Kogatana, Bungaku Kanjincho, Omri Hiko Shichi, Onna Kusunoki, Chuko, Fukitorizuma and *Futari Bakama*. Of all these the first four on Danjuro IX's list are regularly performed today, and one, *Kagamijishi*, is a perennial favourite among dance plays.

Kagamijishi was first staged in 1893. It describes how a young palace maid, Yayoi, is ordered to dance with a *shishi gashira*, or carved ceremonial lion's mask, at the New Year. The play is divided into two parts: first the dancer is a beautiful young maiden whose dance forms, even when seized by the lion's spirit, are feminine in quality. In the second half the dances are masculine in strength, as the lion with long flowing white mane and fierce make-up sports with two butterflies, a couple of dancers who again provide a feminine contrast to the vigour of the lion's movements. There is a famous closing scene in which the lion dancer, head lowered, swings the long mane in ever widening arcs with a quick motion of the neck, increasing in tempo as he moves across the stage, and finally mounts a small platform where he concludes with a forceful pose. The two parts in this play are always taken by the same actor.

Funa Bunkei and *Momijigari* have been discussed in the chapter on dancing. *Takatoki* is not a dance play really, although every opportunity is taken to introduce dance passages into it. It concerns Lord Takatoki, a man noted for his ruthlessness and selfish pride. His pet dog bites an old woman outside his mansion one day, and her *samurai* son Adachi Saburo, appearing on the scene, slays the dog. Takatoki, in a furious rage, orders him to be taken prisoner and executed. The advisers of Takatoki prevail upon him to pardon his captive; he reluctantly agrees and calls for wine and his chief concubine to entertain him and help him to forget his displeasure. While she and her handmaids are dancing, the mansion is plunged into darkness and a fierce storm breaks out; the women retire. A number of long-nosed goblins then appear one by one before the pensive Takatoki. There is some wild dancing in which Takatoki is eventually compelled to join; his strange companions proceed to kick him, pummel him and toss him from one to the other until finally he is left unconscious on the ground. The concubines and attendants rush in with lights and revive their master, whose pride has been humbled. The mocking laughter of the goblins is heard in the distance as Takatoki strikes a pose and the curtain is drawn.

As a rival collection to the eighteen new plays of Danjuro IX, a selection known as the *shinko engeki jusshu*, or ten neo-classical dance plays, was devised by the actor Onoe Kikugoro V. They were as follows: *Tsuchigumo*, *Ayatsuri Sambaso*, *Ibaragi*, *Modori Bashi*, *Hagoromo*, *Hitotsuya*, *Fura Dera no Nako*, *Rakan*, *Kosakabe* and *Kikujido*. Of these the first five are still very popular today; three of them have been described in the chapter on the dance.

Modori Bashi, first staged in 1890, is really the prologue to the play *Ibaraga*. It describes how Watanabe no Tsuna, ordered to search for a fiend which is terrorizing the capital, meets a beautiful woman travelling alone at night. He offers to see her on her way, and reaching the Modori bridge, he looks down into the moonlit water, only to see a reflection of a horrible fiend instead of the fair face of his companion. Later he confronts her with his discovery and she assumes her true shape. A fierce fight ensues in which Watanabe cuts off the fiend's arm, thus leading up to the events which take place in the play *Ibaragi*. *Modori Bashi* is now often performed by the doll theatre where it is possibly better than on the Kabuki stage.

A play called *Migawari Zazen* is sometimes included as one of the ten neo-classical dance plays. It was adapted from *kyogen*, the comic interludes of the Nō drama, and was first staged in 1911. It is a farce which is Kabuki humour at its best. Yamakage Ukyo wishes to go off to a rendezvous with his paramour. He tells his wife he is going to observe a Buddhist vigil, a ceremony in which the participant sits alone in a ceremonial chamber holding a heavy cloak over the head to obscure the face. Yamakage leaves his servant, Kaja Taro, as a substitute, however, and goes off to his rendezvous. The wife of Yamakage discovers his trick and herself takes the place of Kaja Taro to await her husband's return. Yamakage comes back, bibulous and unsuspecting, and blurts out his doings before the shrouded but indignantly trembling form of his wife, who, unable to contain herself any longer, reveals her wrathful countenance to the astonished husband and chases him off the stage.

There are other actors' anthologies besides the ones named, but those that have been described are the most famous ones and the most important. Apart from the various dance pieces and adaptations from the Nō, the Kabuki repertoire may be broadly divided in two, the plays which were originally of doll theatre origin and those which were written specifically for the Kabuki stage; of the two the former are by far the most numerous, but they are rarely played in full today, the most famous scenes being staged as one- or two-act plays. These scenes long ago captured the imaginations of theatregoers and have remained deep rooted in their affections.

The most celebrated of all plays of doll theatre origin is *Chushingura*, or to give it its full title, *Kanadehon Chushingura*, the story of the forty-seven loyal retainers. It is a dramatized version of a historical incident known as the Ako vendetta, which occurred in the first years of the eighteenth century. Lord Asano of Ako became enraged at insults he received from a high official supposed to instruct him in points of court etiquette, and struck him with his sword while on duty in the Shogun's palace. This was a grievous offence and Asano was ordered to commit suicide by *seppuku*. He carried out his sentence and his estates were confiscated in accordance with custom, thus signifying the extermination of his house. His retainers were left without a master and a means of livelihood. Some forty-seven of them pledged themselves to avenge their master's wrongs; after two years of hardship and suffering, during which time they never lost sight of their goal, they raided the residence of their late master's enemy and killed him after a fierce struggle with retainers who outnumbered them. The forty-seven men then awaited the consequences of their deed; they knew they were criminals in the eyes of the law. After considering the case for some time, the authorities served a death sentence, although public opinion was on the side of the forty-seven retainers. As a concession to honour, they were allowed to meet death by committing *seppuku* as their master had done. They died together on February 4, 1703, their remains being buried in the Sengakuji Temple where their tombstones may be seen today.

The play *Chushingura* used this story as a basis for the plot; it was written by Takeda Izumo in collaboration with Namiki Senryu and Miyoshi Shoraku and was first produced at the Takemoto doll theatre in Osaka in 1748. The Ako incident was of such public interest that more than one hundred plays were essayed on the subject at various times, but the work of Takeda Izumo easily proved the most outstanding. In 1706 a drama based on the subject was written by the great Chikamatsu Monzaemon. Called *Gohan Taiheki*, it did not survive, although it served a useful purpose in suggesting preliminary treatment for some of the staging of Takeda Izumo's masterpiece. Between the staging of Chikamatsu's play in 1706 and that of Takeda Izumo in 1748, many other plays dealing with the same theme came and went. It was really the art of a celebrated actor Sawamura Sojuro, renowned in Osaka and Kyoto, which inspired Takeda Izumo to set about writing a play which would do justice to the actor's talents, and he chose the *Chushingura* theme.

The play is a long one having eleven acts altogether. If presented in full today it has to be spread over a daytime and evening performance at the theatre; even so some of the scenes must be cut. Single acts of the play form popular items in Kabuki programmes, the seventh act, Yuranosuke at his revels, and act eight, the bridal journey, are staged very frequently.

There is a common saying in the theatre in Japan that if a manager finds business bad he has only to stage *Chushingura* to draw a full house, so great is the popularity of this tried favourite. The reason for the high position it holds is first and foremost the scope that it gives to the actor's skill; there is no other play in which are combined all the favourite forms and devices of the Kabuki drama as in this one. In *Chushingura* the playgoer can see all that the Kabuki stage has to offer in the way of technique; the roles of this play mark the highest achievements for the art of the actor, once he plays the leading roles of *Chushingura* he has attained that maturity in accomplishment which the Japanese theatregoer expects.

The play, in actual fact, pays no attention to accuracy in the original theme, more than two-thirds of it being additions and inventions introduced to make a good stage story and not a historical account. Names used are all fictitious ones and characters are introduced who certainly were not concerned with the real Ako incident. The basic theme of the play is quite simple and different from the actual event. A man's wife is insulted by his superior. He retaliates, but is punished with death because of his position. His retainers set out to avenge the wrongs of the master. Around this are woven a number of extraneous events and

*Scene from 'Chushingura' (after a print by Toyokuni I) shows
suo costume with eboshi and naga bakama*

happenings in the lives of various people, which all provide extra
stage entertainment according to the traditions of the Kabuki
theatre. A brief outline of the stage story is as follows.

In accordance with the laws in force, which forbade references
on the stage to contemporary events and personages, the period
in which the events of the play *Chushingura* are supposed to take
place is that of the Asikaga Shogunate, some three hundred and
fifty years before the time of the Ako incident. The play opens
with the scene before a new shrine erected at Kamakura, in
commemoration of the defeat in battle of the Shogun's enemy
Yoshida Nitta. The younger brother of the Shogun is present
with a gathering of noblemen to take part in the ceremony,
among them are Lords Enya Hangan and Wakasanosuke,
charged with receiving guests. The helmet of the vanquished
enemy, Nitta, is to be presented to the shrine as a token, but it is
in a chest with many others gathered from the battlefield and
no one can identify it, except the Lady Kaoyo, wife of Hangan,
and formerly a maid of honour to the Emperor, who had presented the helmet to Nitta. She is called to pick it out from among
the others. After the ceremony, when the gathering has broken
up, Moronao, the Governor of Kamakura, slips a love letter into
the sleeve of Lady Kaoyo and when she rejects it makes open love
to her, saying that her husband's fate depends on how she receives his advances. Wakasanosuke returns to interrupt this scene
and angrily orders the lady away; Moronao in a rage tells him

she goes by his permission not Wakasanosuke's, and that she has been secretly conveying her husband's desires to be instructed in the proper discharge of court duties. Wakasanosuke restrains his anger as the official procession returns; the scene closes with the glaring Wakasanosuke and the arrogant Moronao in a battle of looks with Enya, who has remained behind from the procession, sensing trouble.

The next act shows the house of Wakasanosuke in the evening. Two servants are discussing the affair of their master with Moronao when Honzo, chief retainer to Wakasanosuke, sends them about their business. Honzo's wife Tonase enters with their beautiful daughter Konami. Rikiya, the son of Yuranosuke, is announced with a message from Lord Enya about a court reception on the next day; Konami and Rikiya are betrothed. Honzo leaves, telling his wife to offer the young man hospitality after delivering his message. Tonase connives at it so that her shy daughter receives Rikiya; he delivers his message in formal style and draws back, asking her to report it to Lord Wakasanosuke, who himself interrupts the meeting of the young lovers and thanks Rikiya. The young man then goes off with Konami; Wakasanosuke is left alone until Honzo comes in and advises his master to retire early. Wakasanosuke tells Honzo privately that he and Lord Enya have been given the duty of receiving guests during the week devoted to the inauguration of the new shrine and that Moronao had been appointed their adviser on ceremonial matters, but he had become so arrogant and insulting that the situation was unbearable. Wakasanosuke says that he intends to return Moronao's insults in public tomorrow. Honzo is inwardly horrified at his master's rashness but pretends to agree. He lops off a branch from a small pine tree and exhorts his master to cut down Moronao in the same fashion. Wakasanosuke retires then, pleased at Honzo's approval, but the retainer rides off secretly into the night, intent on saving his lord from the consequences of his folly.

The next scene shows the main entrance of a palace where the guests are to be entertained. A palanquin arrives accompanied by the chief retainer Bannai and others. Moronao alights and is engaged in conversation with the flattering Bannai, when a messenger appears to say that Honzo, retainer of Wakasanosuke, wishes to see Moronao immediately. Bannai protests at this intrusion, but Moronao says he will interview him, and there is a comic passage where the retainer instructs the attendants how to prepare for a fight. Honzo arrives with several servants bearing gifts; he states that his master Wakasanosuke desires advice on the duties attached to the post he holds and requests Moronao to accept the following gifts. Bannai reads out the list of rolls of silk and pieces of gold and the astonished Moronao, after a private consultation with his retainer, decides to accept them. Moronao invites Honzo to the festivities that day, the latter, glad that his plan had succeeded enters the mansion with the others. Shortly afterwards, Lord Enya arrives in his palanquin accompanied by his retainer Kampei; they enter the gates on being told that Lord Wakasanosuke has already gone in. Next appears the beautiful maiden O Karu, with servants of the Enya family; she asks for Kampei at the gate. He comes out to her and she presents a letter asking him to give it to his master, Enya Hangan, as it is from his wife. While he is gone, Bannai appears and tries to make love to O Karu, but is forestalled by Kampei who returns and disappears with his sweetheart.

After this the scene shows the interior of the mansion; Moronao and Bannai are seen meeting with Wakasanosuke, whom Moronao greets cordially, and then throws down both his swords at his feet, asking pardon for his rudeness of the other day. Wakasanosuke is dumbfounded by this change of front and unable to vent his anger, to the delight of the hidden Honzo, is finally escorted out by Moronao's men on the plea of illness. Soon after Wakasanosuke's departure, Lord Enya arrives before Moronao, who scolds him for being late. Enya hands over the letter from his wife, brought to him by O Karu through Kampei. Moronao reads it; it is a poem which hints that, as the lady concerned is already a wife, she cannot accept his suit. Annoyed by this snub, Moronao begins to taunt Enya Hangan, who tries to contain his rising anger, but the words of his superior become more and more insulting; finally, unable to control himself any longer, Enya strikes at Moronao with his sword, wounding him in the forehead. Honzo comes out of hiding to restrain his master; guards rush in on hearing the commotion and Enya is seized and carried off. The stage revolves to show a back entrance to the mansion; the uproar can be heard within and Kampei is trying to enter, anxious about his master. The attendants refuse him

turns out to be Senzaki Yagoro, also a former retainer of Lord
Enya Hangan. They discuss the fate of their master. Kampei
expresses shame for his failure to come to his lord's help, but says
that he has heard Yuranosuke is plotting to avenge their master's
death; he begs Senzaki Yagoro's help in getting his name included among the conspirators, in order that he may expiate his
sins to his master. The other man does not reveal the plot directly
to Kampei and pretends to know nothing about it. He says that
as they are all now *ronin*, and poor men, they are trying to
collect money from those grateful for their late master's favours,
in order to erect a monument to his memory. Kampei takes the
hint and says that his position is a pitiful one; he has no means
but the old farmer Yoichibei, father of O Karu, served Lord
Enya and is anxious to see the good name of Kampei, his son-in-
law, restored, and that if he is told of what is required he will
probably sell some of his land and give the money for the cause.
Senzaki Yagoro says that he will pass on Kampei's message to
Yuranosuke and see what can be done; the two men then say
farewell. The rain is coming down more heavily and a storm
raging when along the road comes the tottering figure of the old
farmer Yoichibei, carrying a paper lantern. He stops and out of
the thickets steps a wild-looking character, Sadakuro. He is the
selfsame son of Ono Kudayu, the retainer who refused to join
the pact with the others to avenge their master's death. Since
that time Sadukoro has turned highwayman. Seeing a bulging
purse of money thrust in the old man's *kimono* he brutally kills
him with his sword and seizes the purse, kicking the body to one
side. At this moment a wild boar comes dashing towards the spot;
it is wounded and Sadakuro steps back from its onrush as a shot
rings out; he drops dead immediately. Kampei appears groping
through the dark for the boar he thinks he has killed. He
stumbles over the body of Sadakuro and starts back in astonishment, he puts out his hand again for any sign of life and feels
the purse, stolen from Yoichibei. It is too dark to see the body
and overjoyed with his luck at finding money which will enable
him to join in Yuranosuke's scheme, Kampei makes off into the
night.

The house of Yoichibei, the farmer, is next revealed to the
audience. His wife, O Kaya, and her daughter, O Karu, are seen
arguing with Ichimonjiya, the master of a tea-house and his

The highwayman Sadakuro in 'Chushingura'

assistant, who have arrived to claim O Karu in service, producing as proof a bond of agreement signed by Yoichibei himself. Ichimonjya wants to know where Yoichibei is, complaining that an arrangement was made that half the sum should be paid on the signing of the contract and the other half when O Karu was handed over. O Kaya is at a loss what to say, but exclaims she cannot do anything until her husband returns. The tea-house master grows impatient, he wishes to hand the money over then and there and take the girl. While they are arguing, Kampei appears, gun on shoulder, and the tea house master, guessing he is O Karu's husband, produces his bond of contract and tries to take the girl off at once. O Kaya restrains him and explains to Kampei that her husband, knowing his son-in-law's great need of money to retrieve his honour, had sold his daughter to service in a tea-house for a period, to get the cash required. Kampei replies that he is grateful for his father-in-law's help in this matter, but he himself has now had a piece of great fortune and they had better wait for the return of Yoichibei before doing anything more in the matter. The tea-house master, fearing that perhaps they doubt his word, tells them that the money he paid Yoichibei was contained in a purse made of the same striped material as the *kimono* the farmer was wearing, as they will see when he returns. Kampei starts on hearing these words, stealthily drawing the purse from his pocket he sees it is made of the same material that the tea-house master has described. O Karu meanwhile comes over to Kampei and asks what she must do in the argument with the tea-house master; he finally replies that, as there seems to be no other help for it, she had better go. He also adds that he had seen Yoichibei that morning and it is uncertain when he would return. O Kaya scolds Kampei for not having told them this before while O Karu is carried off in the palanquin of the tea-house master. Soon after her going, two hunters arrive carrying the body of Yoichibei on a shutter; the old woman is overcome with grief. She urges Kampei to seek out the murderers; becoming suspicious of his silence she draws near him and seizes the purse which she had noticed him looking at secretly a little time ago. O Kaya reviles and curses Kampei, and finally strikes him furiously in her anger, but Kampai remains silent. In the middle of it all two *samurai* arrive at the door, they have come from Yuranosuke. They tell Kampei that his subscription towards a monument for their dead lord had been received that morning, but Yuranosuke could not accept it because of Kampei's failure to do his duty to his master in the past. Kampei is stunned by the news; O Kaya comes forward and tells the visitors that he is a thief and a murderer. On hearing her story they reproach him bitterly, until the miserable Kampei, overcome with despair, mortally stabs himself. The dying man then explains how he shot his victim in error; that at the time he could only think of the occurrence as an act of heaven to allow him to get money for his late master's cause. He begs the two men to spare him a little sympathy. One of the *samurai* turns over the body of the dead farmer and notices that it has been gashed with a sword, not shot, the true situation is revealed as they remember the corpse of Sadakuro they passed in a wood on their way there. O Kaya clings to the dying Kampei and begs his forgiveness. Kampei feels his name is cleared and he can go to the next world in peace; his joy is even greater when the two *samurai* inform him that they will now write his name on the list of the faithful, who are sworn to avenge Lord Enya Hangan. Kampei's last words are that his spirit will linger on earth until their task is completed, and he administers himself the *coup de grace* by piercing his throat with the dagger. The two *samurai* leave amidst O Kaya's lamentations, taking the fateful purse as a sign that a faithful companion has joined their league.

Act seven, which follows the last scene, is a favourite one. It shows the stylish Ichiriki tea-house in Kyoto. Here Yuranosuke is seen living a life of gaiety and pleasure, drinking and playing light-hearted games with the waitresses. In the midst of his revels, three of his former companions, Jutaro, Yagoro and Kitahachi arrive, accompanied by Heiyemon, a soldier formerly in the employ of Lord Enya. Heiyemon goes off to the rear quarters, the other three enter the house to find their master in a drunken stupor. They can get no sense out of him and are about to strike him down in their disgust at his betraying the cause when Heiyemon enters; he begs them to stay their hands. He pleads with Yuranosuke to allow him, a common soldier, to join the great conspiracy, but Yuranosuke pokes fun at him and falls asleep again. The four men leave until such time as the effects of the wine shall have worn off their leader.

It is night time now and Yuranosuke's son hurriedly appears; seeing his father asleep he looks fearfully round and rouses him by clashing his sword. Yuranosuke wakes, still feigning drunkenness; humming a tipsy stave he goes to the wicket gate to which Rikiya has retired and here furtively receives a letter. This is a famous scene enacted on the *hanamichi* and contains a depth of dramatic feeling. Yuranosuke takes the letter and Rikiya disappears. The letter is from Lady Kaoyo, containing information regarding the movements of their enemy, Moronao; Yuranosuke is about to read it eagerly when a visitor arrives. It is Kudayu, the former retainer of Lord Enya, who refused to participate in the plot of the others to revenge their lord's death. Yuranosuke pretends to welcome him, the other asks if all this gay life is not mere pretence to cover up a plot against Moronao. Yuranosuke flatly denies it and acts as though the past were best forgotten in wine; he calls on Kudayu to drink a cup with him. Kudayu agrees and takes up a morsel of octopus from a dish to offer it to Yuranosuke. The latter receives it gratefully and is about to eat when Kudayu reminds him that it is the eve of the anniversary of their lord's death, it should be observed by abstaining from food. Yuranosuke quickly replies that it is Lord Enya whose stupidity brought them to their present state, and he has good reason to hate his memory now. With that he eats the fish, to the astonishment of the wily Kudayu. Yuranosuke then staggers from the room, saying he is going to order a fowl to be cooked while they amuse themselves with singing and dancing. He goes off; Kudayu remains behind and Bannai, the chief retainer of Moronao, appears from hiding. They confer and agree that Yuranosuke really seems to be not worth troubling about any longer; even the blade of his sword is rusted and they order Kudayu's palanquin to be brought. When it arrives, Kudayu, unseen by Bannai, slips out at the other side, places a heavy stone in the palanquin and hides under the veranda of the house. The discovery of the stone by Bannai marks one of the humorous incidents of the play; he trots along beside the palanquin chatting and suddenly lifting the curtain discovers the stone. Kudayu calls out from his hiding place; he tells him that he is anxious to find out the contents of the letter which Yuranosuke has received, he is a little uneasy about it, he therefore sends Bannai on his way with the palanquin. Meanwhile O Karu, now a beautiful courtesan, appears at the balcony of a room overlooking the main house, taking the evening air. Yuranosuke re-enters; surprised to find Kudayu gone he commences to read his letter by the light of a hanging lantern above the veranda. O Karu looks down from above, and thinking with a woman's curiosity that it is a love letter, draws out her small toilet mirror; by tilting it above her shoulder she is able to see the reflection of the letter's contents. The missive, like all women's letters of the time, is written on a long scroll of paper which, as Yuranosuke reads, gradually hangs down over the edge of the veranda where the hidden Kudayu begins to read it, tearing off a portion. At this juncture O Karu's *kanzashi*, ornamental hairpin, drops to the ground with a clatter, startling Yuranosuke, who instinctively looks up and hides the letter behind his back. He notices the torn end and calls out to the confused O Karu to come down, bringing a small ladder to the balcony of her room and assisting her to descend. He asks if she saw anything and hesitatingly she replies that he looked much pleased with a letter. On noticing his vexation, O Karu questions him; Yuranosuke answers that he loves her so much he intends to marry her and redeem her from service. Commanding her to stay where she is and on no account to leave, he goes to see the proprietor of the house and make arrangements. O Karu, pleased at the thought of regaining freedom, is suddenly confronted by Heiyemon, who is in reality her brother. She recognizes him and is at first ashamed, but when he tells her that he has heard all about it from their mother she is happy and whispers to him the events that have just happened. Heiyemon realizing that Yuranosuke is only acting a part and that he will now kill O Karu to preserve his secret, draws his sword and strikes at his sister. She springs aside and asks what she has done, saying that if she has committed wrong it is her husband Kampei and her father who should punish her, not Heiyemon. Filled with pity, Heiyemon flings away his sword and tells her the news about Kampei and her father; she is lost in her grief and clings to her brother asking for particulars. Heiyemon explains that Yuranosuke must kill her to save his precious secret, that it was wrong of her to read the letter and that is why she is going to be redeemed, not through infatuation. It is better therefore for her to be killed by her own brother, and this will serve a double purpose, it will also allow him, a man of low birth, to join the others in their conspiracy; he begs O Karu to give him her life. O Karu, in her sorrow, says she has now nothing to live for, she will therefore kill herself and afterwards if her body is of use to her brother, he can do what he choose with it. In the middle of this climax Yuranosuke comes upon the scene; he says that he has heard their conversation and now he is cleared of all doubts regarding them both. O Karu shall be spared to mourn her dead, Heiyemon shall accompany him on their great mission. She replies she would rather join her husband in the next world than mourn for him, but Yuranosuke replies though her husband Kampei has joined the revenge party, he has not yet been able to kill a single enemy and has nothing to report to his master in the other world. O Karu must help him therefore. Yuranosuke, holding O Karu firmly by the hand, in which is clutched the blade with which she was about to kill herself, forces it between the boards of the veranda, piercing the skulking Kudayu below. He orders Heiyemon to drag him out, reviles Kudayu for his treachery and after a long speech tells Heiyemon to cut the traitor down. At this juncture, Jutaro, Yagoro and Kitahachi, the three *samurai* who have been listening behind the partitions in secret, appear and apologise to Yuranosuke, who takes no notice, but orders Heiyemon carry the drunken guest (Kudayu) to the river and cool him off.

Act eight is another *michiyuki*, and shows Konami, who appears in the second act as the lover of Rikiya, Yuranosuke's son, on her way with her mother Tonase, to the home of her sweetheart. Honzo, her father and retainer of Wakasanosuke, is living in Kamakura in prosperity, but Yuranosuke and his family since the death of Lord Enya have retired to Yamashina, near Kyoto, where they live in comparative obscurity. Although there is a love pact between them, Konami feels deserted by Rikiya as their betrothal has never been confirmed by the traditional exchange of gifts, and she begins to pine, until her mother at last decides to take her to give in marriage to Rikiya. The scene, with dance and *joruri*, describes the journey of the two women and expresses the sadness of Konami, especially when they see the bridal train of a *daimyo's* daughter among the pines at Miho; Konami envies it, she herself might have travelled in this fashion had the position been a different one.

Act nine shows the two women at their journey's end arrived at the house of Yuranosuke in Yamashima. They are ushered in and welcomed by O Ishi, Yuranosuke's wife. Tonase pleads with O Ishi to accept Konami in marriage for her son, explaining that as her husband could not come he has sent her as deputy and produces his two swords as proof. O Ishi replies that her husband is away from home but that in any case everything has changed since former days. Konami's father is now high in his lord's service, while Yuranosuke is a poor *ronin*; the match would therefore be an ill suited one and their children as ill balanced together as a lantern and a temple bell. Tonase does not at first understand the other woman's attitude until O Ishi points out that Honzo bettered the fortunes of himself and his master by offering bribes to Moronao; Yuranosuke could not therefore receive the daughter of such a man as his son's wife. Tonase is offended, but says that she will pass over the insult for her daughter's sake; in the eyes of the world she is the legitimate wife for Rikiya. O Ishi will have none of it and goes out as

Konami bursts into tears. The mother tries to comfort her, saying that there are plenty of other good families who will accept her, but Konami refuses crying out that she will never marry any other than Rikiya. Tonase then takes up a sword and is about to kill herself, crying that in that case she cannot return to Honzo as she has failed in the duties of a mother and wife. Konami restrains her, saying that it is she who should die, not her mother, as alive she is such a trouble to her parents. Tonase decides to kill her daughter first and then herself, but is stopped in the act by the wistful notes of a flute outside played by a *komusō*, a wandering Buddhist priest with a large wickerwork head dress concealing his face. Each time that Tonase lifts her sword a voice calls out 'Desist!', each time that she lowers it the plaintive music is heard once more. Tonase is puzzled until O Ishi enters and says it is a sign to stay her hand, Rikiya may now marry Konami. She informs the overjoyed Tonase that in view of her resolute character and the chastity of Konami she will agree to the match, but on one condition. Tonase puts down her sword in relief and asks what the condition is. She starts back speechless when O Ishi replies that she wants the head of Tonase's husband Honzo. When asked why, O Ishi answers that it was Honzo who prevented Lord Enya from dispatching the hated Moronao, who escaped at the expense of their noble lord. If Tonase wants Honzo's daughter to marry the son of Yuranosuke she must produce the head of Honzo. Tonase is at a loss, when the Buddhist minstrel, stepping in from outside, takes off his head dress to reveal himself as Honzo. Astonished, they ask why he is here; he replies that he has heard all that has been said, he will tell them in due course what secret mission brought him here. Turning to O Ishi he says that he foresaw events might turn out in this fashion and so came here disguised to find, as expected, his head is desired as a wedding gift. That is the wish of a real *samurai*, but Yuranosuke is now a drunken good-for-nothing; as a frog's offspring can only become a frog, Rikiya must be no better than his father; it is he, Honzo, therefore, who will have the say and he will refuse Rikiya as a son-in-law. O Ishi in anger takes down a spear from the wall and attacks him with it, he knocks it aside, throws her on the floor and pins her down with his knee. As the other two women look on in fear and trembling, Rikiya rushes in and picking up the spear thrusts it in Honzo who falls groaning to the floor. Yuranosuke enters; speaking to the fallen man he says that he must be happy to die by the hand of his son-in-law as he most desired. Honzo, with failing speech, explains that he has never ceased to regret his past conduct; as atonement he travelled here unknown to his family, in this disguise and lurking about the neighbourhood he had discovered Yuranosuke's real intentions. He felt that if he died by Yuranosuke's hand, the wedding of their son and daughter would be able to take place and he would have expiated his sins. Yuranosuke lays bare his innermost thoughts to the dying man; pushing aside the sliding screen he shows two tombstones made from the snow in the garden. This, he explains, will be their end after they have avenged the death of their master, they will melt away like snow. To make Konami a widow so soon after her marriage would be too cruel, it was this which had prompted family indifference to the match. The dying Honzo extols Yuranosuke for his fidelity, saying that his daughter is more fortunate than anyone to be allowed to marry into such a family. To the husband of his daughter he would like to make a wedding gift before he dies; taking a folded paper from inside his *kimono* he presents it to Rikiya, who receives it with a bow and opens it. To the astonishment of father and son, it is a fully detailed plan of Moronao's mansion; Yuranosuke does not know how to thank him, it was the one thing lacking for the completion of their plans. They excitedly discuss it; Honzo in a weak voice cautions them against over-optimism, Moronao, he explains, has all his sliding doors secured with fastenings and the rain shutters are bolted and barred. Yuranosuke demonstrates by means of a bamboo tree bent beneath the snow in the garden how they can overcome their difficulties. The bamboo resumes its natural position as soon as the weight of snow is taken off; so by using a number of bamboo bows applied between the lintels and sills of the mansion, and by cutting the strings of the bows and using the force with which they straighten themselves, the shutters of the windows will come off their grooves and fall down. Honzo is now rapidly sinking, his sobbing daughter and wife at his side. Yuranosuke puts on the disguise of the wandering priest, saying that he is going to Sakai to await the gathering of the other conspirators; in gratitude to Honzo this one night of love is allowed to the young people. He departs playing a melancholy tune on his pipe which echoes away as the curtain is drawn over the tragic scene in the house.

The next act, the tenth, is generally omitted today being, as it is, less connected with the main plot of the play than any of the others. It concerns Gihei, a merchant of Sakai, who is responsible for shipping off the arms required by the forty-seven loyal retainers in secret. The merchant's loyalty is so great that he is even prepared to divorce his wife if needs be and dismisses all his servants in order that not a soul should find out what he is about. Yuranosuke rewards him for his services by reuniting wife and husband, promising to use the name of Gihei's house as a password when they make their night raid on the mansion of Moronao.

The final act shows the forty-seven *ronin* gathering at night in the snow before Moronao's mansion, intent on achieving the object for which they have suffered and worked so long. All the arrangements are made, the raiders are divided into two parties as the stage revolves to show the interior of the mansion and the attacking party fighting their way through, grappling hand to hand with the retainers of Moronao. The scene is one which gives great scope for the sword fighting technique and acrobatics of the Kabuki stage. Moronao is finally run to earth skulking in an outhouse, dragged out and dispatched with the blade that was used by Lord Enya Hangan to commit *seppuku*.

This outlines the main stage story of *Chushingura*. In cold print it means little, on the stage it makes powerful drama. Its strength lies in the way the playwright has taken a theme, embroidered, developed it, and preserved a connection between the changing scenes to maintain unity in a plot that, at every stage of its unfolding, gives prior consideration to the varied aspects of the actor's forms and technique. Without knowing something about the forms peculiar to the Kabuki drama, it is a difficult play for the foreigner to follow; he tends to be distracted by literary content, which in this case appears tortuous in its ethical reasoning if it is not realized that the dramatist has deliberately exaggerated and expanded the social code of his times, a code undoubtedly severe in its application, to make the best possible material for his actors. It is their entries and exits which matter before all else.

SOME NOTABLE KABUKI PLAYWRIGHTS

CHIKAMATSU MONZAEMON (1653–1724)

The name of Chikamatsu is famous in Japanese literature and familiar to the West if only for the fact that he is often referred to as the Japanese Shakespeare. It is one of those dubious terms which are so often used to designate comparisons between East and West, and why it should be necessary to create a Japanese Shakespeare any more than it is necessary to have an English Chikamatsu is a debatable point.

Many of the details of Chikamatsu's life are obscure, though it is asserted by some authorities that he was a Buddhist acolyte in his youth and studied the scriptures, whilst later on he is said to have served a court nobleman who often composed plays for Uji Kaga, a celebrated *joruri tayu*. Whatever the facts concerning his early life it is certain that in his twenties he commenced to write Kabuki plays for the actor Sakata Tojuro, and continued to do so for a period of twenty-seven years. The number of plays he wrote during this period have been variously attributed by different sources as being between twenty-five and fifty. The majority of them were composed for Tojuro's company and written to suit the leading actors concerned. None of these works remain in their original form today and none were comparable to his later work for the *ningyo shibai* or doll theatre. At the age of fifty-one he became tired of the limitations placed upon him by the Kabuki actors.

Tojuro was now an old man and his successors were not of his stature, so that Chikamatsu abandoned his Kabuki playwriting and went to Osaka. There he devoted himself to writing dramas for the Takemoto za, a doll theatre founded by a master *joruri tayu*, or chanter, Takemoto Gidayu, and here he continued until his death in 1724. By freeing himself from the slavery of the Kyoto actors he was able to give free rein to the genius of his imagination in the doll theatre and so lay the foundations for what paradoxically enough was to be a new Kabuki theatre. He composed more than a hundred plays for the Takemoto za with both historical and domestic backgrounds. His work was characterized by a depth of understanding of the psychology of his fellows and human nature in general. His rhetorical construction was excellent, embodying a cunning use of classical and colloquial styles and poetic narrative. Chikamatsu's work had an untold influence on Kabuki play writing and adaptations of many of his dramas are still acted today.

CHIKAMATSU HANJI (1724–83)

Chikamatsu Hanji was also a playwright for the Takemoto za. He was a follower of the first Chikamatsu and adopted his name in later years. He collaborated with other writers in plays, some of which are still popular today.

CHIKAMATSU TOKUSO (1752–1810)

A pupil of Chikamatsu Hanji, he also wrote for the Takemoto za. He was particularly noted for his adaptations of fiction into plays.

TAKEDA IZUMO (1691–1756)

Takeda Izumo worked with Chikamatsu Monzaemon at the Takemoto za and is second only in name to the master, later succeeding him as chief playwright. He made his individual contribution to plays which were later to become some of the most famous in the Kabuki theatre and are still popular today. He did a great deal to advance the technique of playwriting.

KI NO KAION (1663–1724)

Ki no Kaion was an able author and playwright who collaborated with Toyotake Wakatayu (1680–1764), a pupil of Takemoto Gidayu. He opened a rival theatre to his master's and named it the Toyotake za. Some ten years younger than Chikamatsu Monzaemon he became the latter's keen rival, often choosing the same theme for a play, although he lacks the imaginative power of Chikamatsu. He is credited with about forty plays, some of which survive.

NAMIKI SOSUKE (1694–1750)

Namiki Sosuke succeeded Ki no Kaion at the Toyatake za and gained a considerable reputation. He wrote more than twenty pieces in collaboration with others. His style influenced succeeding dramatists and he had several able pupils who carried on his name.

NAMIKI SHOZO (1730–73)

Namiki Shozo was an Osaka dramatist who wrote many plays for the actor Nakamura Utaemon I, famous for playing villain roles in plays adapted from the doll theatre. Namiki Shozo's chief claim to fame, however, lies in his work in developing stage technique. He was the inventor of the revolving stage and made many innovations in stage construction and arrangement by adapting the technique of the doll theatre for the Kabuki.

NAMIKI GOHEI I (1747–1808)

Namiki Gohei was an Osaka playwright who gained great popularity, later moving to Yedo. He was a disciple of Namiki Shozo and collaborated with the actor Sawamura Sojuro III. He was a prolific writer and was credited with more than one hundred works, some of which are still performed.

MATSUDA BUNKODO (1684–1741?)

Matsuda Wakichi, better known as Bunkodo, was a writer who worked with Chikamatsu Monzaemon and later collaborated with Takeda Izumo in a number of plays, many of which are still being staged.

MYOSHI SHORAKU (1696–1775?)

Myoshi Shoraku collaborated with Bunkodo and Takeda Izumo, whose student he was. Little is known about his personal history and he is said to have been a physician at one time.

SAKURADA JISUKE (1734–1806)

Sakurada Jisuke was a poet and man about town who wrote plays with a social background and dance numbers, some of which are still famous.

SAKURADA JISUKE II (1768–1829)

He succeeded to the title of the first Sakurada Jisuke and was noted for his dance plays, several of which are still famous.

SAKURADA JISUKE III (1801–77)

A disciple of the second Sakurada Jisuke, he succeeded to the title in 1829. He was skilled in rewriting rather than creating, but some of his dance numbers are still staged.

TSURUYA NAMBOKU IV (1755–1829)

Tsuruya Namboku was often referred to as *dai* Namboku, the great Namboku. He was a prolific writer with a long list of plays to his credit, many of which are still staged. He was particularly skilful in writing ghost plays, some of the most famous dramas of this type coming from his pen. He wrote plays for the actors Matsumoto Koshiro IV, Onoe Matusuke and Onoe Kikugoro III. He started life humbly with little education, but his abilities and instinct for the theatre enabled him to play a leading part in the Kabuki of his time, and he ranks as a stage genius of unusual qualities.

SEGAWA JOKO III (1806–81)

Segawa Joko III was a disciple of the great Namboku. He took the themes of the professional storytellers for many of his dramatic subjects. His plays were written in great detail, and in his time many of them broke all records; one at least has survived as one of the most popular *sewamono* plays on the stage.

KAWATAKE MOKUAMI (1816–93)

Mokuami, as he is generally referred to, was a disciple of the great Namboku from whom he learned a great deal. He holds an extraordinary position in the history of the Kabuki theatre for his achievements bridged the Yedo and Meiji eras and he wrote for the audiences of two different ages. He was a prolific writer who tried his hand at every different type of Kabuki plot, and he has some fifty pieces to his credit. It was in *sewamono* plays that he really excelled, especially those dealing with gamblers and thieves and a lower strata of society. He was particularly skilled in witty dialogue and composition. Like everyone he had his failures, but many of his dramas are still exceedingly popular; indeed it is rare to find a Kabuki programme today that does not include one play from his fertile imagination. About twenty-five of his works were written during the Meiji era, several of them being specially designed for Ichikawa Danjuro IX. His dance plays in the tradition of the Nō theatre are still among some of the more outstanding of their kind. Mokuami had a disciple, Takeshiba Kisui (1847–1923), whose work never went beyond that of his master and who is best remembered today by a single dancing play. There were many other distinguished names who followed after these two men, names connected with new developments and new forms in Kabuki play writing. Mokuami, in the legacy that he bequeathed to the Kabuki theatre, belonged to the old style *kyogen sakusha*; he was, as he has so often been described, 'the last of the great Kabuki playwrights'.

CHAPTER X

SIX REPRESENTATIVE KABUKI PLAYS

I. SEKINOTO

A *shosagoto* play

SEKINOTO or, to give its full title, *Tsumoru Koi Yuki no Sekinoto* was first staged in Yedo in 1764 as a new dance piece in the *kaomise* or November performance at the Kiriza theatre. It has a *tokiwazu* musical accompaniment which is a famous example of this school of theatre music. *Sekinoto* is a typical classical Kabuki dance piece, whose original dramatic setting has long ago been forgotten, the play remaining today as an independent dance number, one of the longest on the contemporary stage. Its theme was taken from a literary work entitled 'The World of Komachi and Kuronushi', but the dance play itself is a complete fantasy which ignores all logical reasoning and is only concerned with making a charming stage spectacle, in which dancing and an excellent musical setting are most important. The principal characters are as follows:

Komachi hime: A beautiful lady of high birth.

Yoshimine Munesada: A high ranking official loyal to the Imperial House and the lover of Komachi.

Sekibei: A barrier keeper, in reality Otomo no Kuronushi, usurper to the Imperial throne.

Sumizome: A courtesan of Shumokucho, in reality the spirit of the old cherry tree, called Komachi Zakura.

The name Komachi used in this play has a certain significance for it comes from that of Ono no Komachi, a beauty celebrated in Japanese history.

The theme concerns the struggles between Munesada, a loyal subject of the Imperial House, and Kuronushi, a usurper. After the death of the Emperor Temmei, a fight took place between Munesada and Kuronushi, in which Munesada's side were defeated. During the battle, the brother of Munesada, who was called Yasusada and had as a lover the courtesan Sumizome, sacrificed his own life to allow his brother to escape. He tied a blood-stained sleeve to the leg of a hunting hawk and dispatched it to Munesada to let him know of his death. In the play, Munesada is shown living in exile near the tomb of the late Emperor, his house in which he sits playing on the *koto*, a long zither-like instrument with thirteen silken strings, is built beneath the shade of the ancient cherry tree which continues to blossom even in the depths of snowy winter. His retainer Sekibei is gatekeeper to the barrier close at hand, it is a disguise adopted by the usurper Kuronushi in preparation for his attempts on the throne.

The lady Komachi, lover of Munesada, arrives at the snow-covered barrier on Mount Osaka and discovers him in his retreat. Sekibei admits her through the barrier; after a certain amount of banter over the two lovers, he drops the Imperial Countersign and Privy Seal from his sleeves while dancing and makes them suspicious. Sekibei passes it off and goes away to prepare some *sake* for a wedding celebration. Munesada and Komachi confer and as they do so a white hawk flies in with something tied to its leg, which Munesada discovers is the bloodstained sleeve sent by his brother. A cock crows, although it is night time and beneath a stone they find a precious mirror with a cock engraved on the back. It is a heirloom of an loyal family and thoroughly suspicious of Sekibei, Munesada sends Komachi off to report to the loyalists, while he remains to find out more. Sekibei returns drunk with wine, Munesada tries to search him, but Sekibei is suspicious and Munesada retires to rest. Left alone, in his cups Sekibei decides to cut down the great cherry tree and sharpens his axe. He tests it by cutting Munesada's *koto* in two, from it drops the bloodstained sleeve which Munesada had hidden inside before departing. As Sekibei picks up the sleeve, the Imperial seal flies from his pocket into the cherry tree. He tries to cut the tree but as he lifts the axe he finds himself powerless and after several attempts falls into a doze. The spirit of the tree appears disguised as Sumizome the courtesan, she feigns love for Sekibei and uses her wiles on him until finally he drops the bloodstained sleeve from his *kimono* while dancing. Sumizone picks it up and after accusing Sekibei, assumes her true shape as the spirit of the tree. She attacks Sekibei, who by this time has cast off his disguise as a barrier keeper. The play ends with the two in angry combat, the spiritual powers of Sumizome overcoming the evil but human mind of Sekibei.

The Play

When the play opens the stage is obscured by a blue curtain, the *asagi maku*, which is pulled away to reveal a colourful setting. In the rear centre of the stage grows a huge cherry blossom in full bloom, behind it painted background represents a snow-covered mountainous landscape. A huge axe leans against the tree to the left of which is a notice board inscribed *Komachi Zakura*, the name of the tree, and a small snow-covered trellis fence. To the right, is a small Japanese style house whose interior is concealed by drawn rattan blinds. Towards the front of the stage and near the *hanamichi* is a small portable wooden gate, *shiyorido*, which represents the barrier. The *tokiwazu* musicians are visible at the extreme left of the stage.

Sekibei is sitting dozing behind the barrier, a small axe between his knees. He wears a green *kimono* with a bold white pattern and crimson lining, a black *obi*, deep peacock blue skin-tight breeches, black *tabi* and a persimmon coloured skull cap. A yellow tobacco pouch hangs at his waist. He awakes and rising commences to chop wood; this done he sits down against the tree and lights his pipe. All this time a descriptive *tokiwazu* accompaniment is going on, of course. Then the lady Komachi appears on the *hanamichi*, she wears the *akahime kimono* and *fukiwa* hair style described in the section on costume. Around her shoulders is a short cape made of stranded yellow silk, representing straw, and in her hand she carries a traveller's stave and a hat with a conical crown, made of green silk ribbed with gold and known as an *ichimegasa*. Around the bottom of her *obi*, which is patterned in white and gold, is bound a narrow, yellow silk sash. Komachi poses and dances on the *hanamichi* to the *tokiwazu* music and as she does so, the rattan blinds of the house on the stage are rolled up to reveal Lord Munesada sitting with his *koto* against the wall behind him. There are gold sliding doors patterned with flowered roundels at the rear of the room in which he sits. Komachi comes up to the barrier gate and Munesada orders Sekibei to open it and let the stranger in. Sekibei rises and dances to the words of the *tokiwazu* narration. The whole of the play is carried out in this fashion, a combination of the dance and mime of the actors and narration and music of the *tokiwazu* carries the story along. Sekibei is represented as questioning Komachi and asking her if she has a pass to enter the barrier; he is suspicious of such a beautiful woman alone in this desolate spot. Komachi replies that she is a nun at heart; she too postures and dances on the other side of the barrier; Sekibei stands with folded arms, then they both dance and Komachi goes out on to the *hanamichi* again, returns and is finally pulled through the barrier by Sekibei. Munesada steps down from his house, the rattan blind drops and there is a dialogue between him and Komachi. They recognize each other and after a conversation between them, the rattan blind at the front of the house is drawn up again and Sekibei joins in. He exclaims: 'So you're the Lady Komachi I've heard so much about. Lord Munesada must be glad to see you; well, let me hear your strange story.' Munesada dances with a fan whilst Komachi, seated on the ground in the rear, watches. The *tokiwazu* narration goes: '. . . as for me I have passed through great trouble. Do you remember this cherry tree, transplanted from the palace to the burial place of the late Emperor? It once flowered black in mourning for its master. It has been named Komachi Zakura because it regained its true colour by virtue of your poems. Now I am living here in memory of my late master and of you.' Following Munesada, Komachi rises and does a dance. 'Late last autumn I caught a glimpse of you; unable to restrain myself I wrote letter after letter. . . .' After her dance, which symbolizes her love story with Munesada, Sekibei comes over and cries: '*Yoi, yoi, yoi, o medeto gozaimasu*', 'congratulations', and gives a deep bow. As he does so, the Imperial Countersign and seal drop to the ground from either sleeve. Munesada cries: 'This is . . .', Sekibei replies: 'That is . . .' and snatches it from him. Komachi cries: 'This is . . .' and Sekibei answers: 'That is . . .' but fails to snatch the seal from her. The three do a dance together, followed by Komachi dancing alone between the two men; Sekibei pushes her over to Munesada and they dance once more as a trio. 'It would have been much easier if we hadn't fallen in love, it is our sad fate that we must live apart. The lovers weep with full hearts. To free you from your grief I propose to act as go-between, I'll go now and warm some wine for you in the back room. So saying he hurries out.' Sekibei disappears round the corner of the house, a curtain is raised round the *tokiwazu* players and a white hawk suddenly appears at the right of the stage, and drops a silken sleeve which it carries in its beak. A stage assistant has a replica of a white hawk affixed to the end of a long thin bamboo cane which he manipulates for this scene. Munesada takes the sleeve and reads it. '. . . why, words are written on it in letters of blood . . . it's a line by Koju, a Chinese hero, spoken when he died in place of his elder brother . . . how sad.' He drops the sleeve on the floor as a cock is heard to crow. 'What, a cock crowing at this hour of night?' Munesada takes an axe, lifts a stone and draws out a small mirror covered in crimson silk. The curtain is removed from in front of the *tokiwazu* players again at this point. Munesada and Komachi converse. 'A cock is engraved on the back of the mirror, it has crowed in protest against the bloodstained sleeve. It must be the mirror Hachisei, treasure of the Otomo family. By the way, the countersign of Ono no Takamaru is the same as the one Sekibei dropped just now. The barrier keeper is under suspicion. I'll remain here and try to find out more while you go and tell Lord Takamura to surround the barrier at a signal. Farewell, Komachi, you must hasten now. . . .' Komachi walks to the gate looking back longingly; she goes on to the *hanamichi*, stumbles and falls, rises, poses and then runs down it swinging her sleeves, to the beating of a drum and *samisen* music. Munesada stands at the gate, a bell is heard to strike the hour and he turns, takes up the sleeve and re-enters his house. He sits and says prayers for his dead brother, picks up the sleeve once more and speaks. 'It is discourteous for me to carry this bloodstained sleeve when I am in mourning for the Emperor. What shall I do, oh I know. . . .' He hides it inside the body of the *koto*. Munesada next goes down the steps from the house as Sekibei appears very drunk, holding a flask of wine and a red lacquer *sake* bowl. Then follows a piece of drunken mime to the accompaniment of the *tokiwazu* narration. 'Well, well, wine is the greatest consolation one can have in the world. Oh, are you still here, where's the bride? Ah, I see she's gone to bed, you'd better go to bed too and fall deep in the river of love.' Munesada comes over to the toper and says: 'You are very drunk, Sekibei, it's dangerous, dangerous. . . .' Pretending to support him he tries to extract the seal from Sekibei's *kimono* sleeve. 'What are you, doing putting your hand in my sleeve? . . .' Sekibei does a drunken dance to a folk tune used at weddings. Munesada tries to seize him, but Sekibei pushes him off unsteadily, the two pose and Munesada goes back into the house, standing angrily with his sword as the rattan blind is drawn once more to conceal him from view. Sekibei falls flat on his face on the ground.

Eventually he sits up and there is more drunken miming in time with the *tokiwazu* narration. As he drinks, above the front of the stage a small conventionally designed representation of a cloud, with seven gleaming points within it, is suddenly seen. The blind at the front of the house is raised again to reveal an empty room; there is the beating of a large drum off stage, the tinkling of the small Buddhist handbell and the notes of flute and *samisen* from the *kuromisu*. Sekibei, on his knees, speaks: 'I see the star Chinzei reflected in this wine bowl; I've heard that if one makes a fire of invocation at this hour of night and says prayers to the deity Hansoku Taishi, any wish or desire may be granted. I think I'll cut down this three hundred-year-old cherry tree with my axe.' Sekibei throws away the *sake* bowl and performs *bukkaeri*, that is, he turns down the upper part of his *kimono* to reveal a garment of black and gold with crimson sleeves beneath. He seizes the large axe and poses with it, then going over to a flat stone, he commences to sharpen the axe on it, saying: 'What shall I test the blade with, ah, I'll chop that *koto*.' He goes into the house and breaks the *koto* in two with a single blow, picking up the bloodstained sleeve which drops from the instrument. As he does so, the seal flies from his pocket and lands in the cherry tree. This illusion is created by a quick movement of the actor and an ingenious trick of the small property men. Sekibei goes back on to the stage to the beating of a drum. A *korombo* appears fluttering a paper butterfly at the end of a long cane, and Sekibei tries to chop it in vain. He raises the axe high to strike the tree, but there is a staccato beat of drums and he remains with arm posed in mid air, grimacing. This happens each time he attempts to cut the tree; finally he gives it up and falls asleep over his axe as the lights are dimmed. In this scene, Sekibei remains seated, leaning on the axe, eyes closed and his left hand held upright before his face. There is *samisen* music and singing and a light staccato tattoo on a drum as, to the notes of a melancholy flute, the figure of Sumizome appears inside the trunk of the tree. A ghostly effect is achieved by means of special lighting, the trunk of the tree being made with a transparent aperture. After further mysterious music the courtesan finally appears on the stage. She is attired in a dove grey *kimono* patterned with cherry blossom sprays, which sweep away on the ground. Her *obi* is pale blue with a pink lining, being that of a courtesan in the attire of the inner chamber. Her hair is dressed in *tsubushi shimada* style, described in the section on *katsura*, with long white lacquered wooden pins and ornaments. She poses and dances around Sekibei; there is another tattoo of drums and the sleeper rouses himself. He rises to his feet and adjusting his *kimono* to its original form, carries on a conversation with the vision before him. 'Why, there stands a woman I've never seen before, where did you come from?' Sumizome replies: 'From Shumokucho.' On being asked why she has come, she tells Sekibei it is only to see him and that she wants him for her lover. Sekibei replies that it is kind of her but he does not understand and she answers: 'You are very suspicious, you know this song, "Cherry Blossoms in the Mountains . . .".' Sekibei replies: 'Some flowers are blooming while others fall . . . .' 'Just like those flowers, it depends on how a person thinks,' retorts the courtesan. Sekibei demands her name, on being told that it is Sumizome he exclaims that it was once the name of the old cherry tree; it is a good name but he has never been to the gay quarters and asks to be told about the procedure there. There comes another passage of dancing and mime between the two. Sumizome and Sekibei go out on to the *hanamichi* and act as though a courtesan with an attendant is passing down the road, with appropriate musical accompaniment, and finally go on to the stage where they enact the following scene described in mime and *tokiwazu* narration: 'A gay fellow, face hidden by a kerchief, comes down the dark road and hesitates at the door. The lantern I see there belongs to him, I am sure.' 'But isn't the mistress of the house watching me?' 'Oh, I've waited so long, I am happy to see you but I cannot talk here.' 'When the man complains, the girl beckons to him across the fence, hidden beneath her long outer dress he is taken into her private room and finds himself in bed just at midnight.' 'Why, the sheets are still warm, you've got a young and handsome lover who's much too rich I am sure. How annoying!' 'It's heartless of you to accuse me of something I am innocent of, I'll pinch you.' 'Ouch! All right, I'm going back. Oh, I'm afraid I left my tobacco pouch under the pillow, shall I return? No, I'm going home!'

All this time the two are performing appropriate actions and gestures to the musical narration, until finally they rise and dance together again. While they are gesturing, Sekibei accidentally drops the bloodstained sleeve; Sumizome seizes it and sits down weeping. Sekibei poses, his arms in his sleeves, and Sumizome rises and goes over to him. 'It is cruel of you to have cheated me when all this time you have a pledge from another woman.' 'It is foolish of you to pay so much attention to this sleeve. . . .'

A complex and vigorous passage of action and dancing then follows, and intermingled with it the *tokiwazu* music tells how the two characters reveal their true selves to each other. Sumizome, in sorrow and anger, explains that the blood on the sleeve is that of her husband, that she is the spirit of the cherry tree who became a woman endowed with human feelings. She loved Yasusada, who died instead of his eldest brother, and the sleeve soaked with his blood had drawn her here; moreover, Sekibei had cut her original form, the cherry tree, with his heartless axe.

Sekibei cries out that he is Otomo no Kuronushi, grandson of Yakamochi, the pride of his family. A surprising change is effected in the outward appearance of the two actors before the eyes of the audience. Sekibei performs *bukkaeri* with the aid of a *koken*, or stage assistant. The top half of his costume is lowered to show a black garment with crimson inner sleeves and a wide border of purple and white check on the lower portion draping his legs. His cap is removed to release a bushy mane of black hair. He seizes the large axe and poses with it, doing a *mie*. Then while Sumizome is having her costume adjusted, Sekibei makes up his face with fiercesome markings. To do this he stands with his back to the audience and uses the large axe, which contains a small mirror and a cunning device which allows the actor to use it as a miniature dressing room. Sumizome's costume has been lowered to reveal a pink, sprig-patterned *kimono*, her hair is loosened and let down in flowing locks. The wig worn by the actor in this instance is so constructed as to allow such a procedure to be adopted. These various changes effected, the two actors carry out a dance in which the barrier keeper, now revealed in all his evil, attacks his companion again and again with his huge axe. This provides several opportunities for the rigid poses common to this type of action. Sumizome's dance is at first a sad one, as she caresses the sleeve of her dead lover, weeping and sighing by turn. Then she takes up a sprig of cherry blossom and there is a quick passage by the two of them, wielding the axe and the blossom, and more posing before they pursue each other round the cherry tree. Finally they rush out on to the *hanamichi*, pose, then back on to the stage. Sekibei staggers back as Sumizome mounts a small red dais brought forward by a stage assistant and stands erect with the blossom held aloft, while Sekibei poses with his axe. As the song has it: '. . . and so she disappeared and went back to her original shape, her resentful and reproachful voice lingered in Sekibei's ears. The cherry tree blossomed as though heaped with white snow. So the story of Komachi Zakura has been handed down and this is the end of the story.'

The curtain is drawn on this tableau to the sound of the wooden clappers, the beating of a drum and quick *samiscn* music.

II. KANJINCHO
A *shosagoto* play

Kanjincho is considered one of the masterpieces of the Kabuki theatre, being one of the *juhachiban* dramas listed in the previous chapter. It was first performed in March 1840 by Ichikawa Ebizo, later Ichikawa Danjuro VII (1791–1859), in commemoration of the first Ichikawa Danjuro (1660–1704), his illustrious ancestor, who himself had staged a Kabuki version of the Nō drama *Ataka*, on which the present *Kanjincho* is based. The famous fifth son of Danjuro VII, Ichikawa Danjuro IX (1838–1903) brought some refinements to the 1840 version as originally performed. In 1887 he was asked to play before the Emperor; an auspicious event in the history of the Kabuki, and *Kanjincho* was the play chosen.

Kanjincho, which was devised by the playwright Namiki Gohei III (1789–1855), preserves a timeless quality which more than a hundred years later still makes it one of the best loved dance dramas on the Kabuki stage. It has a *nagauta* musical accompaniment. It is interesting to compare it with the *shosagoto* play *Sekinoto*, described previously, for while both may be defined under the same main classification of dance drama, yet both are very different in content, each being representative of dif-

ferent periods in the history of the theatre. The principal characters of *Kanjincho* are as follows:

Togashi: Barrier keeper.

Yoshitsune: Younger brother of Yoritomo, leader of the
powerful feudal clan of Genji. In the play, disguised as a
mountain guide, or *goriki*.

Benkei: Warrior priest and Yoshitune's inseparable companion
and loyal follower. In the play, disguised as the leader of
a band of *yamabushi*, itinerant priests of a special Buddhist
sect.

Kamei, Kataoka, Suruga and Hitachibo: Retainers of Yoshitsune, also disguised as *yamabushi*.

Gunnai, Gennai and Heinai: Soldiers of Togashi.

The story of *Kanjincho* concerns two of the most celebrated
figures in Japanese history, Yoshitsune and his follower Benkei.
The tales of Yoshitsune's prowess are legion and he won battle
after battle on his brother's behalf in the great struggles of the
Genji and Heike clans for the mastery of Japan. His successes
only aroused the enmity of his brother Yoritomo, who refused to
receive his kinsman fresh from his victories, and Yoshitsune,
after waiting three weeks in vain for a sign of friendship, left for
the capital to try and raise forces against Yoritomo. He was unsuccessful and was compelled to go into hiding. Accompanied by
Benkei, his trusted follower, and a handful of men, he set off
north into the mountains, the whole party disguised as *yamabushi* or wandering priests. Yoritomo got wind of their ruse,
however, and ordered barriers to be set up at every province, with
strict orders for every wandering priest to be examined. It is from
this point that *Kanjincho* takes up the tale.

When the curtain is drawn at the beginning of the play, a full
nagauta orchestra is revealed seated at the rear of the stage.
Togashi strides on to the stage followed by his page and announces himself to the audience; his movements are slow and
dignified, betraying their origin in the stage technique of Nō
actors. He is an imposing figure in *suo* costume boldly patterned
in blue and white and he wears a high black hat, a *tateboshi*, on
his head. After making his speech, he seats himself at the right
of the stage. Next Yoshitsune, disguised as a mountain guide,
appears on the *hanamichi* and poses dramatically. He carries a
stave and a large circular straw hat in one hand; a brocade-

covered *oizuru*, a container used in former times to hold a
Buddhist image, is strapped to his back. His costume, too, shows
close affinity with that of Nō players, as does that of all the
actors in *Kanjincho*. Yoshitsune is followed on to the *hanamichi*
by his three followers and lastly Benkei. The dialogue and posing
of the actors at this stage symbolize Yoshitsune and his men on
the highway approaching the first of the mountain barriers; they
have heard that Yoritomo has discovered their disguise as wandering priests. To counteract this, Benkei disguises his master as
a mountain guide and tells him to keep well in the rear of the
bogus priests' party of which he assumes the leadership. At first,
the others argue, but Yoshitsune commands them to obey every
order given by Benkei and the whole party proceeds forward
towards the barrier which, in the play, means they proceed on to
the stage. There is no realism in the stage setting which is the
same as that used in all plays of Nō derivation. A large conventionalized pine tree is painted on the rear portion of a simple
cream-coloured set designed to represent planking. Bamboo trees
are painted on the right and left portions. The actors make their
entry at the right of the stage through a curtain striped in
purple, ochre, red, green and white, and exit through a small
trap door at the left, i.e. left of the audience.

When Benkei and his party reach the barrier, it is evident
that they are suspect, and Togashi has them halted by his men
and questions Benkei closely. Benkei replies that they are wandering priests collecting contributions for the reconstruction of
the Todai Temple at Nara. Togashi is still adamant, and Benkei's
party recite their rosaries to convince the barrier guards they are
genuine priests. The suspicious Togashi then tells Benkei that,
if he is indeed a genuine priest, he must be following the customary practice of carrying a *kanjincho*, or subscription scroll,
with him, and commands him to read it. This is a very famous
scene in the play, providing an opportunity for some bold posing
and expressive gesture on the part of the actors. Benkei's costume and that of his companions is based on Nō stage dress and
is unique in design. A small black pillbox-shaped hat is set on the
front of the head and in the case of Benkei, secured round the
chin with a thick white braided cord. He wears a black half-length
garment patterned in gold, with wide sleeves which stand out
stiffly from the shoulders. Beneath this is visible an inner *kimono*

in broad orange, blue and white check; his wide, cream-coloured trousers are angular in cut and stand out stiffly from the ankles, and they are designed with a flat panel at the rear which imparts a bulky squareness to his figure. Below his shoulders on either side, hang two large white pom-poms with two more at his back. A Buddhist rosary, or *juzu*, is twisted round his left wrist; it consists of a circlet of one hundred and eight wooden beads with two crimson tassels attached. Benkei carries a fan and wears the customary white dancing *tabi* of the actor on his feet.

When Togashi calls upon Benkei to read the *kanjincho*, he answers, a little put out: 'What, do you wish me to read the *kanjincho?*' and Togashi replies ironically: 'That's what I mean!' Benkei grunts 'All right!' The *nagauta* musicians are playing a song: 'Of course he has no *kanjincho* but taking out a scroll he pretends to read loudly.' Benkei goes to the rear of the stage and returns with a scroll which he slowly unrolls and commences to read loudly. Togashi, who is sitting upright and motionless at the right of the stage, rises slowly and dramatically; he begins to move towards Benkei, his fan uplifted. Every movement of the actor is deliberate, and part of an effect which seems to emphasize the mounting tension. The audience waits expectantly, the atmosphere of the theatre is hushed. Togashi stops, he is leaning forward in an attitude of suspicious inquiry, suddenly he starts forward, glances at the scroll in Benkei's hand and draws back hastily. Benkei turns aside and assumes a rigid pose, clutching the false *kanjincho*. The scene is a triumph of facial expression, which plays such an important part in Kabuki technique.

In the case of Togashi, the actor must portray a man whose suspicions are confirmed, but who at the same time makes the decision to ignore his discovery in deference of his admiration of the way in which his quarry dares all for his master's cause. Benkei, on the other hand, is a man whose ruse has been discovered but is prepared to bluff it out to the end and match his mental skill with that of his adversary.

After hearing Benkei's feigned reading to the end, Togashi then, as a further test, questions Benkei on the significance of the different articles of dress he and his party are wearing and on the Buddhist scriptures. This, too, is a notable scene in which the dialogue between the two men increases in pace as Togashi hurls one question after another at Benkei. The latter answers them all satisfactorily, however, in a manner equal to the occasion; he had once been a real priest so they presented no difficulty to him. Togashi then apologises saying: 'I was wrong to suspect so reverent a priest, even for a moment. Now I will be a contributor to your subscription fund.' He presents Benkei with gifts and sends him on his way with his party. Just as they are leaving, one of Togashi's soldiers recognizes the disguised Yoshitsune, and Togashi calls the whole party back. With great presence of mind, Benkei rushes up to his master and seizing the stave from his hand belabours him with it, upbraiding him the while for his slothful gait which has brought suspicion on them. He then turns to Togashi and offers to beat the guide to death on the spot. It being inconceivable that any retainer could strike a master like Yoshitsune in such a fashion, Togashi again gives the party permission to proceed and retires from the scene to bring *sake* as a token of apology to the wronged victims. Inwardly, Togashi is overwhelmed by anguish as well as surprise; he realizes what it must have cost Benkei to strike his master in this fashion. This passage on the stage is the occasion for some particularly dramatic and bold poses on the parts of all the actors concerned, including a powerful tableau as the two parties face each other when Benkei and his men are called back. The opposing sides surge back and fore across the stage to the accompaniment of a striking musical passage, which in conjunction with the slow dance of the actors, creates a scene full of superb stagecraft.

While Togashi has gone for the *sake*, Yoshitsune thanks Benkei for his prompt action in saving their lives; Benkei, overcome by the enormity of what he had done, is in tears for the first time in his life. Togashi reappears with the *sake* and invites Benkei to drink. Warmed with the wine and relieved that the crisis is past, Benkei is in happy mood and feels grateful towards Togashi. He rises and pretends to play the game of 'the winding stream' in a dance. As he dances, he thinks of incidents in his past; he realizes their escape is due to the mercy of Buddha, and lifts his rosary in his hand and prays. Suddenly, he lifts his fan and gives a signal to his party to leave; they rise and depart hurriedly as the song in the play says: 'As though treading on the tail of a tiger, or escaping from the fangs of a poisonous serpent.' Then Benkei himself leaves; as his party vanishes in the distance he prays and tenders thanks to heaven for their deliverance and joyfully follows in their wake. The final scene of the play is the occasion for some relief to the preceding tension as Benkei lightheartedly drinks wine and performs his solo dance. At the end, Benkei makes his exit down the *hanamichi* performing *tobi roppo*. Performed to the beating of a drum, it constitutes a stirring finale and symbolizes a spirit of joy and exultation.

Kanjincho contains elements which appeal readily to the Japanese imagination. It depicts a hero who extricates himself and his companions against all odds from a difficult situation by his presence of mind and ready wit. It is a theme which is universal in appeal. Beneath it there is a more subtle play on psychological elements; the loyalty of a man to the master he serves and the recognition of his loyalty in the minds of his opponents.

There is nothing realistic about the play, which is a superb piece of formal design. From the first entry to the last exit, the imagination of the spectator is led along from one climax to another by a series of dance movements and postures which are skilfully co-ordinated in an abstract pattern of movement. The musicians who accompany the action identify the story in outline as the play proceeds, assisted by a certain amount of more intimate dialogue between the actors themselves. In its dignity and power and the quality of its dancing, *Kanjincho* is entitled to rank among the dramatic masterpieces of the world.

III. SAKAYA

A *sewamono* play

This one-act play is actually a scene from a longer and more complex drama called *Hadesugata Onna Maiginu*, which is not acted in full today. It was written for performance in the doll theatre and was first staged in 1772 at the Toyotake Theatre in Osaka. The author was Chikamatsu Monzaemon (1653–1724), but the play was rearranged by Chikamatsu Hanji (1724–83); later it was adapted for Kabuki performance. Both doll theatre and Kabuki versions are staged today. The part of Osono in the play is one of the favourite roles of Yoshida Bungoro, the grand old man of the Bunraku theatre. The title is taken from that of the most famous scene in the full play, *Akaneya Sakaya*, which means the Red Chamber *Sake*, or Wine, Shop. The name *Sakaya* by itself simply means *Sake* Shop.

This play is a classical *sewamono* drama in the purest sense of the term, and possibly one of the more difficult for the layman to follow. Being a *sewamono* play, in theory it is more realistic than other types but, as it is of doll theatre origin, the technique is bound by a symbolism which requires more than superficial knowledge to appreciate the finer qualities of the play. The costume and stage settings are realistic in that they are faithful period reproductions, but the movements and speech of the actors are based on the technique of the doll theatre. The musical accompaniment is of course *gidayu*.

The theme deals with parental love and the duties of a wife as dictated by the family code of a society which was essentially feudalistic. It requires some mental adjustment and a knowledge of Japanese character on the part of Western people to appreciate why, for instance, Osono is regarded as the pattern of virtuous stage wives by Kabuki audiences; and it is necessary to understand the rigid dictates which conditioned her behaviour in a situation which could only be considered intolerable today.

Lastly, the fact that the plot is a continuation of events not depicted or referred to on the stage, may give an impression of starting in mid air and constitute something of a puzzle to the uninitiated. It does not worry the Japanese playgoer at all. He is already familiar with preceding events and if he is not, and this may often be so today, at any rate he has an instinctive knowledge of the kind of happening required to produce a certain type of situation and he accepts things without too much attention to logic. His real interest lies in the way the actor uses a traditional technique to render the many emotional passages which a play such as this contains.

The principal characters in the play are as follows:

Hambei: A wine merchant.
Sayo: His wife.
Hanshichi: Their son.
Osono: Hanshichi's wife.
Sankatsu: A courtesan and Hanshichi's mistress.
Otsu: Small daughter of Hanshichi and Sankatsu.
Sogan: Father of Osono.

Hanshichi, son of Hambei the wine merchant, has been accused of murdering a man in a brawl. Previous to this, Hanshichi has deserted his wife Osono, and left his parent's home to live with Sankatsu, a courtesan, by whom he has a child. As a result of his behaviour Sogan, father of Osono, has taken her away forcibly from the house of her parents-in-law, while Hambei has disinherited his son. In spite of all this Hambei, unknown to his wife, goes to the magistrate's court on hearing of Hanshichi's crime and enters bail for his son, being released on parole and in chains. Hanshichi is still at large and in this way Hambei hopes to prolong the young rake's life.

When the play opens it is evening, and the stage set shows the *sake* shop, both interior and exterior, in the customary fashion of the Kabuki; a dozing apprentice is seen at the entrance to the store and a second one makes an appearance with an empty wooden wine container and they go off. Then Hambei is seen coming down the lane towards his house, i.e. the actor makes his entry on the *hanamichi*; he is accompanied by two of his acquaintances who see him to the entrance of the house and then depart. All three wear the sober coloured *kimono* of elderly citizens, and *haori*, the wide sleeved three-quarter length coat worn over the *kimono*. Sayo, wife of Hambei, comes out to receive him, and he enters an inner room whilst she goes off to prepare the lamps.

Then as the *gidayu* narration tells us in the play: 'When the evening bell is tolling, Sogan brings his daughter to her husband's home for, young wife though she is, she has been separated.' Sogan appears outside Hambei's house, his daughter following respectfully behind. Sayo comes to the door and gives an exclamation of surprise on seeing her daughter-in-law again. They greet each other. Father and daughter enter the house, Osono remaining modestly near the entrance in accordance with correct etiquette. Sogan takes off the skull cap he wears to reveal that his head is shaven, a sign of repentance. He asks to see Hambei, who comes out still wearing his *haori* and demands angrily why they have returned, saying that since Sogan took his daughter away by compulsion, they must continue to remain as strangers. Sayo is about to apologise for her husband's hasty words, but Sogan stops her saying that Hambei's conduct is natural enough under the circumstances. He then tells them that he took Osono back because he considered Hanshichi had forfeited her love by his conduct. He was thinking only of Osono's future, he con-

tinues, but realizes now that it was an error on his part. Ever
since he had taken Osono away, she had wept and refused to eat
until at last he became concerned about her health. Now he
wished to return their daughter-in-law to them and apologise
for his mistake.

Sayo wants to take Osono back immediately, but Hambei still
refuses, saying that since they have disinherited their son, they
have now no need of a daughter-in-law. Sogan retorts that the
disinheritance is only temporary, and on Hambei refuting the
suggestion, asks why in that case he had taken his son's place at
the tribunal that very day. Both the women start on hearing this.
Hambei is seized with a paroxysm of coughing; they rush over
to assist him and taking off his *haori* they see, to their horror,
that he is bound by chains which up until now have been concealed by the outer garment. They are even more horrified when
they learn the reason from Sogan and hear of Hanshichi's crime
which has brought suffering on his father in this way.

Sogan turns to Hambei and says that he now understands the
depths of his love for his son and that, more than ever, does he
realize how wrong his own conduct has been in taking Osono
away. He points out that his daughter is a motherless child whom
he loves as Hambei loves his son; he pleads for Osono to be received back into the house of her parents-in-law to save her
reason and to avoid destroying the true love of fathers.

Hambei, his heart touched, replies that he realizes that Osono
has been a dutiful daughter-in-law and a pattern of virtue. He
now has no great regrets in parting with Hanshichi, but to lose
Osono is a mortal blow; however, if she stays in his house she is
likely to become a widow. He turns to Osono and tells her that
she must not grieve because he appears too hard on her, he is
only thinking of her future; he excuses himself to discuss matters
with Sogan in the next room. The three elders go off leaving
Osono to herself. Next follows a very famous scene, one of the
climaxes of the play. Like a dutiful housewife, Osono commences
to tidy up the room, folds away her father-in-law's *haori*, clears
away the teacups and attends to the lamp. As she carries out this
series of homely actions, she soliloquizes on her present unhappiness. This is known as *kudoki*, the technique already
described in Chapter VII.

'If I die,' cries Osono, 'the parents will receive Sankatsu as his wife because there is a child between them. I tried to please Hanshichi, although I realized it was hopeless to expect his love. Forgive me, Hanshichi, I was never angry with you; the more I think of you, the greater is my sorrow, and though you do not love me, I shall die for you in your house.' The whole time that Osono has been speaking, her words have been accompanied with a series of poses and gestures in time to the music of the *samisen*, showing the strong influence of puppet technique. It is an exceedingly emotional passage and as an example of *kudoki* is one of the more famous renderings of its kind.

At the conclusion of her soliloquy, Osono has taken out a small dagger and is about to stab herself, when a small child enters the room crying out for milk. It is Otsu, the daughter of Hanshichi and Sankatsu. Osono is surprised and calls Otsu to her; at this moment the three elders come back into the room. Hambei, on seeing his son's child, cries out that she surely must bear a letter with her; his intuition is correct, and as they search the child a folded letter drops from an amulet case worn by her. They all cluster round and Hambei commands Osono to read it. There follows an emotional scene in which Osono, Sayo, Hambei and Sogan read from the letter aloud in turn.

In the missive, Hanshichi thanks his parents for their devotion and upbringing and commands his child to their care as a symbol of the love he should have borne his parents. He goes on to apologize to Osono for failing to respond to her selfless devotion to him, but explains that he had already been in love with Sankatsu before his marriage; perhaps, however, they could become husband and wife in a future life. He concludes by asking Osono to comfort his parents after the death of their undutiful son and to take care of his daughter Otsu. They are all very moved by the letter; the grandparents take Otsu in their arms and try to comfort Osono.

The stage revolves, Hanshichi and Sankatsu are seen outside the house attired as for a midnight journey. Sankatsu, who wears the long flowing *kimono* of the courtesan, has a silken scarf draped over her high coiffure, one point of the drapery being held between her teeth to shroud her face. A kerchief is bound round Hanshichi's head. Sankatsu is weeping and cries out that she would like to hold her child to her breast again. Hanshichi on his knees begs his parents' forgiveness. Then rising he tells San-

Michiyuki—the young lovers on the way to commit suicide

katsu they must tarry no longer; taking her by the hand they flee down the lane, Sankatsu calling a sorrowful farewell to her child as they hasten towards a double suicide. This is a typical and dramatic finale as the two lovers run down the *hanamichi*, Hanshichi pulling Sankatsu by the hand as she looks backward over her shoulder. It is worth noting that the actor who plays Osono very often takes the part of Hanshichi as well, constituting one of those lightning changes characteristic of the Kabuki stage. The part of Sankatsu hastening to another world may be said to have had a sombre significance for the late Ichimura Uzaemon XVI (1905–52), for it was his last stage appearance shortly before his death.

The stage set is a faithful representation of the interior of a house of a merchant of the period, the name of the shop being seen in large characters on the curtain over the entrance to the shop at the side. The action takes place within the main room of the house, the set only being changed at the end to show the exterior of the building when Hanshichi makes his entry with his paramour. In its entirety this play is an excellent example of one of the early *sewamono* dramas.

IV. GENYADANA
A *sewamono* play

This play is an example of a *sewamono* drama of a different style and a much later period than the previous one. It belongs to the class referred to as *kizewamono*, that is to say, plays dealing with gamblers, thieves and the inhabitants of the underworld in general. *Genyadana* again is a part of a longer play entitled *Yo Wa Nasake Ukina No Yokugushi*, which is occasionally given in full today. The *Genyadana* scene, however, long ago established itself as a favourite among theatre goers and is one of the most popular *sewamono* dramas of its kind. It was written by Segawa Joko III (1806–81), who is said to have developed his theme from a tale told by the professional storytellers. It was first staged in 1853 with Ichikawa Danjuro VIII (1823–54) as Yosaburo. Within living memory it was one of the favourite roles of Ichimura Uzaemon XV (1874–1945), who brought great distinction to the part. To a multitude of playgoers in Japan the names of Uzaemon and Yosaburo are synonymous. Ichikawa Arajiro II (1889), who still plays the part of Tohachi in a way that no one else can, is the last surviving member of the group of older actors who performed in this play with Uzaemon XV.

The only musical accompaniment is *ohayashi* singing and playing in the *kuromisu*. Certain songs mark the entry of the actors on the *hanamichi*, and there is an intermittent *samisen* accompaniment in a low key to passages of dialogue, but the emphasis in a play like this is on the dialogue and posing of the actors; the music, such as it is, is subsidiary to everything else.

Genyadana was a district in old Yedo where the gay ladies of the period resided; it is sometimes referred to as *Genjidana*, the original name of the district in the Kamakura era. This is in deference to the official rule which in former times forbade plays to deal with the contemporary scene, and the rather transparent device in this case sets the scene of the play back some hundreds of years. Older people still call the play *Genjidana*, while another title commonly heard is *Kirare Yosa*, or 'Yosa of the Cuts'.

The chief characters in the play are as follows:

Yosaburo (Kirare Yosa): A young man of good family who has come down in the world and whose handsome looks are marred by the scars of knife cuts.

Komori Yasugoro (Yasu the Bat): A petty thief and black-mailer who has a bat tattooed on one cheek and is Yosa-buro's companion in crime.

Otomi: A good-looking young lady who was Yosaburo's lover formerly, but is now being kept in the household of a prosperous merchant.

Tazaemon: The merchant.

Tohachi: A shop clerk to Tazaemon.

A handsome young man named Yosaburo, son of a good family, was recuperating from a long illness at the seaside resort of Kisarazu in Chiba Province. Walking on the seashore one day he fell in love with a beautiful girl named Otomi. They soon became intimate and Yosaburo's departure from Kisarazu was delayed.

Otomi was actually a ransomed *geisha* who belonged to the household of Akama Genzaemon, a prominent gambler in the locality. He became furiously jealous on hearing of Otomi's lover and surprising the couple together one day, he ordered his hench-men to disfigure Yosaburo with knife cuts and throw him into the sea to drown. Otomi, in despair at the fate of her lover, and being pursued by one of Genzaemon's followers, cast herself into the ocean too.

Yosaburo, who escaped death by a lucky chance, was after-wards disowned by his parents and reduced to the gutter. Trading on his disfigured features, he resorted to a vagabond's life and became nicknamed *Kirare Yosa*, 'Yosa of the Cuts'. His com-panion in misfortune was a petty thief and blackmailer called Yasugoro, nicknamed Komori, the bat, because of a tattooed design of this creature on his cheek.

Otomi also escaped death; she was rescued by a traveller in a passing fishing boat. He took her to his home and gave her shelter; she continued to live with him ostensibly as his kept mistress, ignorant both of the fate of her lover Yosaburo and the fact that her rescuer was her own brother from whom she had been parted since childhood. Three years have elapsed since these events when the play *Genyadana* opens.

In the first scene the curtain is drawn to reveal a deserted stage. In the centre is a latticed, gabled wooden gate with a high black fence on either side, the entrance to a house in Genyadana. Suddenly Tohachi, the shop clerk, appears running from the right and crouching down beside the gate, places a kerchief over his head and complains bitterly that it is raining again. Next, Otomi and her maid appear from the right holding paper umbrellas over their heads. Otomi's hair is down and tied in a loose knot, for she is returning from the public bath house. Recognizing Tohachi as her protector's employee, she invites him indoors for a smoke until the rain stops.

The stage revolves and the next scene reveals the elegant interior of Otomi's dwelling. She seats herself on the *tatami* before a small dressing mirror and proceeds to do her hair whilst the maid goes off for some tea. A considerable amount of humorous chit-chat ensues between Otomi and Tohachi in which the shop clerk makes sheep's eyes at her until, in some final byplay, she daubs his face with her white make-up, giving Tohachi's face the appearance of a circus clown.

At this juncture, the musicians in the *kuromisu* strike up a song and two figures appear on the *hanamichi*, spotlighted against the darkened auditorium. They are Yosaburo and Yasugoro, represented as walking down the lane towards Otomi's house. Yosaburo is tall and pale, his arms are folded across his chest, his face is half covered by a white, blue-spotted kerchief bound round his head and fastened round his upper lip in the fashion of the period. Called *hokaburi*, this style of head covering was commonly worn by the more disreputable citizens of Yedo and those who wished to conceal their identity. It is often seen on the Kabuki stage, where it is used with peculiarly dramatic effect. A large criss-cross scar is visible on Yosaburo's left cheek beneath the kerchief. Yasugoro is in direct contrast to his companion; short in comparison, he wears a dingy, old woman's *kimono* much too large for him, which is tucked up around his legs. A bat is tattooed on his right cheek.

The two men stop before they reach the stage and Yasu points out the house to his companion who merely nods. They arrive at the entrance where Yosaburo is instructed to wait outside until he is called, and to remember that the evening's job is only a sideline. Yosaburo nods in silence once more; with his arms still folded, he proceeds to juggle a stone with his foot, while Yasu goes inside and bowing low, introduces himself in oily tones. Tohachi turns and sits with his back to the newcomer, and, incidentally, the audience. Otomi calls out to inquire what Yasu is after. Recognizing him as a man who has recently been im-

Yosaburo in play 'Genyadana' showing hokaburi (kerchief round head)

portuning her, she disgustedly tries to send him away. Yasu in wheedling tones then tells her that it is not for himself he has called tonight, but for a friend of his who has been badly injured in a quarrel and for whom he is collecting subscriptions, to enable him to go to the hot spring resort and recover. He then calls Yosaburo in and introduces him. Yosaburo without so much as a glance at anybody sinks to his knees in a deep bow and finally goes and seats himself near the entrance, back to the others with hands clasped round his knees.

Otomi tells Yasu that she cannot help him any more, whereupon he begins to get impudent and make insinuations about her position. Otomi becomes very indignant and Tohachi, who until this time has remained silent, takes a hand in the conversation. He assumes a comically bold air and taking a small sum of money wrapped in paper from Otomi, who has decided to give it to preserve the peace, throws it down before Yasu and tells him to be off. Yasu looks at the money and throws it back, saying that it is not enough and finally utters violent threats towards the shop clerk, who in terror bolts behind a screen and remains hidden. Fearing to create a further scene, Otomi gives Yasu the final sum he demands.

While the wrangle has been going on, Yosaburo suddenly becomes restless, he pushes open the outer door and peers through, then looks back into the room again and surveys the furnishings of the house; finally he turns round and sees Otomi's face for the first time; he gives a violent start and turns back quickly again, his hand trembling, his indifference changed to an emotional realization. This is one of the key moments in the play. Yasu, pleased with the night's work, takes the money from Otomi and with unctuous thanks sidles over to Yosaburo. Yosaburo looks at it and orders him to return it. Yasu, thunderstruck, and thinking that his companion has gone crazy, tries to protest but it is of no avail, Yosaburo insists. With bad grace Yasu throws the money down and retires to the rear of the room.

Then follows another highlight in the play. Yosaburo draws himself up, pulling his arms from within the sleeves of his *kimono*, which are left hanging loose. He walks quickly over to Otomi and bending towards her, speaks in a voice which rises in crescendo and emphasis. 'Er—Madam?—Madam Otomi—once it was Otomi! It's a long time since we parted from each other!' Otomi asks who he is; Yosaburo whips the kerchief off his head and curtly gives his name. Otomi is taken aback and Yosaburo, drawing back the ends of his *kimono* to expose scarred legs, sits down quickly, legs crossed and hands clasped in front of them, palms outward. A characteristic piece of posing, emphasizing the most dramatic denouement of the play. After this, Yosaburo commences one of the best known speeches in the play, if not in the Kabuki theatre. His lines are spoken in the *shichi go* metre described in the section on the actor's *serifu*; a single *samisen* acts as accompaniment in the *kuromisu*.

Otomi denies that she has forgotten him and tries to explain her present circumstances, but Yosaburo will not listen and demands to know the name of the man who is keeping her. Noticing Tohachi peeping above a screen, he calls to Yasu to seize him and make him confess who Otomi's protector is. The terrified Tohachi refuses and finally, escaping from Yasu's rough grasp, bolts from the room. At this moment Tazaemon, Otomi's rescuer, appears outside the door and hearing the altercation inside stops to listen before entering. He goes in just as Yosaburo is once more demanding the name of Otomi's protector in a brusque tone and remarks loudly that the information had better come from him. Yasu, back turned towards Tazaemon, turns round threateningly on hearing the words; on coming face to face with the newcomer his mouth falls open in astonishment and he bolts quickly behind a screen.

Tazaemon strides past the surprised Yasu, seating himself he asks Otomi whether Yosaburo is a relative or acquaintance; she becomes a little confused. Noticing this, Tazaemon asks Yosaburo the purpose of his visit. Yosaburo says that he is a relative and demands to know how Tazaemon comes to be Otomi's patron. Tazaemon explains how he rescued Otomi and that he has since behaved towards her only as a relative; they have no other feelings towards each other. Yosaburo disbelieves this and starts abusing Otomi once more. Tazaemon interrupts and asks what relationship exists between Yosaburo and Otomi. After some hesitation and with prompting from Otomi, Yosaburo replies that he is her brother, 'a brother of unusually deep connections'.

Tazaemon thereupon asks Yosaburo to wait a little while he calls Yasu out from behind his screen. Yasu crawls out like a whipped cur and Tazaemon reproaches him, remarking that Yasu's father was a loyal employee of his store and calls upon him to repent of his unfilial conduct before it is too late. Turning to Yosaburo again, Tazaemon exhorts him to start life anew as he seems a man of good breeding. He adds that if he wishes to take Otomi away he may do so at a later date, meanwhile he will give him money to start an honest trade. Tazaemon gives Yasu a generous sum in gold coins, asking him to hand it to Yosaburo. Yasu, bubbling over with their good fortune, goes over to Yosaburo who surlily orders him to return the money to Tazaemon. But this time Yasu has had enough; he gets angry with Yosaburo and reminding him of the debt of gratitude he owes him, Yasu, his mentor and partner in crime, he threatens to drag him off with the money if he will not go quietly. Yosaburo finally reluctantly agrees to go, followed by Yasu bowing and scraping to Tazaemon. Otomi half rises as if to follow, Tazaemon restrains her.

Once outside, Yasu heaves a sigh of relief and accuses Yosaburo of giving him a lot of trouble, explaining how awkward it was to be recognized by Tazaemon, a benefactor of his father. In the last scene, the stage has revolved to show a street; the two men are standing in the centre engaged in rapid conversation. Yosaburo says that he has a call to make and will be back later. Just as he is departing, Yasu stops him and asks with an anxious air if he has not forgotten something. Yosaburo thinks hard but can remember nothing. Yasu becomes more and more agitated. Finally feeling the gold coins within the sleeve of his *kimono*, Yosaburo gives a hearty laugh and tells Yasu to hold out his hand. The relieved Yasu receives five gold pieces, but complains that it is not enough. After considerable argument Yosaburo threatens to take the money back; Yasu, seeing that it is of no avail to hold out for more, accepts with good grace, remarking that he has not had an altogether unprofitable evening. They part with expressions of farewell, Yosaburo reminding Yasu to have the *sake* ready when he returns. The curtain is drawn.

Genyadana holds a unique place in the affections of Japanese theatre lovers and Yosaburo and Otomi are among some of the best known characters on the Kabuki stage. Some of Yosaburo's lines have become immortal and there is not a teashop mistress in the land but can quote them by heart.

The play is characterized by realism, but even so, to a Westerner, it contains a formality strangely at variance with the reality of his own stage. *Genyadana* is marked by a series of climaxes which are built up with a great deal of stylized gesture and speech on the part of the actors. Every movement that Yosaburo makes is familiar to a Kabuki audience: the way he sits, walks and gestures follow a set formula which has been adhered to by generations of actors, who have been judged by the particular skill with which they render a particular scene. The main dialogue in the play is colloquial speech which, although it is readily understood today, contains expressions no longer heard in everyday life. In its essence, *Genyadana* is a piece of dramatic storytelling, so designed as to allow the actor to weave around it his finished performance of formal expression, movement and dialogue.

V. TERAKOYA
A *jidaimono* play

Terakoya is one of the notable tragedies of the Kabuki theatre and is actually one of the most famous scenes from a much longer play in five acts, entitled *Suguwara Denju Tenerai Kagami*. Several of the other scenes from this drama are still staged, either singly or on occasion together, but of them all *Terakoya* remains probably the most celebrated. The full play was the joint work of four playwrights and was first staged at the Takemoto Theatre in Osaka in 1746. The *Terakoya* scene was the work of the playwright Takeda Izumo (1691–1756), a name second only to that of Chikamatsu Monzaemon in the quality of the work he produced.

The drama was written as a doll play and later adapted for the Kabuki, the musical accompaniment therefore is *gidayu*. Both doll theatre and Kabuki versions are staged today; although there are slight variations between the two, this is a case in fact where the Kabuki version can be said to be considerably better than the original in a number of ways.

Terakoya has for its theme the old Japanese conception of loyalty by which a man must sacrifice even his life or that of a family member for the cause he serves. In this instance, a *samurai*, Matsuo Maru, causes his own son to be beheaded in order to save the life of the son of his master and benefactor.

The action of the play takes place in a period corresponding to A.D. 887 in European history, but the settings and costumes are by no means accurate from a period point of view, being considered only for stage effect and devices are used which, in fact, belong to the Tokugawa era (1603–1868). The play *Sugawara Denju Tenerai Kagami* is actually a dramatic version of the life of Lord Sugawara Michizane, a high ranking scholar of the earlier period named. He was raised to a post of great responsibility by the Emperor, in order to help restrain the subversive influence on the state of the powerful Fujiwara family. However, he fell victim to a plot by Fujiwara Tokihara, who in the play is spoken of as Shihei. Michizane was disgraced in the eyes of the court and banished to exile as a minor official. He died in exile, but eventually his innocence came to light, his honour was restored and posthumous court rank awarded him. Michizane was an accomplished calligrapher among his other qualifications, and Genzo Takebe, who features in *Terakoya*, was his trusted pupil and loyal servant. In order to protect Kanshushai, the son of his exiled master, from arrest by Shihei, he kept him hidden away as his own son in his private village school of calligraphy, *Tera-*

koya. The story of the play is as follows: Shihei found out that Genzo Takebe was concealing the young Lord Kanshushai, and decided to have the boy killed in order to ensure no possibility of Michizane's succession being preserved. Shihei ordered his lieutenant, Shundo Gemba, to summon Genzo to the office of the village headman in order to cross-examine him and trap him into agreeing to present them with the head of Kanshushai.

Chief characters in the play are as follows:

Genzo Takebe: A village schoolmaster.

Tonami: His wife.

Matsuo Maru: Retainer of Lord Shihei.

Chiyo: His wife.

Kotaro: His son.

Kanshushai: Son of the exiled Lord Michizane.

Shundo Gemba: Lieutenant of Lord Shihei.

Yodarekuri: A rustic schoolboy.

Midai: Mother of Kanshushai.

When the play opens, Genzo is on his way back from the fatal meeting. He has no real intention of killing Kanshushai but is trying to think of a plan to find a substitute from among his pupils. On scrutinizing them again he realizes that there is no hope of any of them being able to deceive Shihei, who had ordered a certain Matsuo Maru, familiar with Kanshushai by sight, to act as a witness when the head was finally produced. Genzo knew this Matsuo well and regarded him as a traitor. Matsuo, the pine, was one of three brothers, the sons of Shiratayu, a retainer of Michizane, Genzo's own master. The other two brothers were named Umeo Maru and Sakura Maru, the plum and the cherry, the father having called his three children after the favourite trees of Michizane, his master. Umeo Maru and Sakura Maru were in the employ of Michizane, and on his banishment Sakura committed suicide while Umeo Maru disappeared, awaiting a chance to better his master's fortune. Their father, Shiratayu, followed his master into exile. Only one member of the family, Matsuo Maru, appeared to be disloyal to the cause, for he remained in the service of the enemy Shihei.

Matsuo refers to these facts in the course of the play and they also explain the symbolism of the pine twig which he throws in at the door of the village school, when he returns to explain matters to Genzo.

When Genzo saw Matsuo at the cross-examination by Shihei's followers, he realized that he would not be able to deceive him with the head of a country pupil as he had planned. Genzo regarded it as an act of fate, therefore, that just at this moment a new pupil named Kotaro, of aristocratic features, should have been enrolled in his school that day by his mother. He decided to kill Kotaro and substitute his head for Kanshushai's.

Kotaro was in fact the son of Matsuo. Though in the employ of Shihei, Matsuo had been waiting for an opportunity to show his real loyalty to Michizane. He realized what type of a man Genzo was and that he would never sacrifice Kanshushai but would try to find a substitute; he realized too what a dilemma Genzo would be in with only country bred boys to choose from. He arranged with his wife to take their son as a new pupil in the school, knowing that Genzo must inevitably choose him to take the place of Kanshushai. In this way Matsuo, according to the code of the time, discharged the highest debt of personal loyalty a man can pay.

After the followers of Shihei had departed in triumph with what they thought was the head of Kanshushai, Matsuo returned to the school house, where his wife had preceded him, revealed the whole story and finally called in Kanshushai's mother, whom he had secretly brought back from exile. Mother and son were reunited in a scene in which everything was overshadowed by the great personal tragedy of Matsuo and his wife, Chiyo. Genzo and Tonami, already labouring under great mental stress, were overcome when they learnt the true state of affairs. Finally, obsequies were performed for the dead Kotaro in which everyone took part.

When the curtain is first drawn in the play, the village school is seen with all the children busy at their desks. As the *chobo* tells us in the prologue: 'It is worth one thousand or even two thousand gold coins to learn each character well, it is of untold value in the present and the future. The teacher encouraged his pupils with these words, among them was Kanshushai. Genzo Takebe and his wife guarded him well as though he were their own son. Genzo moved to Seriu village and gathered many boys as pupils, some were skilled in handwriting and some were not. Some daubed the faces of other boys and some their hands instead of writing in their copybooks. Others drew dolls instead of writ-

Scene from 'Terakoya' (showing kokumochi costume and katsuyama wig)

ing Chinese characters, and when discovered by their master scratched their heads. Among the pupils was Gosaku's son, older than the rest. . . .'

On the stage the little Lord Kanshushai is seen sitting in the rear of the schoolroom apart from the others, his hair style marking him as different in rank to the other pupils. Yodarekuri, a bumpkin older than the rest, is trying to incite them to put down their brushes while the master is absent. He is a boisterous character who provides the touch of comic relief to the intensity of the main theme. Eventually, Genzo is seen returning down the lane, symbolized by the *hanamichi*, and the pupils become quiet immediately.

Genzo is walking slowly, with bent head and his arms folded across his chest. He looks pale and appears troubled by his innermost thoughts. He stops and looks up at the school, and then quickening his pace hurries to the entrance, where he is greeted by the pupils who rush towards him and bow deeply, except Kanshushai, who remains in his seat. Genzo stands looking at them and says aloud to himself: 'There is a proverb which says breeding will tell. These country boys brought up far away from a city background are useless for our purpose.'

He turns away in disgust, and then Tonami, his wife, appears and scolds him for being heartless to the boys. She tells him that a new pupil Kotaro has joined the school, and asks Genzo to see him. Kotaro is brought in to greet Genzo, who at first scarcely notices him, until suddenly looking up he remarks on the boy's good looks and greets him affably. Tonami tells Genzo that Kotaro's mother went to a neighbouring village after leaving her son at the school. Genzo then asks Tonami to dismiss all the pupils to an inner room and the children leave noisily, only Kanshushai being ushered into a separate room. After they have all gone, Tonami returns and questions Genzo on his distraught appearance and strange behaviour. Genzo tells her that Shihei has ordered him to behead Kanshushai, and that the treacherous Matsuo, a former member of their Lord's family, is being sent to identify the head. He explains that the only solution he could think of was to substitute a head of one of the village pupils, but on seeing their rustic looks he realized that he could not hope to deceive Matsuo with such a ruse. The arrival of a new pupil with aristocratic looks must be regarded as an act of fate, therefore, to save Kanshushai. Tonami is at first distressed by her husband's intentions, but he convinces her there is no alternative. While they are talking, the sounds of Shihei's men are heard outside and Genzo and Tonami hastily disappear into another room.

The beating of a large drum is heard from the *kuromisu*, and a procession of actors appear down the *hanamichi*. First comes Gemba, a fierce but colourful looking figure, who struts slowly along with a sideways step like a large turkey cock. His face is painted a ruddy hue with heavy eyebrows outlined in black. His hair is dressed in two large tufts at either side of his shaven crown, and on the back of his head he wears a small conical black hat at a backward angle. His upper *kimono* is of green and gold with an orange lining; he wears a black doublet and orange-coloured hose with canary-yellow ankle socks, *tabi*, and *zoori*, or sandals. A monstrous black square silk panel embroidered with a crest is affixed to his left sleeve, his right arm encircles a *kubi oke*, a plain, cylindrical wooden box with a lid, for the head of the victim. After him come eight *torite*, a bodyguard, who wear white headbands and white shoulder straps over a plain black *kimono*, a white girdle over which is knotted a purple cord encircles each waist. In their right hands they carry a short, metal rod called *jutte*, to which is attached a crimson tassel. After the *torite* comes a palanquin with drawn blinds carried by two bearers. This procession winds its way on to the stage. As they form up, eight villagers dressed in sober coloured *kimonos* and *haoris*, their formal dress, rush out in a file on the *hanamichi* and prostrate themselves, crying out in chorus. By this time, Gemba has seated himself astride a stool outside the gate of the house and sits in an arrogant manner as a voice is heard from the palanquin and Matsuo steps out. He wears a long ornate *kimono* embroidered in black, white and gold and leans heavily on a long sword as though very weak. His theatrical wig represents the headdress of a sick man, the hair having been allowed to grow thickly on the shaven crown. A white paper band is fixed round it ending in a large bow at the back, symbol of an invalid. The whole effect is of some elaborate fur hat rather than natural hair, and it is typical of the manner in which theatrical hairdressing ignores realism for the sake of stage effect. Matsuo's facial make-up is a deathly white, his mien is that of a man who is desperately ill.

The villagers, anguished fathers of the pupils, have heard what is afoot and have come to beg to be allowed to take their children away. Gemba, addressing them with contempt, orders them to call out their brats one by one. They do so and as each child comes out in turn he is stopped by Gemba at the gate, who waits for Matsuo's verdict. There is an amusing passage when the lout Yodarekuri, struck on the head by the disgusted Gemba's fan, runs blubbering to his parent who attempts to take him on his back; being a small man he is taken up by his unwieldy son instead, who overstrides his father and takes him off pick-a-back down the *hanamichi*. After all the pupils have gone with their parents, Gemba's party enter the school house to confront the angry Genzo and the trembling Tonami. The latter, throughout the play, is dressed in the *kokumochi*-style *kimono* and *katsuyama* wig, described in the section on the costume of the actors. After a passage of conversation between Matsuo and the scornful Genzo, the schoolmaster is brusquely ordered to go and return with the head of Kanshushai by the arrogant Gemba. Genzo goes off with defiant steps carrying the empty box. While he is away, Matsuo tries to trap Tonami by pointing out that there is an extra desk in relation to the number of pupils they have just

counted. As they are talking, the sound of a blow is heard from
the back of the house and the party become rigid with expectation, though each of them for a different reason. Genzo returns
slowly with his grim burden and places the box before Matsuo.
This is the most tense moment in the play as Matsuo seats himself and slowly, slowly begins to take off the lid of the box.
Behind him, Gemba's men are poised ready to strike should
Matsuo declare the head false, whilst Genzo is trembling with
hand on sword, ready to strike at Matsuo in the same instant.
The suspense is held for some moments, to be relaxed as Matsuo
finally declares the head genuine. Gemba is triumphant and gives
permission for Matsuo to go off on the sick leave which he has
asked for himself. Gemba flings some scornful words at Genzo and
goes stalking off down the *hanamichi*, stopping first to perform a
mie and beating the box containing the trophy and carried under
one arm with a bold swagger. His men follow him.

When they have gone, Genzo and his wife are completely
overcome with emotional relief after the ordeal; they bring out
Kanshushai from the cupboard where they have hidden him.
They are rejoicing when the voice of Kotaro's mother is heard
calling outside for admittance.

This scene, too, utilizes the *hanamichi* to advantage; the drum
beats and Chiyo, Kotaro's mother, comes running with hasty
steps, a figure of tragedy thrown into bold relief and emphasizing
a coming climax. Chiyo knocks agitatedly at the gate and looks
this way and that while waiting. Inside, Genzo pushes Tonami
and Kanshushai out of the room and goes to admit Chiyo, who
introduces herself with the phrase: 'I am the mother of the boy
who entered this school a little while ago.' They are words full
of great meaning when spoken by the master actor. Genzo asks
her in and answering her query tells her that Kotaro is playing
with the other boys in an inner room. She calls him by name; as
she turns to go and find him Genzo attacks her from behind
with his sword. He has decided that there is nothing to be done
but slay her in order to preserve their secret.

Chiyo defends herself by taking up the small writing desk of
Kotaro as a shield. Genzo's blade comes down on the desk, which
is split apart and from it drops a child's burial clothing. Chiyo
asks Genzo point blank if he has substituted Kotaro for Kanshushai. He stands back astonished, and at this moment Matsuo

is seen outside the entrance to the house. He slides the door aside and tosses a pine twig, to which is attached a written poem, into the room. Genzo picks it up and reads aloud: 'In a world in which the plum blossom was blown away and the cherry blossom perished. . . .' 'How can the pine remain coldhearted,' finishes Matsuo, stepping inside. Genzo is about to attack him but Matsuo throws down his own swords at the schoolmaster's feet. Then the whole story comes out how Matsuo and his wife deliberately sacrificed their son in order to save Kanshushai. Matsuo understood the character of Genzo and foreseeing the course of action he would try to take in his dilemma, played his tragic part in assisting him and so paid his long outstanding debt of honour to his master. The scene is now one pregnant with sorrow; Genzo and Tonami are overcome at the enormity of the sacrifice as the grieving Matsuo consoles the weeping Chiyo and is at last himself overcome by tears as he hears how bravely his son met his end. Their grief is shared by Kanshushai who enters dressed in costume indicative of his high rank. Suddenly, Matsuo rises and going to the entrance blows a whistle which he takes from his pocket, and summons a palanquin which appears from behind the shrubbery. Out of it steps Midai, the mother of Kanshushai, whom Matsuo has secretly brought back from exile, and there is a happy reunion in the midst of sadness. Finally there is a moving scene in which *kadobi*, a funeral ceremony, is performed to the dead Kotaro. All join in. The play closes with a tableau: Midai and Kanshushai, two colourful figures, are standing together in the schoolroom, and therefore above the level of the others on the stage. Genzo and Tonami are on their knees with bowed heads on the front stage, whilst Matsuo and Chiyo in mourning costume of white and pale blue, are on the extreme right. Chiyo is on her knees beside Matsuo, who holds his sword and the twig of pine at his right side. His feet are astride, while his left arm is lifted at shoulder height with outstretched palm. The *chobo* sings 'they are departing', and the curtain is drawn.

In *Terakoya*, the Kabuki convention whereby different sets of actions are shown going on simultaneously within and without a building, is seen to the best advantage, while the *hanamichi* provides several extremely dramatic interludes. The child actor also plays an important part in the development of a plot such as this.

The scene in which the head has to be viewed, *kubijikken*, has its counterpart in several other Kabuki plays. The formality of the stage technique provides an abstract quality which mitigates the audience's apprehensions. Indeed the whole drama which carries everything to extremes, even if judged by the ethics it embodies in its plot, is characterized by this same abstract feeling. Most foreigners who see it are moved by its power and tragic intensity; it is excellent theatre.

VI. DOMO MATA
A *jidaimono* play

This drama is a part of a longer play called *Meihitsu Keisei Kagami*, which was first staged at the Takemoto doll theatre in Osaka in 1752. It was devised by Yoshida Kanshi and others, but is actually an adaptation of a play by Chikamatsu Monzaemon, called *Keisei Hangonko*. A *jidaimono* of a very different type to the preceding one, *Domo Mata* is an interesting and unusual drama from a psychological point of view. It is as well to understand the old Japanese system of *deshi*, in following the plot. In all the arts and crafts, no matter what they were, it was the custom for pupils to attach themselves to a certain master and become his disciple or *deshi*. They would follow his instruction and when they reached a certain stage of proficiency they were allowed to take the name of their teacher. It was regarded as a signal honour and a test of their competence as an artist, a badge of professional recognition in fact. This is the principle underlying the intensity of the relationship between Matahei and his master, which might at first seem somewhat puzzling to the foreigner. Chief characters in the play:

Tosa Shogen: A master painter.
Kita no Kata: Shogen's wife.
Matahei: Pupil of Shogen (later Tosa Mitsuoki Matahei).
Otoku: Matahei's wife.
Shurinosuke: Pupil of Shogen.
Utanosuke: Another pupil of Shogen.

Domo Matahei was a painter and the pupil of the famous Tosa Shogen. He was cursed with a physical affliction, a stammer which caused him to be despised by everyone. He had a faithful and devoted wife, however, Otoku, who spoke on behalf of her husband and did her utmost to achieve recognition for his talents

A doll theatre puppet: Matahei

by asking Shogen to bestow the name of the Tosa School on
Matahei.

When the play opens, the house of Tosa Shogen is seen. It is a
country residence surrounded by bamboo thickets and under-
growth. A party of farmers appears down the lane, i.e. on the
hanamichi, armed with a miscellany of weapons and talking excitedly. It turns out they are looking for a tiger which has been
seen in the neighbourhood and they are searching in the thickets
round the house when Shurinosuke, favourite pupil of Shogen,
appears and scolds them for disturbing the peace of a famous
painter. When he hears their reason, he laughs them to scorn
by saying that tigers do not live in Japan. Hearing the altercation
Shogen himself comes out and tells Shurinosuke to allow the
farmers to carry on their their search, as the absence of tigers in
Japan cannot be proved.

Suddenly the tiger appears in a thicket and the farmers call Shogen to come and see it. Shurinosuke steps down from the house with a lighted candle and leads his master to the spot where the tiger is lurking. On seeing it, Shogen informs them that it is obviously a tiger which has escaped from a painting by the famous artist Genki, and that he will make it disappear in their presence. Shurinosuke interrupts and begs Shogen to let him test his prowess instead. Shogen agrees, the pupil takes a large paint brush and standing before the tiger makes several flourishes and the animal disappears. The farmers are astonished and praise the skill of the young man, while Shogen is delighted with his pupil. He tells Shurinosuke that he may now adopt the title of Tosa as a reward; Shogen then goes indoors to prepare the coveted certificate of merit.

After this incident the stage is deserted once more and Matahei appears on the *hanamichi* preceded by his wife, Otoku, who leads the way with a lighted paper lantern. Matahei carries a package containing cooked eels, a delicacy in Japan, to give to his master. When they reach the house, Shurinosuke intercepts them and on learning who they are calls Shogen out to meet his guests. The painter and his wife appear; Kita no Kata thanks Otoku for the gift while Matahei's wife apologizes for her garrulous tongue, but explains that she has to do all the talking for Matahei as he has such an affliction. All this time Matahei is gulping and trying to form words which he cannot get out. Otoku turns to Shogen and says that on the way they met a party of farmers, who told them that Shurinosuke had received the honoured title of Tosa. Matahei, her husband, is senior to Shurinosuke and is very discouraged by the news, she continues, as she pleads fervently for her husband, begging Shogen to bestow the title on Matahei.

Shogen replies that Shurinosuke received the award for meritorious service; Matahei has achieved nothing yet and as he cannot speak properly it is unlikely that he ever will. He advises them to return home quickly.

Matahei is overcome with distress, he clutches his throat wildly and tries to force the words out again, and finally bursts into tears in his anguish. At this juncture a dishevelled figure comes flying down the *hanamichi* brandishing a sword, and running up to the front of the house collapses on the ground. It is Utanosuke, another of Shogen's followers. When he is brought round, he

Matahei keeps watch: scene from 'Domo Mata'

tells them that the wife of the nobleman who is Shogen's patron
and master has been carried off by a rival faction, while her
husband is missing. He recites the events using the *gochushin*
technique, described in the chapter on the actor's techniques.
From a literary point of view this scene may appear to bear little
relation to the plot of *Domo Mata*, the theme of course is connected with the main play of which *Domo Mata* is a part. As a
stage device it introduces a variation into the main action on the
stage and provides a contrast in techniques which pleases the eye
of the audience.

When Utanosuke has finished his story he is sent off with
further instructions while Shogen ponders their next step.
Previous to this Matahei has been told off to wait at the gate;
he sits like a faithful watchdog, eyes fixed on the distance all the

time the recital has been going on. On the stage, this is symbolized by Matahei sitting gazing up the *hanamichi*. When Utanosuke leaves he brushes roughly past Matahei without even noticing him, emphasizing the indifference of his colleagues to Matahei's presence.

Matahei goes back to the house to plead with Shogen to allow him to go on a mission to assist the wife of their noble master. Shogen brusquely thrusts him aside and orders Shurinosuke to set out on the task. Matahei clings to Shurinosuke and pleads with him to change places and allow him to go in his stead. Shurinosuke, angered by Matahei's persistence and restraining grip, threatens to strike him if he does not let go, whereupon Matahei begs him to cut him down, saying that he prefers to die. Shogen now takes a hand and ordering Shurinosuke off quickly, rails angrily at Matahei. Matahei tries to follow Shurinosuke; Otoku detains him and Matahei, seized with a passion of vexation and frustration, strikes his wife and throws her down roughly. Sadly Otoku gets to her feet and makes a last impassioned plea to Shogen on her husband's behalf; Shogen remains absolutely adamant and goes angrily indoors.

Matahei is now weeping bitterly. Otoku turns to him and says: 'I am sorry for you, Matahei, but you must give up your cherished desires. You have two hands with ten fingers, but it is unfortunate that you stammer.' She goes on to say that the only thing he can do now is to commit suicide, then perhaps he will be granted the Tosa title after his death. Before he dies, he must paint his portrait on a stone fountain in the garden and this will serve as his tombstone. Matahei sadly agrees and Otoku brings over his brushes and prepares his ink. This done, Matahei walks over to the fountain which is rectangular in shape and as high as his shoulder; squatting down behind it he commences to paint his portrait on the side facing his teacher's house. As he works, the painting is seen to appear simultaneously on the front of the fountain as well, in full view of the audience. This is achieved by an ingenious device of the small property men, one of whom is hidden in the fountain.

After he has finished, Matahei goes back to his wife and sinks down in despair on the ground. The sorrowing pair have not yet noticed the miraculous occurrence. Otoku rises and walks to the fountain to bring back a bamboo ladle of water for her husband to drink before he kills himself. Then she sees the double portrait and is overcome with her discovery. Tremblingly she approaches Matahei and drags him over; she is speechless for once. Matahei looks at the fountain agitatedly, back and front, then looks again. They are both transported with joy at what has happened and cannot contain themselves at the sight of Matahei's skill, his painting is so wonderful that it can even penetrate stone!

Shogen, hearing their excited cries, comes out; on being shown what has happened he is astounded; he turns to Matahei and tells him that he may now really adopt the name of Tosa. Matahei's cup of happiness is full. Shogen's wife brings him ceremonial costume to put on and he dances triumphantly as Otoku plays on the shoulder drum, or *kotsuzumi*. As the curtain is drawn, Matahei is seen posing bravely with a large brush held aloft, the other characters grouped in tableau around him.

The doll theatre version has a somewhat different ending, for Shogen cleaves the stone fountain, on which the portrait is painted, in two with his sword. As he does so Matahei immediately regains his powers of speech and there is an amusing scene where the doll Matahei recites the vowels of the Japanese syllabary, then suddenly realizes he is speaking normally. The scene where Matahei knocks a cup of tea out of his wife's hand and roughly strikes her is a masterpiece of puppet technique; the expression and movement of Otoku would touch anyone's heart at this moment.

The Kabuki version relies to a great extent on the symbolism and formal technique of the doll theatre and pays little attention to logical reality, as the reader will gather. An important feature is the miming of the actor playing Matahei, an exceedingly difficult role to act convincingly yet within the limits of prescribed convention. The part of Otoku is also one of the more important in the repertoire of the *onnagata* actor and is only taken by a seasoned player. Otoku is regarded as the model of a faithful wife by Japanese people; in real life the name is often applied to a woman whose character contains those qualities symbolized in this celebrated stage personality.

CHAPTER XI

THE PLAYHOUSE
AND ITS DEVELOPMENT

⚶

BEFORE the birth of O Kuni's Kabuki, the ordinary people amused themselves in the open with various diversions such as puppet shows and dance spectacles, which were held in specified areas. It was these areas which were the forerunners of the special quarters in the towns where the playhouse came into being. After O Kuni's entertainment was received with such acclaim by the public, a stage was built for her performance, largely modelled on the one used by the Nō theatre and modified somewhat to suit more popular requirements. This was the beginning of the modern Kabuki playhouse. Eventually it passed through a series of changes in design, during which time all traces of the Nō influence were gradually eliminated and it became the unique type of stage construction it is today. The Nō stage proper has remained to all intents and purposes fundamentally the same as it was then, except that it is now always indoors instead of in the open.

In the earliest style of Kabuki theatre there was no roof over the audience and greenroom, but only the stage. Later the site of the playhouse was enclosed with a bamboo fence built in a crosswise pattern with a tower at the front called a *yagura*. The *yagura* was originally a symbol of the Shogun's authority to perform. In the top of the tower sat a drummer who beat a tattoo to open the day's performance, and this is the origin of the beating of a drum offstage which still opens and concludes a Kabuki performance. The *yagura* came to be draped with a curtain decorated with the *mon*, or crest, of the theatre. At the foot of the tower was a narrow opening called the *nezumi kido*, literally mouse door, through which the audience had to stoop to enter the auditorium.

The most significant feature of the Nō stage is the *hashi-gakari*, or bridge, along which the actors make their entries and exits. This was adapted into the early Kabuki theatre, more or less in its original form, then gradually changed, first being set at right angles to the main stage then in front of it. It seems fairly obvious that the Nō *hashigakari* was the origin of the present day *hanamichi*, or flower way. There is a school of thought which believes the *hanamichi* had its origin in a temporary walk that audiences used in the old days when they made a practice of carrying flowers to the actors. It makes a pretty story, but in the writer's opinion, the relationship between the *hanamichi* and *hashigakari* is so obvious and logical that it refutes any other theory.

During the period of the Wakashu, Onna and Yaro Kabuki, a considerable number of theatres sprang up; about 1620, permission was given for the construction of seven in Kyoto, which became known as the seven *yagura*. Later on *za* became a generic term for theatre and was generally used. Literally it means a seat, or meeting place, and from this came to mean a company of players and was used by dancers attached to the great shrines.

In 1624, the Saruwaka za was opened by a man called Kanzaburo, at Nakabashi in Yedo. He was the first actor manager of the period and his name is still perpetuated on the Tokyo stage. Later the Saruwaka za became the famous Nakamura za, one of the four historic Yedo theatres founded in the Genroku era. In 1633 the Myako za and in 1634 the Murayama za were founded, both in Sakaicho, Yedo. The theatre made one development after another during this period, but it also underwent many trials and tribulations for it was subject to strict Government controls and constant interference from the authorities. The lives of actors and managers were precarious in the extreme, the Kabuki was in constant financial distress and these facts influenced theatre construction for a long time, so that playhouses were simply bare barracks constantly exposed to the dangers of fire.

Only eight years after the Saruwaka za was built, it was ordered to move to Negicho district in Yedo, along with the puppet theatre and other diversions which clustered round the main theatre. The reason given was that it was considered to be too near headquarters; the Shogunate officials preserved an inflexible policy in keeping entertainments away from the city and in one place, to facilitate easy vigilance. Other theatres were ordered to move to Sakaicho, Fukiyacho and Kobikicho districts, areas where the Yedo theatre was to have its being for more than two hundred years. The three areas named were chosen by the Government after a fire which destroyed Yedo in 1657, and following this conflagration, several places of entertainment were closed permanently. Four large theatres were allowed to rebuild, besides a number of small puppet shows and the like. The theatres were the Saruwaku za, the Miyako za, the Murayama za and the Yamamura za. Following the official definition of licensed theatre quarters, two other famous theatres, the Morita za and the Kiri za, were built in Kobikicho in 1660 and 1661 respectively, and there were signs of revived prosperity in the Kabuki world. Then occurred an affair famous as a scandal which had far reaching effects on the theatre in general; it concerned the amorous relations of Ejima, a high ranking lady-in-waiting in a nobleman's house, and Ikushima Shingoro, an actor of the Yamamura za. It was the signal for drastic intervention on the part of the authorities. The Yamamura za was closed for good and theatres other than the Saruwaka za, Murayama za and Morita za were banned, while actors and all theatre people were ordered to move into the districts in which the three playhouses were situated. Strict regulations were brought into force regarding their relationship with the outer world and every detail of their lives became subject to control. It was this policy which created a theatre society unique in customs and habits. The ban was extended to Kyoto and Osaka as well as Yedo, theatres being limited to five in Kyoto and four in Osaka.

During the Genroku era, the Saruwaka za and the Murayama za were renamed the Nakamura za and Ichimura za respectively, and these two together with the Morita za became the three most celebrated theatres in Yedo. In spite of difficulties, the Kabuki eventually prospered and went from strength to strength. The theatre quarter of Sakaicho remained in being for two hundred years; the district adjoined Fukiyacho and in these two areas the Nakamura za and Ichimura za were situated, while the Morita za was separate in the Kobikicho district. The three theatres were the only ones allowed to possess a *yagura*, or drum tower, decorated with their crests. Before dawn, the spectators used to flock to these playhouses anxious to arrive with the first drum beats, and the play season must have been an occasion for lively and colourful happenings as the crowds thronged the streets. The theatres were surrounded by tea-houses, called *chaya*; they were divided into four classes, *ojaya*, *maejaya*, *kochaya* and *mizujaya*, according to the rank and class of people they served. It was through these tea-houses that the theatregoers of better class purchased their tickets; they were also used as retreats and meeting places during intervals. People stayed in the theatre from early morning until late evening in those days; intervals were very long, and as there were no facilities and conveniences in the playhouse itself, the tea-houses served a very practical purpose and they prospered accordingly. The tea-house has ever since been intimately connected with the theatre, actors often coming from tea-house families. Long after the theatres were no longer segregated in quarters the *chaya*, or tea-house, continued to exist and serve its many purposes in the vicinity of the playhouse.

The quarters of Sakaicho and Fukiyacho were separated by a *kido*, or gate, around which were situated the *geisha* quarters. During the theatre season, the tea-houses and neighbouring buildings were gaily decorated and this applied particularly during *kaomise*, the opening of the new theatrical season in November. Lanterns were hung from the eaves of houses and theatre buildings, together with sprays of artificial blossom. In front of the theatres stood the *ekamban*, or signboards, on which were painted pictures of the actors; the tradition is still carried on in front of modern Kabuki theatres. There were also the *onadai*, name boards containing the titles of the actors in order of rank, together with large decorative casks of *sake* presented to the players, while red and white bunting was everywhere; these decorations are seen in front of playhouses today at the opening of a season or on special occasions. *Geisha* entertained the crowds, and the atmosphere was one of festivity and lightheartedness.

The theatre quarters continued in this fashion until the occasion when a great fire broke out in the Nakamura za in 1841 and a high official, Mizuno Echizen no Kami, attempted to abolish the Kabuki once and for all. His efforts only succeeded in changing the theatre quarters to Shoten cho in Asakusa, later called Saruwaka cho, and this was the last of the special theatre quarters of old Yedo, with the three playhouses, the Nakamura za, Ichimura za and Morita za flourishing as before.

With the Meiji Restoration of 1868, special theatre quarters were abolished and the playhouses moved into the town; the Morita za went to Shintomicho, the Nakamura za to Shintorigoe cho and the Ichimura za to Nichomachi. An older generation in Japan still remembers the Shintomi za, or former Morita za, and the Ichimura za. The new Shintomi za was founded in the fifth year of Meiji, 1872, by Morita Kanya, a manager with fertile ideas. He enlarged the size of the theatre, both in breadth and width, used stone for construction and introduced many innovations into the auditorium. As a result of his influence, theatre construction changed considerably, although even so many of the old fundamentals were retained. In the Meiji era, three famous theatres were built in Tokyo, the Kabuki za, the Meiji za and the Imperial Theatre. The last was in purely Western style.

The great earthquake of 1923 swept away the last vestiges of old playhouse construction in Tokyo; the Kabuki za, which had been destroyed, was rebuilt and became the principal theatre of the city. Next to it were the Meiji za at Hama cho, the Shimbashi Embujo, together with the Tokyo Gekijo and the Imperial Theatre, at all of which Kabuki seasons were staged. There was also a theatre in the suburbs, the Shinjuku Daiichi Gekijo, where the younger Kabuki actors regularly appeared.

The last war changed the situation once more. The Kabuki za and Meiji za were destroyed by bombing, but restored in 1951 and 1950 respectively. The Tokyo Gekijo and the Shinjuku Daiichi have become cinemas and the Imperial Theatre is devoted chiefly to revue. The Shimbashi Embujo remains as before, but it was never a theatre used entirely for Kabuki in any case and there are only two or three performances each year. Among all the present Tokyo theatres, the Kabuki za is the only one devoted solely to Kabuki all the year round. This theatre has a capacity of about 2,000 as compared with the 1,700 of the Meiji za. A traditional feature which disappeared with war was the double *hanamichi* of the old Kabuki za, now reduced to one in the interests of seating requirements and expenses, a concession to business which would have been howled down by the audiences of old Yedo! What then would they have said to a performance of *Chushingura* by Osaka actors at the Imperial Theatre in November 1953! This Western-style theatre, which suddenly had the urge to produce the great Kabuki classic, possesses no *hanamichi* at all; a temporary construction a few feet long was connected from a side exit to the stage. *Chushingura* without a *hanamichi*, a feature absolutely indispensable to this particular play; one imagines a horrified Morita Kanya looking down from a shadowy auditorium. With all his reforms he never conceived anything like that!

Other large theatres staging Kabuki outside Tokyo are the Kabuki za in Osaka, seating 2,000, the Minami za in Kyoto, and the Misono za in Nagoya, the two last with a capacity of about 1,500. Besides these there is of course the Bunraku za in Osaka which is used solely for the doll theatre. Of the Tokyo theatres, the Kabuki za and Meiji za still retain something of the atmosphere of the old Kabuki, an atmosphere with marked characteristics which every modern innovation cannot completely dispel. In describing physical features which do so much to preserve this atmosphere, it is necessary to go back a little and trace their development.

The development of stage construction was synonymous with that of the play. In 1644 the Ichimura za first used two different types of stage curtain. One, the *hikimaku*, was pulled across the stage to open and close a performance. This principle is still observed, for the main stage curtain in a Kabuki theatre is drawn across by hand and not raised and lowered as in the Western theatre. The second, the *kiriotoshi*, an auxiliary curtain, was suspended to cover the stage and released suddenly by a sharp pull of supporting cords, thus creating an element of surprise in the proceedings. This too is used today. These developments assisted in the transformation of the Kabuki stage from its Nō prototype into the frame stage, or *gaku bachi butai*, which became the finally accepted form.

In 1668, the new Kawarazaki za used for the first time an element of construction which, in fact, was the forerunner of the modern *hanamichi*. Eventually, two *hanamichis* were customary in every theatre, the main one on the left being called *hon* and the one on the right *kari*, or temporary *hanamichi*, this being narrower in width than the main construction. The double *hanamichi* became common around 1760, if we are to go by the various *ukiyoe* prints of the period. Prior to this, a platform was built on to the centre of the *hon hanamichi*; it was called the *nanori dai* and was used by the actor to recite special dialogues. It was a device to break the division between audience and stage, a principle which has always been emphasized in Kabuki technique.

The mid-eighteenth century was a fruitful period in the development of theatre construction; the revolving stage, or *mawari butai*, was originated in 1757 by the dramatist Namiki Shozo (1730–73); he is also credited with having introduced many ideas and arrangements from the doll theatre into the Kabuki. The revolving stage was therefore in use in Japan long before it was experimented with in the Western theatre, and has played a vital part in the development of the actor's technique; it has been consistently used in every theatre since its inception. The fundamental feature of the revolving stage is the fact that it allows a whole scene to be changed before the eyes of the audience: time, place and atmosphere can be altered and the sequence of a story carried forward without a break. On the other hand, the audience can be transported back to a point where the story was left off so that it is possible to gain a three-dimensional understanding of the play and its action.

The revolving stage works on the turn-table principle and of course varies in size according to the dimensions of the stage as a whole. The one at the Kabuki za in Tokyo is sixty feet in diameter, while that of the Meiji za is forty-two feet. Nowadays it is driven by electric power, but in former times it was worked solely by manpower. This is well shown in *Gekijo Kummo Zue*, an old book published in the Tokugawa era which is a veritable Bible of the Kabuki. The turn-table was attached by ropes to windlasses at either side of the stage and worked by several men.

The area beneath the main stage of a theatre is known as *naraku*, a Buddhist term meaning the bottomless pit, where much effort goes unrewarded and is seen by none. Nevertheless, the men who worked in the depths of *naraku*, if invisible, often had their more spectacular efforts applauded by the audience just as though they were actors, and audiences will still show their appreciation of a skilful piece of stagecraft by the various workers behind the scenes.

A later development of the *mawari butai* was the *janome butai*. In this, the revolving stage is in two parts so that an inner portion can revolve in an opposite direction to an outer portion. The word *janome* refers to the Japanese paper umbrella known as *janomen gasa*, which was designed with a broad circular pattern to which the plan of the double revolving stage bears some resemblance. All kinds of ingenious effects could be produced with this device, such as, for instance, a boat sailing under a bridge. Prior to its destruction in the war, the Tokyo Kabuki za possessed a *janome butai*, but it has disappeared from the theatres today.

Other inventions of the same period as the revolving stage were the *seriage* and *serisage* devices. These, by means of trap door arrangements built in the stage, allow the actors slowly to appear and disappear from view. A similar arrangement on the *hanamichi* is called the *suppon*; this is situated in a position referred to as *shichi san*, because it is seven units of measurement from the rear of the threatre and three units from the stage. It is a device used with particular effect for the appearance of ghosts and spirits. In the present Kabuki za, there are three *seriage* of different sizes built into the stage and known as *seri, chuzeri* and *okiseri* respectively; they are chiefly used for spectacular effects in dancing plays. Like the revolving stage, *seriage* devices were formerly worked by hand but are now driven by electric power.

By the middle of the eighteenth century, the architectural interior of the theatre had begun to assume an appearance which remained typical until after the Meiji Restoration. It was some time before the old gable roofed stage, *hafu yane hon butai*, a relic of Nō influence, was done away with, and it was the Miyako theatre that first abolished it in 1796, after that it was not long before other theatres followed suit. The nineteenth century saw no further inventions, but all previous developments were now incorporated as the accepted stage form.

A print by Toyokuni III (1786–1864), published in the middle of the nineteenth century, shows the interior of the famous Nakamura za of Yedo, and it is a lively representation of the typical Kabuki theatre and its audience. An earlier print of the Nakamura za published in 1771, by Utagawa Toyuhara, is also of interest for it still shows the old gabled roof stage, but the main features of the auditorium appear to be more or less similar except that the earlier print does not show the centre of the auditorium divided into little pen-like enclosures separated by cat walks, which were a feature of the later theatre.

In the Toyokuni print, the form which the theatre took in the early nineteenth century is very clearly shown. The building was rectangular in shape and made of unpainted natural wood. The stage stretched the width of the auditorium, but was apron fronted and so surrounded on three sides by audience. The space in the centre between the two *hanamichis* was called the *hira doma* and consisted of square pens bounded by wooden cat walks. The audience sat inside the pens, the floors of which were covered with straw matting. On the far side of each *hanamichi* were what were called the *taka doma*, consisting of a single row of enclosures at the side of the *kari hanamichi*, and a double one by the main *hanamichi*. Behind the stage above the *taka doma* at this side, further seating for the audience called *rakandai* was built. Judging by the various prints extant, six seems to have been the maximum number of people squeezed into the *doma* enclosures, although according to one Japanese authority seven was the official number.

The seating in the *doma* went by various names according to their position in the theatre, some examples are *maedoma*, *nijudoma*, *kiridoma*, along with picturesque terms like *okubi*, big neck, or *takotsubo*, octopus pot. The seating adjoining the stage seems to have varied from time to time according to the size of the theatre, and went by various special names too. Beyond the *naka doma* at either side was the seating called *sajiki*. First came a row of open boxes above the level of the centre *doma* and at *hanamichi* height, extending the length of the auditorium. Behind this was a row of enclosed boxes with barred fronts and above this, on the second storey, ran a railed gallery also arranged for seating. Behind the *sajiki* was the *tsumbo sajiki*, literally deaf man's gallery, and here extra members of the audience were squeezed in. In the modern Kabuki theatre, the influence of the old *sajiki* is still to be seen in the seating at the sides of the auditorium.

It is extremely interesting to look at the audience in a print like the one described here. Everyone is there. The married lady, the connoisseur, the young blood, the *geisha*, the shopkeeper; all are accurately portrayed in the costumes and hairstyles of their period. They are laughing, exchanging glances or engrossed in the play, whilst attendants bring round tea and *bento*, the lunch boxes which still play such an important part in Japanese life. The significant thing is that one can pick out from the throng all the characters one sees on the Kabuki stage in the

The Kabuki Horse, after an illustration in 'Gekijo Kummo Zue'

later *sewamono* plays. The happy jostling audiences of the Yedo theatre little dreamed as they hurried through the *nezumi kido* that one day they themselves would be immortalized.

Members of the audience in the old theatre, by no means negligible, were those people popularly referred to as *omuko*, literally, 'great beyond or opposite'. They were theatre lovers of narrow means who occupied back seats, far behind the front gallery which contained more fortunate spectators. They were real connoisseurs, so that no sensible actor would treat them with less respect than the wealthier of his audience. Witty and apposite cries, *kakegoe*, issuing from this quarter during a performance were prized by the actors themselves, hence the current expression borrowed from the stage, *omuko wo unaraseru*, literally, 'make *omuko* groan', i.e. 'take their breath away'. If an actor succeeded in doing this, he counted it a triumph of his art.

The pillars at the two sides of the Yedo stage were called *daijin bashira*, a symbol of the connection with the Nō stage. At the right of the stage to the audience was fixed the *kurofuda*, a black tablet on which was written the name of any member of the audience urgently wanted outside. A Japanese writer records that if someone was required to leave the theatre, his name was first of all called three times, even if the play was in progress;

if there was no response the *kurofuda* was hung up, but for this privilege there was a set charge. Today visitors are called from the auditorium by modern microphone systems, but only during the intervals of a performance!

Suspended above the stage was the famous *joshikimaku*, the curtain patterned with vertical bars of green, black and persimmon, a combination of colouring which is striking in its simplicity and somehow redolent of the very atmosphere of the Kabuki theatre. Its colour scheme is invariably seen used for advertising, wrapping papers and other articles which for any reason at all wish to suggest the Kabuki.

In former days the colour scheme used in some theatres was black, persimmon and white, and in a print of the Meiji era showing a small theatre called the Hisamatsu za, the curtain is depicted in stripes of green, black and pale blue. It was the green, black and persimmon scheme which survived all the others though and became a tradition which has been handed down.

In the Yedo theatre, the *joshikimaku* was customarily suspended to run from the left side of the stage to the audience, while from the right a second curtain could be pulled in front and this was generally indigo with the crest of the theatre in white.

Behind the stage were the greenrooms, built in three stories. The entrance to them was called the *urakido* and the first floor contained bathrooms for the actors; *hayashi beya* or musician's room; *sakusha beya*, playwright's room; and *kodogu beya*, small properties room. On the second floor were rooms called *naka nikai* for the use of the *onnagata* actors, and on the third floor were rooms for *zagashira*, the leader of the troupe, together with others for *nadai shita*, the lower actors, and a large room with a planked floor used as a meeting-place for full rehearsals. The greenrooms of a theatre are still built in three stories, but there have been many changes in them dictated by modern stage procedure.

The *hanamichi*, as already explained, was divided into ten units of measurement which fixed the *shichisan* as seven from the rear of the theatre and three from the stage, and at this point the *suppon*, literally tortoise, was constructed. The *hanamichi* connects the stage to a small room at the back of the auditorium known as *toya*, or chicken coop, another example of

The Yedo Theatre (after a contemporary print) showing kyogen kata using the hyoshigi. Note the kurofudo described in this chapter

the humorous nomenclature so often found in the old Kabuki. The *toya* is the room from which the actors make their entry on to the *hanamichi,* and it is shut off by a curtain, the *age maku,* bearing the crest of the theatre. It is almost the same as it was in the old days, the main innovation being that it now contains the switch to operate the concealed lighting which is a feature of the modern *hanamichi.*

From the foregoing descriptions, it is possible to trace the development of some of the most salient features of theatre construction and their final appearance in forms which impart such an individual appearance to the Kabuki playhouse. The Kabuki za in Tokyo is the best example of the traditional Kabuki playhouse in modern style. It is the fifth theatre to bear this name, having been twice destroyed by fire and once by earthquake in addition to the bombing of the last war. The first Kabuki za was built in 1889 and was the scene of many of the stage triumphs of Ichikawa Danjuro IX. The present building was rebuilt on the site of the old, retaining the former façade with its traditional curved roof gables and ornate entrance. It embodies all the luxuries and services provided by modern decoration, lighting and plumbing. Within its carpeted foyers are restaurants, shops and kiosks of every description; there is a lounge with a picture gallery and even a television set! A far cry from the old Nakamura za. The auditorium and the stage retain the natural wood construction of tradition and there are *tatami* boxes down both sides of the theatre on the sites of the old *sajiki*, but the bulk of the seating is in Western style. Square in its proportions, the auditorium has two tiers of galleries above it. At the very rear of the topmost one lies the *tachimi*, literally, 'stand to see'. Here for a modest sum the true Kabuki enthusiasts are allowed to enter for one particular play and watch their favourite actor. The *habituè* of the *tachimi* is regarded as the true connoisseur, the man who understands all the finer points, for he is so far away from the stage that at times it is difficult to hear the words of the players.

Back stage and beneath stage exists that unique society which pursues its own way, consisting of craftsmen and workers to whom the word Kabuki spells universe. There is one difference today, modern lighting, machinery and technical advances demand space and workers never needed in the old theatre.

The Tokyo Kabuki za is the centre of Kabuki activities now, and although there are other theatres, it is here that one finds, in spite of its being a tripper's paradise, a link with the theatre of old. Here the spirits of the mighty are still recalled, as for example when in October 1953, a full scale ceremony was held to commemorate the fiftieth anniversary of the death of Danjuro IX, and a packed house was a reminder that the light still burns if not so brightly as of old.

The playhouse of Yedo was, and its continuation in Tokyo still is, in many ways, a world within a world, a self-contained unit in which work people of many different kinds. They live for one thing only, the theatre in which they have their being, their only object in life is to see the curtain drawn at the appointed hour. Formerly on the other side of that curtain sat audiences to whom the Kabuki was their supreme relaxation; they were as familiar with its colourful characters and their customs as they were with their own mothers. There is a difference today, and to the old theatre hands there is a wide gulf between present audiences and those of pre-war years even. The traditions which were handed down so faithfully and for so long from the three great theatres who queened it over old Yedo are becoming lost in the cinema queues of twentieth-century Tokyo.

GLOSSARY OF JAPANESE TERMS

THE many technical expressions which must be given in romanized Japanese form in a book of this nature are apt to be confusing to the general reader if only by virtue of their number. Unfortunately the problem is an insoluble one.

A writer on Western ballet, for instance, must use French for his technical description, but he is secure in the knowledge that a large proportion of his readers have a nodding acquaintance with the language, or, if not, are at least familiar enough with the ballet to be able to relate technical terms with the minimum of difficulty.

The reverse is true in the case of English people and the Kabuki theatre of Japan, yet it is quite obviously impossible to get round the difficulty by inventing English substitutes for Japanese names; it would only result in confusion and inaccuracy.

This glossary provides an alphabetical list of every Japanese term used in the book together with a description in English; by the use of this it is hoped that the reader may be able to check up his facts in as simple and rapid a fashion as possible. The terms are given in the standard romanized forms used in the Hepburn system.

Agemaku: Striped curtain used on the Nō stage and through which the actors make their entry from the green room. The curtain is pulled upwards from the ground by two poles attached to the bottom. The name is also used to describe the curtain which separates the *hanamichi* and the *toya*. A similar curtain to the Nō *agemaku* is used on the stage in Kabuki plays of Nō derivation; it is also called *kirimaku*.

Aibiki: Stage property like a high stool, used in *jidaimono* plays to support the actor in a pose which simulates sitting in a dignified fashion.

Aiguma: Painted face make-up used for demons, evil spirits, etc. Indigo is the predominating colour.

Aikata: Passage of *samisen* playing inserted in the middle of dialogue to provide dramatic effect. Also used to describe music played in the *kuromisu* at the beginning and end of a play or at the entry and exit of an actor.

Akahime: Crimson patterned *kimono* worn in *jidaimono* plays by princesses and young heroines of high rank irrespective of time and place. The name is also used to describe the role itself.

Andon: Standard lamp.

Aragoto: Acting technique embodying exaggerated posture, make-up and costume. Devised by Ichikawa Danjuro I (1660–1704).

Asagi maku: Stage curtain, turquoise blue in colour, used independently of the main curtain.

Ashi jun: Dancing term, a principle meaning 'good order of steps'.

Ashi zukai: Manipulator who works the legs and feet of the puppet in the doll theatre.

Awase: Process of fitting an actor's wig to his head measurements.

Baba boshi: Small silk attachment worn on the front of the wig of actors playing old women of higher rank.

Bachi: Large plectrum of ivory or wood used in playing the *samisen*.

Bachi oto: Sound made when the *bachi* strikes the skin face of the *samisen*.

Bakama: Costume formerly used by *samurai* and persons of high rank, best described as a form of divided skirt. Also called *hakama*, of which it is an onomatopoetic derivation.

Beni: Rouge.

Bin: Sweep of hair on either side of the coiffure of both men and women.

Bira: Metal ornament used to decorate women's coiffures.

Bokashi: Lines of colour with one of their edges softened; used in *kumadori* make-up.

Bōshi tsuki no katsura: Small patch of coloured silk worn attached to the fronts of certain wigs used by *onnagata* actors.

Bōzu: Buddhist priest.

Bugaku: Ancient dance performance still preserved in the Imperial Household.

Bungobushi: Prototype of *tokiwazu* music.

Busho: Wigs worn by the puppets in the doll theatre; a general term.

Butai: Stage.

Buyo: General term for Japanese dancing.

Chari: Comic roles of the doll theatre.

Chasengami: Hair style fashionable among men in the early Yedo period.

Chirashi: Term used in dancing and *samisen* playing to describe a final passage in quick tempo.

Chōbō: Name used to describe the combination of a *samisen* player and a *tayu* or narrator, in *gidayu* music.

Chō mage: General hair style of men in the late Tokugawa period until the Meiji revolution of 1868.

Chonin: All people below the rank of *samurai* in former days.

Chuzao: Medium *samisen* arm.

Chuzeri: Centre of the three trap door arrangements by which the actors appear and disappear on the Kabuki stage.

Dai: Wooden platforms of various sizes used in stage settings.

Daijin bashira: One of the supporting pillars at the front of the Nō stage to the left of the audience. Also used to describe the two pillars to the right and left of the old Kabuki stage.

Daimon: Stage costumes decorated with an outsize crest representing family coats of arms.

Daimyo: Feudal chief; the highest rank of the *samurai* class, directly responsible to the Shogun.

Daito: Longer of the two swords worn by *samurai* and always taken off indoors.

Dammari: Pantomime or dumb show.

Dangiri: Concluding passage used in *samisen* playing, and in dancing.

Deba: Posture technique used when an actor makes his entry by the *hanamichi*.

Debayashi: Nagauta orchestra.

Dedōgu: Small properties left on the stage during a performance.

Degatari: Name used to describe *kiyomoto* and *tokiwazu* orchestras visible on the stage.

Degatari dai: Raised platform on a swivel base on which *gidayu* musicians sit when performing.

Dengaku: Dramatic entertainment popular in the Middle Ages.

Deshi: Disciple.

De tsukai shiki: Technique of handling puppets on the stage while in full view of the audience.

Dō: Framework of the body of a *samisen.*

Dogushi: Wooden grip used to control the mechanism of puppets.

Dōke kata: Comic roles in the Kabuki.

Dokuhaku: Monologue.

Doma: Seating in the auditorium of the old style theatre.

Dozō: Small white plastered stone buildings used as warehouses in former times. Examples may still be found today.

Ekamban: Signboards placed outside the theatre entrance showing pictures of the actors in plays. They were actual paintings and the custom is still perpetuated.

Ekiro: Musical effect used in the *kuromisu* to represent the sound of an old highway with the tinkling of pack horse bells.

Eri: Collar of a *kimono.*

Fukeyaku: Roles of the aged in the doll theatre.

Fukiwa: Wig worn by actors when dressed for the *akahime* roles.

Furi: A dance movement with expression and slow tempo.

Furidashigasa: Small property used in stage dancing. It consists of three small flat circular hats fitted one inside the other by a device which enables the actor to fling them out as a trio. He has one in either hand while performing.

Furitsukeshi: Choreographer in a Kabuki theatre.

Futozao: Thick *samisen* arm.

Gabu: Puppet head which can be changed from that of a beautiful woman into that of a fiend.

Gegi ongaku: Music and effects in the *kuromisu.*

Geisha: Women trained from childhood as professional entertainers for social occasions. The genuine *geisha* is accomplished in singing, dancing, playing the *samisen* and is not a prostitute. Artistic standards of *geisha* have degenerated today, however, and the name is often wrongly applied.

Geta: Wooden clogs of various sizes worn by both men and women in Japan.

Geza: Another name for *kuromisu.*

Gidayu: Style of *joruri* music devised by Takemoto Gidayu (1650–1714) which afterwards became the music exclusively used in the doll theatre and all Kabuki plays of doll theatre origin.

Gigaku: Early dance entertainment which came from China to Japan in the seventh century.

Giri: Samurai code of obligation.

Gochushin: Special technique used when actors play young warriors returning from battle to make a report.

Habutae: Silk or cotton skull cap worn by actors under their wigs. Also used to describe the silk fitted over the metal foundation of a wig.

Hada nugi: Lowering of the *kimono* sleeves to emphasize an emotional or aggressive passage of acting.

Hafu yane hon butai: The roofed stage supported by pillars which was adapted into the early Kabuki theatre from the Nō.

Hakama: See *bakama.*

Hanagasa: Paper umbrella covered with blossoms used as a property in dancing.

Hanamichi: Long wooden gangway which connects the Kabuki stage to the rear of the theatre and used by the actors for exits, entrances and dancing.

Hanaya: Original design from which developed all face make-up for female devils or fiends.

Hanayoten: Supernumeraries who wear gay clothing and carry cherry blossom sprigs. They appear as a bodyguard to an official and attempt to seize some principal character at his request. Their technique is quite unrealistic and they serve to add to the general stage spectacle often in a comic fashion.

Haori: Three-quarter length garment worn over the *kimono* generally out of doors, although it is also worn indoors on formal occasions.

Harakiri: Suicide by piercing the stomach with a short sword. Also called *seppuku* by the Japanese.

Harikata: Men who do the pasting of paper on to wooden constructions in the making of large stage properties and sets.

Harimono: Process of pasting paper mentioned above.

Hashigakari: Gangway of Nō stage.

Hatamoto: High ranking *samurai* next to *daimyo*.

Hayawagari: Quick change technique used in dancing on the stage.

Henge: Nō play masks used for fiends and monsters.

Hengemono: Stage dance in which several changes of costume and character are made by the same actor.

Hibachi: Portable container for a charcoal fire common to Japanese dwellings.

Hidari zukai: Manipulator who works the left arm of the puppets in the doll theatre.

Hikidōgu: Scenery mounted on runners which is pulled offstage to give the appearance of movement to a stationary puppet.

Hikimaku: Stage curtain pulled across from left to right and vice versa.

Hikinuki: Technique by which an actor wears several layers of clothing, each held together by threads, which can be ripped away to reveal a different costume underneath.

Hime: Young unmarried woman of good birth and family.

Hinadan: Two-tiered platform for musicians.

Hippari no mie: Pose taken by two or more actors in the finale of a play in which they appear to be straining against one another.

Hira butai: Name used to describe a set built flat on the stage instead of on a raised platform.

Hitatare: Nō stage costume based on ceremonial dress of former times.

Ho ho beni: Face rouge.

Hon hanamichi: Main *hanamichi* in the old style theatre, to the left of the auditorium facing the stage.

Honjoshi: One of the three basic methods of tuning the *samisen.*

Hosozao: Thick *samisen* arm.

Hyakusho: Farmer or peasant in feudal times.

Hyōgo mage: Wig style worn by actors playing *oiran* or courtesan roles.

Hyōshigi: Quadrangular sticks of hardwood which are clapped together in the hands or downwards on a wooden board, to mark the opening and close of a performance, and to provide special stage effects.

Ichimegasa: Hat made of silk on a bamboo frame with a circular brim and a conical crown used in certain plays by actors playing a lady of high rank.

Idaten: Musical effect used in the *kuromisu* to express haste and urgency.

Idokoro no fudo: Centre of movement for a dancer while performing.

Iemoto: Leader of a school of dancing.

Ippon kuma: Painted face make-up representing a young hero.

Ishō: Stage costume; a general term.

Ishō kata: The men who look after the costumes, the wardrobe masters.

Itchubushi: School of *samisen* music from which the present *tokiwazu* style was developed.

Ito ni noru: Acting technique; keeping time with the strings, the rhythm, and the timing of the actor's movements are controlled by the *samisen* music.

Jamisen: Original instrument from which the *samisen* was developed.

Janome butai: Revolving stage so constructed as to allow an inner portion to revolve in an opposite direction from an outer portion.

Janomen-gasa: Paper umbrella patterned in broad circles.

Jidaimono: Plays with a historical background dealing with the warrior and upper classes.

Jiuta: Old song form originating in Kyoto.

Jō no mai: 'Woman's dance'; term used in Nō dancing.

Jōruri: Music based on narration with a *samisen* accompaniment. The term is used specifically to mean *gidayu* music now.

Joshikimaku: Stage curtain patterned in vertical stripes of green, black and persimmon which is a feature of all Kabuki theatres.

Juzu: Buddhist rosary.

Juhachiban: Eighteen best plays compiled by Ichikawa Danjuro VII (1791–1859).

Kadobi: Funeral ceremony.

Kagura: The oldest dance form in Japan, associated with the sun goddess legend.

Kaidan mono: Ghost plays.

Kaishi: Wad of Japanese paper carried in the *kimono* as a handkerchief.

Kake: Outer robe worn by a courtesan.

Kakko: Small ornamental drum used in dancing and worn fastened to the chest of the performer.

Kamiko: Paper clothing, special stage costume.

Kamikoma: Upper bridge on a *samisen.*

Kami o sabaku: Technique by which an actors lets down the hair of his wig.

Kamishimo: Ceremonial dress of the *samurai.*

Kan: Nō flute.

Kanekyo: Bell festival.

Kanjincho: Subscription scroll.

Kanzashi: Ornament used in the decoration of women's coiffures.

Kaomise: November ceremony to open the new theatrical season in the Yedo theatre. Homage is still rendered to the tradition today.

Karami: Acrobatic technique used in stage fighting.

Karaori: Kabuki stage costume worn by women and based on the Nō costume of the same name.

Kari: Secondary *hanamichi* in the old style theatre, situated at the right of the auditorium to the audience.

Kashira: General term for the heads of the puppets in the doll theatre.

Kataginu: Shoulder pieces of the *kamishimo* costume.

Kataki yaku: Male roles representing the bad characters.

Katarimono: One of the two main divisions of vocal music, recitative being the most important feature.

Katobushi: Musical form now only used on the Kabuki stage in one play, *Sukeroku.*

Katsura: General term for theatrical wigs.

Katsureki geki: 'Plays of living history', written for Ichikawa Danjuro IX.

Katsuyama: Wig worn by actors playing *samurai's* wives in *jidaimono* plays.

Kazari: General term for scenery used in the doll theatre.

Keisei: Courtesan.

Keisei mono: Plays featuring courtesans.

Keshō: General term for make-up.

Ki: Wooden clappers also called *hyoshigi.*

Kido: Wooden gateway used in stage settings.

Kine: Name given to wooden clappers used in the doll theatre.

Kiridoma: Special seating in the old style Kabuki theatre.

Kiriotoshi: Stage curtain suspended to cover the actors and swept away by attached cords.

Kitsune roppo: Technique used by actors playing the spirit of a fox.

Kiyomoto: One of the principal musical styles used in the Kabuki.

Kizewamono: Sewamono plays with thieves, gamblers, etc., as principal characters.

Kochaya: Tea house situated near the theatre in former times.

Kodōgu: Small properties used on the Kabuki stage.

Kodōgu beya: Room backstage where the small stage properties are kept.

Kogai: Bar used as an ornament in the coiffures of courtesans and others.

Kōjō: Announcement made by an actor on the stage at a naming ceremony or on other special occasions.

Kōken: Assistant who helps a leading actor with his clothing and general requirements while dancing.

Kokumochi: Kimono worn by a *samurai's* wife in *jidaimono* plays.

Kokyu: Stringed instrument used in *geza.*

Komusō: Wandering priest of a Buddhist sect who wears a large basket head-covering and plays the flute.

Kosakubu: Department which makes the small properties used in the theatre.

Kōshi: Check patterns used on Japanese dress.

Koshioke: Lacquered cylindrical tube used as a stage property in the No theatre.

Kotoba: Prose forms in Nō drama plays.

Kotoji: Hair ornament used in the coiffure of a courtesan.

Kotsuzumi: Hand drum, shaped like an hour glass, which is played supported on the right shoulder.

Kouta: Japanese song form.

Koyaku: Child roles of the Kabuki and doll theatres.

Kubijikken: Technique of inspecting the head of a decapitated warrior.

Kubi oke: Cylindrical wooden box in which a head is placed prior to *kubi-jikken.*

Kuchi beni: Lipstick.

Kudoki: Actor's technique for depicting women's sighs, tears and regrets for the past. The term is also used of a musical form to accompany such a situation.

Kugutsu mawashi: The most ancient form of puppet entertainment in Japan.

Kumadori: Painted face make-up of Kabuki actors.

Kurofuda: Blackboard hung at the side of the stage in the Yedo theatre to convey messages to the audience.

Kuromaku: Black curtain used independently of the main stage curtain for certain effects.

Kurombo: Stage assistants who wear black clothing with a hood whilst moving about during a performance.

Kuromisu: Black, boarded enclosure at the side of the Kabuki stage which houses musicians responsible for sound effects and special musical accompaniments. Another term for it is *geza*.

Kuruma bin: Side pieces of an exaggerated style of wig worn in many of the older plays.

Kushi: Comb.

Kyakubun: Guest playwright of equal standing to the chief resident writer in the old theatre.

Kyara abura: Hair pomade introduced during the Genroku period.

Kyogen kata: Stage assistants who help the actors in *jidaimono* plays, manipulate the *hyoshigi*, and who act as prompters and carry out a variety of other stage duties.

Maedoma: Special seating in the old style Kabuki theatre.

Maegami: Front portion of the hair in a theatrical wig.

Maejaya: Tea house situated at the front of the old theatres.

Mage: 'Top knot' or chignon in men's and women's hair styles.

Mai: Name used to describe Nō dancing and the type of Kabuki dancing developed from the Nō.

Manaita obi: Broad *obi* worn by courtesans.

Manjitsunagi: Blue and white pattern of Buddhist derivation used in Kabuki stage sets.

Marubōzu: Hair style of a Buddhist priest on the stage; a shaven crown.

Marumage: Hair style of a married woman.

Matoi: Standard carried by the firemen of old Yedo.

Matshame mono: Kabuki dance plays of Nō inspiration and derivation.

Matsuri: Festival.

Mawari butai: Revolving stage.

Meriyasu: Cloth coverings fitting closely to the legs and arms of the actor, painted with stylized muscular patterns.

Miarawashi: Phrase used in *samisen* playing.

Michiyuki: Dance form in which a young couple are shown on the way to committing suicide. There are, however, variations to the theme.

Minarai: Lowest ranking assistant in the playwright's room in the old Kabuki theatre.

Misu Uchi: Alcove for *gidayu* musicians.

Mitu ori: Hair style for men in the early Yedo period.

Mizu jaya: Tea-house situated near the old theatres.

Mochidōgu: Small properties carried by actors including hats and head-dresses.

Mokugyo: Red painted, wooden, shell-like instrument used by a Buddhist priest when chanting the *sutras.*

Mon: Family crest worn on Japanese clothing.

Monogatari: Actor's technique in which he relates past happenings and events by means of gestures and movements timed by a musical accompaniment of *samisen* and narrator. It is also used as a musical term.

Monso: Musical phrase.

Mukimi: Painted face make-up for a youthful and handsome hero.

Musume: Girl of unmarried status; daughter.

Nadai: Qualified to play main roles; an actor's ranking.

Nadai shita: Ordinary actors in the old theatre.

Nagauta: One of the principal musical styles used in the Kabuki theatre.

Naka doma: Special seating in the old style theatre.

Naka nikai: Rooms on the second floor of the old theatres for the use of *onnagata* actors.

Namimaku: Stage curtain with waves painted on it to represent a marine background in certain plays.

Nani nani zukushi: Repeating the same phrase with variations and double meanings as in the Kabuki dialogue.

Naraku: Area beneath the stage containing the machinery.

Nembutsu odori: Old Buddhist ceremonial dance.

Nezumi kido: Small entrance through which the audience had to duck when entering the old style theatre one by one.

Niagari: One of the three basic methods of tuning the *samisen*.

Niju butai: Platform on which a stage set representing a building of some kind is constructed.

Nimaime: Playwright's ranking in the old style theatre. Also used to describe the second *samisen* player, or singer, in a theatre orchestra.

Nimaime wagoto: Male role portraying young men, lovers and husbands; of gentle and unaggressive disposition in direct contrast to *aragoto* style.

Ningyo ni naru: Actor's technique, literally 'becoming a doll'.

Ningyo shibai: Doll theatre.

Ningyo tsukai: Doll manipulator.

Nirami: Actor's technique by which the eyes are slowly crossed to emphasize an emotional passage.

Nyobo: Middle class wife.

Obi: Sash worn round the *kimono* by both men and women.

Oborozome: Special dyed cloth used in former times.

Ōdōgu: Large stage properties such as sets.

Odori: Japanese dancing.

Ohaguro: Substance used by married women to blacken their teeth in former times.

Ohayashi: Musicians of the *kuromisu* or *geza*.

Oiemono: Plays belonging to the *jidaimono* class, and dealing with the struggles of *daimyo* families in the Yedo period.

Oiran: Courtesan.

Oizuru: Box containing a religious image carried on the back of the disguised Yoshitsune in the play *Kanjincho*.

Ojaya: Teahouse outside the old theatre.

Oji: Wig worn by evil characters in *jidaimono* plays.

Okedaiko: Barrel-shaped drum used in the *kuromisu*.

Oki: Musical prelude to the actor's entry.

Okizeri: Largest of the three trap door arrangements used on the Kabuki stage.

Okubi: Special seating in the old style theatre.

Omozukai: Manipulator who works the head and right arm of a puppet in the doll theatre.

Oni: Fiend or demon.

Onnagata: Female impersonator; the actors who play female roles.

Oshiroi: White cream used by actors in their make-up.

Otaiko: Large drum used in the *kuromisu*.

Otoko: Man.

Otokodate: Chivalrous commoners who formed a society in the Yedo period.

Otsuzumi: Waist drum used in the Nō *hayashi* and also by the *nagauta* players.

Oyama: Another term for *onnagata*.

Rin: Small handbell used in Buddhist services.

Rojin: Nō masks representing aged people; a general term.

Ronin: *Samurai* who forfeited his rank because his superior was deprived of his estates or position, or for reasons of personal disgrace.

Roppo: Vigorous posture technique used by Kabuki actors.

Ryujin maki: Stage costume worn by actors who play lieutenants and chief retainers of high officials in *jidaimono* plays.

Sajiki: Tatami floored boxes at the sides of the auditorium of a Kabuki theatre.

Sakusha beya: Playwright's room in the old style theatre.

Sambaso: Ceremonial Nō dance adapted to the Kabuki dance repertoire.

Samisen: Three-stringed instrument used as accompaniment in all styles of theatre music.

Samurai: Member of the warrior or governing class whose badge of distinction was the right to carry two swords.

Sandan: Flight of three steps seen at the front of stage sets representing buildings.

Sanmaime: Playwright's rank in the old theatre, still used for theatrical musicians.

Sansagari: One of the three basic methods of tuning the *samisen*.

Sao: Arm of a *samisen*.

Sarugaku: Ancient dramatic form which influenced the Nō drama.

Saru kuma: Painted face make-up which resembles a monkey's face.

Sashidashi: Long candle holders used by stage assistants in the old days to provide special illumination on the stage.

Senjo jiki: Painted stage background representing a perspective view of the hall in a palace or mansion.

Senkai: Circling motion of the head when an actor performs a *mie.*

Seppuku: Suicide by piercing the stomach with a sword; *hara kiri.*

Seriage: Trap door devices in the Kabuki stage by which actors appear and disappear.

Serifu: General term for the actor's speech.

Sewa kido: Wooden gate used as stage property representing an entrance to a town dwelling, teahouse, etc.

Sewa mono: Plays dealing with the lives of commoners in the Yedo period.

Shamisen: Popular pronunciation of *samisen.*

Shichi go cho: Seven-five syllabic metre.

Shigusa: Mime in dancing.

Shikata banashi: Actor's use of a fan when performing a *monogatari.*

Shinbari: Cymbals.

Shinbutsu: Noh plays concerning deities or Buddhas.

Shin juhachiban: New eighteen best plays compiled by Ichikawa Danjuro VII and IX.

Shinju mono: Plays dealing with the double suicides of lovers.

Shinko engeki jusshu: Ten neo-classical dance plays compiled by Onoe Kikugoro V.

Shinnai bushi: Musical style used occasionally in the theatre.

Shirabyoshi: Women entertainers of old, the precursors of the *geisha.*

Shishi gashira: Wooden lion's mask carried by the actor in certain dance plays.

Shite: Principal actor in Nō plays.

Shōgun: Military head of the State, and supreme Government authority.

Shokunin: Craftsman in feudal society.

Shonin: Merchant or tradesman.

Shosa butai: Special platforms added to the stage in Kabuki dancing plays.

Shosa dai: Platforms laid in sections on the *hanamichi* for a Kabuki dance play.

Shosagoto: Dancing plays.

Shoto: Shorter of the two swords worn by a *samurai.*

Shumei hiro: Ceremony in which an actor succeeds to a new title.

Sode: Sleeve of a *kimono.*

Soga no sekai: 'The world of Soga'; term used to describe the cycle of plays based on the story of the Soga brothers' revenge.

Suji kuma: Painted face make-up representing a courageous warrior.

Sumo: Japanese wrestling.

Suo: Formal dress of *samurai* of old.

Su odori: Dancing in ordinary costume.

Suppon: Trap door in the *hanamichi.*

Suso: Hem of a *kimono.*

Suzudaiko: Kind of tambourine used in dancing.

Suzuri: Japanese ink stone.

Tabako bon: Container for pipe-smoking materials which stood on the floor of all Japanese dwellings in former times.

Tabi: Japanese style sock, used for ordinary formal wear and in dancing.

Tabo: Portion of the hair of a theatrical wig which covers the nape of the neck.

Tachimawari: Sword fighting technique used by actors.

Tachimi: Equivalent of the 'gods' in the Kabuki theatre.

Tachioyama: Leading *onnagata* roles.

Taihaku: Dialogue.

Taiko: Drum beaten with two sticks used in *nagauta* playing and in the Nō theatre.

Taka shimada: Hair style for young unmarried women on formal occasions.

Takotsubo: Special seating in the old style theatre.

Tanzen roppo: Actor's technique supposed to have developed from the posturings of men about town in the late seventeenth century.

Tatami: Finely woven straw matting in sections used as flooring in Japanese interiors.

Tate: Actor's technique which simulates aggressive action.

Tateboshi: High, curved hat worn by the former *samurai*, used as a stage costume in both the Kabuki and the Nō dramas.

Tateyaku: Principal male roles in the Kabuki and doll theatres.

Tayu: Narrator in *gidayu* music.

Tegoto: Musical phrase used to give variation to the main theme and to relieve narrated passages.

Tengu: Long-nosed goblin of Japanese legend.

Tennodate: Music played for solemn scenes by the *kuromisu.*

Teoi no jukkai: Actor's technique to portray the recollections and repentance of a dying man.

Tobi: Firemen of old Yedo.

Tobi roppo: Technique of vigorous postures.

Tokiwazu: One of the principal musical styles used in the Kabuki.

Tokonōma: Alcove containing a painting and a flower arrangement found in every traditional Japanese room.

Tokoto o fumo: Stamping the stage wearing wooden clogs; technique used in the doll theatre.

Tokoyama: Craftsmen who look after the wigs in the Kabuki theatre.

Tombo: Somersault performed by actors.

Torite: Supernumeraries who act as watchmen or a bodyguard, and come to seize or arrest someone on higher authority.

Toya: Room from which the actors make their entry on the *hanamichi.*

Tsuke: Beating the *hyogishi* or wooden clappers downwards on a square board to emphasize an actor's posing.

Tsuke uchi: Stage assistants who carry out the process described above.

Tsukiage: Bamboo rod attached to the body of a puppet in the doll theatre.

Tsubushi shimada: Hair style worn by young unmarried women, courtesans and *geisha.*

Tsugi no ima: Room which is invariably situated on the right of the stage set representing a dwelling of some sort; i.e. to the right of the audience.

Tsume: Puppets used for minor roles in the doll theatre.

Tsuri eda: Sprays of artificial blossom suspended above the stage in a Kabuki theatre.

Tsurigane: Bell.

Uchikake: Outer robe worn by ladies of rank.

Ukiyoe: Japanese wood block prints.

Urakido: Entry to the green rooms in the old theatre.

Urizane gao: Melon seed face; the old Japanese ideal of beauty.

Usuberi: Thin straw matting used on the Kabuki stage.

Uta: Song.

Utaimono: Main division of vocal music whose emphasis is on rhythm and melody as against recitative.

Wakashu kabuki: Young men's Kabuki.

Wakashu kata: Young men's roles.

Waki: Secondary actor in Nō drama.

Waki kyogen: Ceremonial dance performed on the Kabuki stage in Yedo times.

Warizerifu: Reciting a speech in sequence with several actors taking part.

Yago: Shop name of an actor.

Yagura: Drum tower outside the old theatres.

Yakusha: Actor.

Yakusha hyobanki: 'Remarks on the Actors'; a journal published annually in Yedo times.

Yamabushi: Sect of wandering priests.

Yamadai: Dais on which the *nagauta* players sit when on the stage.

Yama kido: Stage property gate representing an entrance to a country dwelling.

Yari yakko: Dancing with spears and other weapons.

Yari kabuki: Adult man's *kabuki;* an early development in theatre history.

Yoten: Costume worn by actors performing the *gochushin* technique.

Yotsudake bushi: Geza musical style.

Yoyoku: Vocal music of the Nō drama.

Yubikawa: Leather thong attached to the right hand of a puppet to enable the manipulator to simulate the gripping of an article by a doll.

Yukioroshi: Light tattoo on a drum which accompanies falling snow on the Kabuki stage.

Zabuton: Silk cushions used by guests when sitting on the *tatami.*

Zagashira: Leader of a group of Kabuki actors or theatre doll manipulators.

INDEX

Actors are listed under their *zokumei*, or personal names,
instead of their *myōji*, or family names.

A CATALOG OF SELECTED
DOVER BOOKS
IN ALL FIELDS OF INTEREST

A CATALOG OF SELECTED DOVER
BOOKS IN ALL FIELDS OF INTEREST

CONCERNING THE SPIRITUAL IN ART, Wassily Kandinsky. Pioneering work by father of abstract art. Thoughts on color theory, nature of art. Analysis of earlier masters. 12 illustrations. 80pp. of text. 5⅜ x 8½.   23411-8 Pa. $4.95

ANIMALS: 1,419 Copyright-Free Illustrations of Mammals, Birds, Fish, Insects, etc., Jim Harter (ed.). Clear wood engravings present, in extremely lifelike poses, over 1,000 species of animals. One of the most extensive pictorial sourcebooks of its kind. Captions. Index. 284pp. 9 x 12.   23766-4 Pa. $14.95

CELTIC ART: The Methods of Construction, George Bain. Simple geometric techniques for making Celtic interlacements, spirals, Kells-type initials, animals, humans, etc. Over 500 illustrations. 160pp. 9 x 12. (USO)   22923-8 Pa. $9.95

AN ATLAS OF ANATOMY FOR ARTISTS, Fritz Schider. Most thorough reference work on art anatomy in the world. Hundreds of illustrations, including selections from works by Vesalius, Leonardo, Goya, Ingres, Michelangelo, others. 593 illustrations. 192pp. 7⅛ x 10¼.   20241-0 Pa. $9.95

CELTIC HAND STROKE-BY-STROKE (Irish Half-Uncial from "The Book of Kells"): An Arthur Baker Calligraphy Manual, Arthur Baker. Complete guide to creating each letter of the alphabet in distinctive Celtic manner. Covers hand position, strokes, pens, inks, paper, more. Illustrated. 48pp. 8¼ x 11.   24336-2 Pa. $3.95

EASY ORIGAMI, John Montroll. Charming collection of 32 projects (hat, cup, pelican, piano, swan, many more) specially designed for the novice origami hobbyist. Clearly illustrated easy-to-follow instructions insure that even beginning papercrafters will achieve successful results. 48pp. 8¼ x 11.   27298-2 Pa. $3.50

THE COMPLETE BOOK OF BIRDHOUSE CONSTRUCTION FOR WOODWORKERS, Scott D. Campbell. Detailed instructions, illustrations, tables. Also data on bird habitat and instinct patterns. Bibliography. 3 tables. 63 illustrations in 15 figures. 48pp. 5¼ x 8½.   24407-5 Pa. $2.50

BLOOMINGDALE'S ILLUSTRATED 1886 CATALOG: Fashions, Dry Goods and Housewares, Bloomingdale Brothers. Famed merchants' extremely rare catalog depicting about 1,700 products: clothing, housewares, firearms, dry goods, jewelry, more. Invaluable for dating, identifying vintage items. Also, copyright-free graphics for artists, designers. Co-published with Henry Ford Museum & Greenfield Village. 160pp. 8¼ x 11.   25780-0 Pa. $10.95

HISTORIC COSTUME IN PICTURES, Braun & Schneider. Over 1,450 costumed figures in clearly detailed engravings–from dawn of civilization to end of 19th century. Captions. Many folk costumes. 256pp. 8⅜ x 11¾.   23150-X Pa. $12.95

STICKLEY CRAFTSMAN FURNITURE CATALOGS, Gustav Stickley and L. & J. G. Stickley. Beautiful, functional furniture in two authentic catalogs from 1910. 594 illustrations, including 277 photos, show settles, rockers, armchairs, reclining chairs, bookcases, desks, tables. 183pp. 6½ x 9¼. 23838-5 Pa. $11.95

AMERICAN LOCOMOTIVES IN HISTORIC PHOTOGRAPHS: 1858 to 1949, Ron Ziel (ed.). A rare collection of 126 meticulously detailed official photographs, called "builder portraits," of American locomotives that majestically chronicle the rise of steam locomotive power in America. Introduction. Detailed captions. xi + 129pp. 9 x 12. 27393-8 Pa. $13.95

AMERICA'S LIGHTHOUSES: An Illustrated History, Francis Ross Holland, Jr. Delightfully written, profusely illustrated fact-filled survey of over 200 American lighthouses since 1716. History, anecdotes, technological advances, more. 240pp. 8 x 10¾. 25576-X Pa. $12.95

TOWARDS A NEW ARCHITECTURE, Le Corbusier. Pioneering manifesto by founder of "International School." Technical and aesthetic theories, views of industry, economics, relation of form to function, "mass-production split" and much more. Profusely illustrated. 320pp. 6⅛ x 9¼. (USO) 25023-7 Pa. $9.95

HOW THE OTHER HALF LIVES, Jacob Riis. Famous journalistic record, exposing poverty and degradation of New York slums around 1900, by major social reformer. 100 striking and influential photographs. 233pp. 10 x 7⅞. 22012-5 Pa. $11.95

FRUIT KEY AND TWIG KEY TO TREES AND SHRUBS, William M. Harlow. One of the handiest and most widely used identification aids. Fruit key covers 120 deciduous and evergreen species; twig key 160 deciduous species. Easily used. Over 300 photographs. 126pp. 5⅜ x 8½. 20511-8 Pa. $3.95

COMMON BIRD SONGS, Dr. Donald J. Borror. Songs of 60 most common U.S. birds: robins, sparrows, cardinals, bluejays, finches, more—arranged in order of increasing complexity. Up to 9 variations of songs of each species.
Cassette and manual 99911-4 $8.95

ORCHIDS AS HOUSE PLANTS, Rebecca Tyson Northen. Grow cattleyas and many other kinds of orchids—in a window, in a case, or under artificial light. 63 illustrations. 148pp. 5⅜ x 8½. 23261-1 Pa. $5.95

MONSTER MAZES, Dave Phillips. Masterful mazes at four levels of difficulty. Avoid deadly perils and evil creatures to find magical treasures. Solutions for all 32 exciting illustrated puzzles. 48pp. 8¼ x 11. 26005-4 Pa. $2.95

MOZART'S DON GIOVANNI (DOVER OPERA LIBRETTO SERIES), Wolfgang Amadeus Mozart. Introduced and translated by Ellen H. Bleiler. Standard Italian libretto, with complete English translation. Convenient and thoroughly portable—an ideal companion for reading along with a recording or the performance itself. Introduction. List of characters. Plot summary. 121pp. 5¼ x 8½. 24944-1 Pa. $3.95

TECHNICAL MANUAL AND DICTIONARY OF CLASSICAL BALLET, Gail Grant. Defines, explains, comments on steps, movements, poses and concepts. 15-page pictorial section. Basic book for student, viewer. 127pp. 5⅜ x 8½. 21843-0 Pa. $4.95

BRASS INSTRUMENTS: Their History and Development, Anthony Baines. Authoritative, updated survey of the evolution of trumpets, trombones, bugles, cornets, French horns, tubas and other brass wind instruments. Over 140 illustrations and 48 music examples. Corrected and updated by author. New preface. Bibliography. 320pp. 5⅜ x 8½. 27574-4 Pa. $9.95

HOLLYWOOD GLAMOR PORTRAITS, John Kobal (ed.). 145 photos from 1926-49. Harlow, Gable, Bogart, Bacall; 94 stars in all. Full background on photographers, technical aspects. 160pp. 8⅜ x 11¼. 23352-9 Pa. $12.95

MAX AND MORITZ, Wilhelm Busch. Great humor classic in both German and English. Also 10 other works: "Cat and Mouse," "Plisch and Plumm," etc. 216pp. 5⅜ x 8½. 20181-3 Pa. $6.95

THE RAVEN AND OTHER FAVORITE POEMS, Edgar Allan Poe. Over 40 of the author's most memorable poems: "The Bells," "Ulalume," "Israfel," "To Helen," "The Conqueror Worm," "Eldorado," "Annabel Lee," many more. Alphabetic lists of titles and first lines. 64pp. 5³⁄₁₆ x 8¼. 26685-0 Pa. $1.00

PERSONAL MEMOIRS OF U. S. GRANT, Ulysses Simpson Grant. Intelligent, deeply moving firsthand account of Civil War campaigns, considered by many the finest military memoirs ever written. Includes letters, historic photographs, maps and more. 528pp. 6⅛ x 9¼. 28587-1 Pa. $12.95

AMULETS AND SUPERSTITIONS, E. A. Wallis Budge. Comprehensive discourse on origin, powers of amulets in many ancient cultures: Arab, Persian Babylonian, Assyrian, Egyptian, Gnostic, Hebrew, Phoenician, Syriac, etc. Covers cross, swastika, crucifix, seals, rings, stones, etc. 584pp. 5⅜ x 8½. 23573-4 Pa. $12.95

RUSSIAN STORIES/PYCCKNE PACCKA3bl: A Dual-Language Book, edited by Gleb Struve. Twelve tales by such masters as Chekhov, Tolstoy, Dostoevsky, Pushkin, others. Excellent word-for-word English translations on facing pages, plus teaching and study aids, Russian/English vocabulary, biographical/critical introductions, more. 416pp. 5⅜ x 8½. 26244-8 Pa. $9.95

PHILADELPHIA THEN AND NOW: 60 Sites Photographed in the Past and Present, Kenneth Finkel and Susan Oyama. Rare photographs of City Hall, Logan Square, Independence Hall, Betsy Ross House, other landmarks juxtaposed with contemporary views. Captures changing face of historic city. Introduction. Captions. 128pp. 8¼ x 11. 25790-8 Pa. $9.95

AIA ARCHITECTURAL GUIDE TO NASSAU AND SUFFOLK COUNTIES, LONG ISLAND, The American Institute of Architects, Long Island Chapter, and the Society for the Preservation of Long Island Antiquities. Comprehensive, well-researched and generously illustrated volume brings to life over three centuries of Long Island's great architectural heritage. More than 240 photographs with authoritative, extensively detailed captions. 176pp. 8¼ x 11. 26946-9 Pa. $14.95

NORTH AMERICAN INDIAN LIFE: Customs and Traditions of 23 Tribes, Elsie Clews Parsons (ed.). 27 fictionalized essays by noted anthropologists examine religion, customs, government, additional facets of life among the Winnebago, Crow, Zuni, Eskimo, other tribes. 480pp. 6⅛ x 9¼. 27377-6 Pa. $10.95

FRANK LLOYD WRIGHT'S HOLLYHOCK HOUSE, Donald Hoffmann. Lavishly illustrated, carefully documented study of one of Wright's most controversial residential designs. Over 120 photographs, floor plans, elevations, etc. Detailed perceptive text by noted Wright scholar. Index. 128pp. 9¼ x 10¾. 27133-1 Pa. $11.95

THE MALE AND FEMALE FIGURE IN MOTION: 60 Classic Photographic Sequences, Eadweard Muybridge. 60 true-action photographs of men and women walking, running, climbing, bending, turning, etc., reproduced from rare 19th-century masterpiece. vi + 121pp. 9 x 12. 24745-7 Pa. $10.95

1001 QUESTIONS ANSWERED ABOUT THE SEASHORE, N. J. Berrill and Jacquelyn Berrill. Queries answered about dolphins, sea snails, sponges, starfish, fishes, shore birds, many others. Covers appearance, breeding, growth, feeding, much more. 305pp. 5¼ x 8¼. 23366-9 Pa. $8.95

GUIDE TO OWL WATCHING IN NORTH AMERICA, Donald S. Heintzelman. Superb guide offers complete data and descriptions of 19 species: barn owl, screech owl, snowy owl, many more. Expert coverage of owl-watching equipment, conservation, migrations and invasions, etc. Guide to observing sites. 84 illustrations. xiii + 193pp. 5⅜ x 8½. 27344-X Pa. $8.95

MEDICINAL AND OTHER USES OF NORTH AMERICAN PLANTS: A Historical Survey with Special Reference to the Eastern Indian Tribes, Charlotte Erichsen-Brown. Chronological historical citations document 500 years of usage of plants, trees, shrubs native to eastern Canada, northeastern U.S. Also complete identifying information. 343 illustrations. 544pp. 6½ x 9¼. 25951-X Pa. $12.95

STORYBOOK MAZES, Dave Phillips. 23 stories and mazes on two-page spreads: Wizard of Oz, Treasure Island, Robin Hood, etc. Solutions. 64pp. 8¼ x 11. 23628-5 Pa. $2.95

NEGRO FOLK MUSIC, U.S.A., Harold Courlander. Noted folklorist's scholarly yet readable analysis of rich and varied musical tradition. Includes authentic versions of over 40 folk songs. Valuable bibliography and discography. xi + 324pp. 5⅜ x 8½. 27350-4 Pa. $9.95

MOVIE-STAR PORTRAITS OF THE FORTIES, John Kobal (ed.). 163 glamor, studio photos of 106 stars of the 1940s: Rita Hayworth, Ava Gardner, Marlon Brando, Clark Gable, many more. 176pp. 8⅜ x 11¼. 23546-7 Pa. $12.95

BENCHLEY LOST AND FOUND, Robert Benchley. Finest humor from early 30s, about pet peeves, child psychologists, post office and others. Mostly unavailable elsewhere. 73 illustrations by Peter Arno and others. 183pp. 5⅜ x 8½. 22410-4 Pa. $6.95

YEKL and THE IMPORTED BRIDEGROOM AND OTHER STORIES OF YIDDISH NEW YORK, Abraham Cahan. Film Hester Street based on Yekl (1896). Novel, other stories among first about Jewish immigrants on N.Y.'s East Side. 240pp. 5⅜ x 8½. 22427-9 Pa. $6.95

SELECTED POEMS, Walt Whitman. Generous sampling from *Leaves of Grass*. Twenty-four poems include "I Hear America Singing," "Song of the Open Road," "I Sing the Body Electric," "When Lilacs Last in the Dooryard Bloom'd," "O Captain! My Captain!"–all reprinted from an authoritative edition. Lists of titles and first lines. 128pp. 5$\frac{3}{16}$ x 8¼. 26878-0 Pa. $1.00

THE BEST TALES OF HOFFMANN, E. T. A. Hoffmann. 10 of Hoffmann's most important stories: "Nutcracker and the King of Mice," "The Golden Flowerpot," etc. 458pp. 5⅜ x 8½. 21793-0 Pa. $9.95

FROM FETISH TO GOD IN ANCIENT EGYPT, E. A. Wallis Budge. Rich detailed survey of Egyptian conception of "God" and gods, magic, cult of animals, Osiris, more. Also, superb English translations of hymns and legends. 240 illustrations. 545pp. 5⅜ x 8½. 25803-3 Pa. $13.95

FRENCH STORIES/CONTES FRANÇAIS: A Dual-Language Book, Wallace Fowlie. Ten stories by French masters, Voltaire to Camus: "Micromegas" by Voltaire; "The Atheist's Mass" by Balzac; "Minuet" by de Maupassant; "The Guest" by Camus, six more. Excellent English translations on facing pages. Also French-English vocabulary list, exercises, more. 352pp. 5⅜ x 8½. 26443-2 Pa. $9.95

CHICAGO AT THE TURN OF THE CENTURY IN PHOTOGRAPHS: 122 Historic Views from the Collections of the Chicago Historical Society, Larry A. Viskochil. Rare large-format prints offer detailed views of City Hall, State Street, the Loop, Hull House, Union Station, many other landmarks, circa 1904-1913. Introduction. Captions. Maps. 144pp. 9⅜ x 12¼. 24656-6 Pa. $12.95

OLD BROOKLYN IN EARLY PHOTOGRAPHS, 1865-1929, William Lee Younger. Luna Park, Gravesend race track, construction of Grand Army Plaza, moving of Hotel Brighton, etc. 157 previously unpublished photographs. 165pp. 8⅞ x 11¾. 23587-4 Pa. $13.95

THE MYTHS OF THE NORTH AMERICAN INDIANS, Lewis Spence. Rich anthology of the myths and legends of the Algonquins, Iroquois, Pawnees and Sioux, prefaced by an extensive historical and ethnological commentary. 36 illustrations. 480pp. 5⅜ x 8½. 25967-6 Pa. $10.95

AN ENCYCLOPEDIA OF BATTLES: Accounts of Over 1,560 Battles from 1479 B.C. to the Present, David Eggenberger. Essential details of every major battle in recorded history from the first battle of Megiddo in 1479 B.C. to Grenada in 1984. List of Battle Maps. New Appendix covering the years 1967-1984. Index. 99 illustrations. 544pp. 6½ x 9¼. 24913-1 Pa. $16.95

SAILING ALONE AROUND THE WORLD, Captain Joshua Slocum. First man to sail around the world, alone, in small boat. One of great feats of seamanship told in delightful manner. 67 illustrations. 294pp. 5⅜ x 8½. 20326-3 Pa. $6.95

ANARCHISM AND OTHER ESSAYS, Emma Goldman. Powerful, penetrating, prophetic essays on direct action, role of minorities, prison reform, puritan hypocrisy, violence, etc. 271pp. 5⅜ x 8½. 22484-8 Pa. $7.95

MYTHS OF THE HINDUS AND BUDDHISTS, Ananda K. Coomaraswamy and Sister Nivedita. Great stories of the epics; deeds of Krishna, Shiva, taken from puranas, Vedas, folk tales; etc. 32 illustrations. 400pp. 5⅜ x 8½. 21759-0 Pa. $12.95

BEYOND PSYCHOLOGY, Otto Rank. Fear of death, desire of immortality, nature of sexuality, social organization, creativity, according to Rankian system. 291pp. 5⅜ x 8½. 20485-5 Pa. $8.95

A THEOLOGICO-POLITICAL TREATISE, Benedict Spinoza. Also contains unfinished Political Treatise. Great classic on religious liberty, theory of government on common consent. R. Elwes translation. Total of 421pp. 5⅜ x 8½. 20249-6 Pa. $9.95

MY BONDAGE AND MY FREEDOM, Frederick Douglass. Born a slave, Douglass became outspoken force in antislavery movement. The best of Douglass' autobiographies. Graphic description of slave life. 464pp. 5⅜ x 8½. 22457-0 Pa. $8.95

FOLLOWING THE EQUATOR: A Journey Around the World, Mark Twain. Fascinating humorous account of 1897 voyage to Hawaii, Australia, India, New Zealand, etc. Ironic, bemused reports on peoples, customs, climate, flora and fauna, politics, much more. 197 illustrations. 720pp. 5⅜ x 8½. 26113-1 Pa. $15.95

THE PEOPLE CALLED SHAKERS, Edward D. Andrews. Definitive study of Shakers: origins, beliefs, practices, dances, social organization, furniture and crafts, etc. 33 illustrations. 351pp. 5⅜ x 8½. 21081-2 Pa. $8.95

THE MYTHS OF GREECE AND ROME, H. A. Guerber. A classic of mythology, generously illustrated, long prized for its simple, graphic, accurate retelling of the principal myths of Greece and Rome, and for its commentary on their origins and significance. With 64 illustrations by Michelangelo, Raphael, Titian, Rubens, Canova, Bernini and others. 480pp. 5⅜ x 8½. 27584-1 Pa. $9.95

PSYCHOLOGY OF MUSIC, Carl E. Seashore. Classic work discusses music as a medium from psychological viewpoint. Clear treatment of physical acoustics, auditory apparatus, sound perception, development of musical skills, nature of musical feeling, host of other topics. 88 figures. 408pp. 5⅜ x 8½. 21851-1 Pa. $11.95

THE PHILOSOPHY OF HISTORY, Georg W. Hegel. Great classic of Western thought develops concept that history is not chance but rational process, the evolution of freedom. 457pp. 5⅜ x 8½. 20112-0 Pa. $9.95

THE BOOK OF TEA, Kakuzo Okakura. Minor classic of the Orient: entertaining, charming explanation, interpretation of traditional Japanese culture in terms of tea ceremony. 94pp. 5⅜ x 8½. 20070-1 Pa. $3.95

LIFE IN ANCIENT EGYPT, Adolf Erman. Fullest, most thorough, detailed older account with much not in more recent books, domestic life, religion, magic, medicine, commerce, much more. Many illustrations reproduce tomb paintings, carvings, hieroglyphs, etc. 597pp. 5⅜ x 8½. 22632-8 Pa. $12.95

SUNDIALS, Their Theory and Construction, Albert Waugh. Far and away the best, most thorough coverage of ideas, mathematics concerned, types, construction, adjusting anywhere. Simple, nontechnical treatment allows even children to build several of these dials. Over 100 illustrations. 230pp. 5⅜ x 8½. 22947-5 Pa. $8.95

DYNAMICS OF FLUIDS IN POROUS MEDIA, Jacob Bear. For advanced students of ground water hydrology, soil mechanics and physics, drainage and irrigation engineering, and more. 335 illustrations. Exercises, with answers. 784pp. 6⅛ x 9¼. 65675-6 Pa. $19.95

SONGS OF EXPERIENCE: Facsimile Reproduction with 26 Plates in Full Color, William Blake. 26 full-color plates from a rare 1826 edition. Includes "TheTyger," "London," "Holy Thursday," and other poems. Printed text of poems. 48pp. 5¼ x 7. 24636-1 Pa. $4.95

OLD-TIME VIGNETTES IN FULL COLOR, Carol Belanger Grafton (ed.). Over 390 charming, often sentimental illustrations, selected from archives of Victorian graphics—pretty women posing, children playing, food, flowers, kittens and puppies, smiling cherubs, birds and butterflies, much more. All copyright-free. 48pp. 9¼ x 12¼. 27269-9 Pa. $7.95

PERSPECTIVE FOR ARTISTS, Rex Vicat Cole. Depth, perspective of sky and sea, shadows, much more, not usually covered. 391 diagrams, 81 reproductions of drawings and paintings. 279pp. 5⅜ x 8½. 22487-2 Pa. $7.95

DRAWING THE LIVING FIGURE, Joseph Sheppard. Innovative approach to artistic anatomy focuses on specifics of surface anatomy, rather than muscles and bones. Over 170 drawings of live models in front, back and side views, and in widely varying poses. Accompanying diagrams. 177 illustrations. Introduction. Index. 144pp. 8⅜ x11¼. 26723-7 Pa. $8.95

GOTHIC AND OLD ENGLISH ALPHABETS: 100 Complete Fonts, Dan X. Solo. Add power, elegance to posters, signs, other graphics with 100 stunning copyright-free alphabets: Blackstone, Dolbey, Germania, 97 more–including many lower-case, numerals, punctuation marks. 104pp. 8⅛ x 11. 24695-7 Pa. $8.95

HOW TO DO BEADWORK, Mary White. Fundamental book on craft from simple projects to five-bead chains and woven works. 106 illustrations. 142pp. 5⅜ x 8. 20697-1 Pa. $4.95

THE BOOK OF WOOD CARVING, Charles Marshall Sayers. Finest book for beginners discusses fundamentals and offers 34 designs. "Absolutely first rate . . . well thought out and well executed."–E. J. Tangerman. 118pp. 7¾ x 10⅝. 23654-4 Pa. $6.95

ILLUSTRATED CATALOG OF CIVIL WAR MILITARY GOODS: Union Army Weapons, Insignia, Uniform Accessories, and Other Equipment, Schuyler, Hartley, and Graham. Rare, profusely illustrated 1846 catalog includes Union Army uniform and dress regulations, arms and ammunition, coats, insignia, flags, swords, rifles, etc. 226 illustrations. 160pp. 9 x 12. 24939-5 Pa. $10.95

WOMEN'S FASHIONS OF THE EARLY 1900s: An Unabridged Republication of "New York Fashions, 1909," National Cloak & Suit Co. Rare catalog of mail-order fashions documents women's and children's clothing styles shortly after the turn of the century. Captions offer full descriptions, prices. Invaluable resource for fashion, costume historians. Approximately 725 illustrations. 128pp. 8⅜ x 11¼. 27276-1 Pa. $11.95

THE 1912 AND 1915 GUSTAV STICKLEY FURNITURE CATALOGS, Gustav Stickley. With over 200 detailed illustrations and descriptions, these two catalogs are essential reading and reference materials and identification guides for Stickley furniture. Captions cite materials, dimensions and prices. 112pp. 6½ x 9¼. 26676-1 Pa. $9.95

EARLY AMERICAN LOCOMOTIVES, John H. White, Jr. Finest locomotive engravings from early 19th century: historical (1804–74), main-line (after 1870), special, foreign, etc. 147 plates. 142pp. 11⅜ x 8¼. 22772-3 Pa. $10.95

THE TALL SHIPS OF TODAY IN PHOTOGRAPHS, Frank O. Braynard. Lavishly illustrated tribute to nearly 100 majestic contemporary sailing vessels: Amerigo Vespucci, Clearwater, Constitution, Eagle, Mayflower, Sea Cloud, Victory, many more. Authoritative captions provide statistics, background on each ship. 190 black-and-white photographs and illustrations. Introduction. 128pp. 8⅞ x 11¾. 27163-3 Pa. $14.95

EARLY NINETEENTH-CENTURY CRAFTS AND TRADES, Peter Stockham (ed.). Extremely rare 1807 volume describes to youngsters the crafts and trades of the day: brickmaker, weaver, dressmaker, bookbinder, ropemaker, saddler, many more. Quaint prose, charming illustrations for each craft. 20 black-and-white line illustrations. 192pp. 4⅝ x 6. 27293-1 Pa. $4.95

VICTORIAN FASHIONS AND COSTUMES FROM HARPER'S BAZAR, 1867–1898, Stella Blum (ed.). Day costumes, evening wear, sports clothes, shoes, hats, other accessories in over 1,000 detailed engravings. 320pp. 9⅜ x 12¼. 22990-4 Pa. $15.95

GUSTAV STICKLEY, THE CRAFTSMAN, Mary Ann Smith. Superb study surveys broad scope of Stickley's achievement, especially in architecture. Design philosophy, rise and fall of the Craftsman empire, descriptions and floor plans for many Craftsman houses, more. 86 black-and-white halftones. 31 line illustrations. Introduction 208pp. 6½ x 9¼. 27210-9 Pa. $9.95

THE LONG ISLAND RAIL ROAD IN EARLY PHOTOGRAPHS, Ron Ziel. Over 220 rare photos, informative text document origin (1844) and development of rail service on Long Island. Vintage views of early trains, locomotives, stations, passengers, crews, much more. Captions. 8⅞ x 11¾. 26301-0 Pa. $13.95

THE BOOK OF OLD SHIPS: From Egyptian Galleys to Clipper Ships, Henry B. Culver. Superb, authoritative history of sailing vessels, with 80 magnificent line illustrations. Galley, bark, caravel, longship, whaler, many more. Detailed, informative text on each vessel by noted naval historian. Introduction. 256pp. 5⅜ x 8½. 27332-6 Pa. $7.95

TEN BOOKS ON ARCHITECTURE, Vitruvius. The most important book ever written on architecture. Early Roman aesthetics, technology, classical orders, site selection, all other aspects. Morgan translation. 331pp. 5⅜ x 8½. 20645-9 Pa. $8.95

THE HUMAN FIGURE IN MOTION, Eadweard Muybridge. More than 4,500 stopped-action photos, in action series, showing undraped men, women, children jumping, lying down, throwing, sitting, wrestling, carrying, etc. 390pp. 7⅞ x 10⅝. 20204-6 Clothbd. $27.95

TREES OF THE EASTERN AND CENTRAL UNITED STATES AND CANADA, William M. Harlow. Best one-volume guide to 140 trees. Full descriptions, woodlore, range, etc. Over 600 illustrations. Handy size. 288pp. 4½ x 6⅜. 20395-6 Pa. $6.95

SONGS OF WESTERN BIRDS, Dr. Donald J. Borror. Complete song and call repertoire of 60 western species, including flycatchers, juncoes, cactus wrens, many more–includes fully illustrated booklet. Cassette and manual 99913-0 $8.95

GROWING AND USING HERBS AND SPICES, Milo Miloradovich. Versatile handbook provides all the information needed for cultivation and use of all the herbs and spices available in North America. 4 illustrations. Index. Glossary. 236pp. 5⅜ x 8½. 25058-X Pa. $7.95

BIG BOOK OF MAZES AND LABYRINTHS, Walter Shepherd. 50 mazes and labyrinths in all–classical, solid, ripple, and more–in one great volume. Perfect inexpensive puzzler for clever youngsters. Full solutions. 112pp. 8⅛ x 11. 22951-3 Pa. $4.95

PIANO TUNING, J. Cree Fischer. Clearest, best book for beginner, amateur. Simple repairs, raising dropped notes, tuning by easy method of flattened fifths. No previous skills needed. 4 illustrations. 201pp. 5⅜ x 8½.   23267-0 Pa. $6.95

A SOURCE BOOK IN THEATRICAL HISTORY, A. M. Nagler. Contemporary observers on acting, directing, make-up, costuming, stage props, machinery, scene design, from Ancient Greece to Chekhov. 611pp. 5⅜ x 8½.   20515-0 Pa. $12.95

THE COMPLETE NONSENSE OF EDWARD LEAR, Edward Lear. All nonsense limericks, zany alphabets, Owl and Pussycat, songs, nonsense botany, etc., illustrated by Lear. Total of 320pp. 5⅜ x 8½. (USO)   20167-8 Pa. $7.95

VICTORIAN PARLOUR POETRY: An Annotated Anthology, Michael R. Turner. 117 gems by Longfellow, Tennyson, Browning, many lesser-known poets. "The Village Blacksmith," "Curfew Must Not Ring Tonight," "Only a Baby Small," dozens more, often difficult to find elsewhere. Index of poets, titles, first lines. xxiii + 325pp. 5⅜ x 8¼.   27044-0 Pa. $8.95

DUBLINERS, James Joyce. Fifteen stories offer vivid, tightly focused observations of the lives of Dublin's poorer classes. At least one, "The Dead," is considered a masterpiece. Reprinted complete and unabridged from standard edition. 160pp. 5³⁄₁₆ x 8¼.   26870-5 Pa. $1.00

THE HAUNTED MONASTERY and THE CHINESE MAZE MURDERS, Robert van Gulik. Two full novels by van Gulik, set in 7th-century China, continue adventures of Judge Dee and his companions. An evil Taoist monastery, seemingly supernatural events; overgrown topiary maze hides strange crimes. 27 illustrations. 328pp. 5⅜ x 8½.   23502-5 Pa. $8.95

THE BOOK OF THE SACRED MAGIC OF ABRAMELIN THE MAGE, translated by S. MacGregor Mathers. Medieval manuscript of ceremonial magic. Basic document in Aleister Crowley, Golden Dawn groups. 268pp. 5⅜ x 8½.
23211-5 Pa. $9.95

NEW RUSSIAN-ENGLISH AND ENGLISH-RUSSIAN DICTIONARY, M. A. O'Brien. This is a remarkably handy Russian dictionary, containing a surprising amount of information, including over 70,000 entries. 366pp. 4½ x 6⅛.
20208-9 Pa. $9.95

HISTORIC HOMES OF THE AMERICAN PRESIDENTS, Second, Revised Edition, Irvin Haas. A traveler's guide to American Presidential homes, most open to the public, depicting and describing homes occupied by every American President from George Washington to George Bush. With visiting hours, admission charges, travel routes. 175 photographs. Index. 160pp. 8¼ x 11.   26751-2 Pa. $11.95

NEW YORK IN THE FORTIES, Andreas Feininger. 162 brilliant photographs by the well-known photographer, formerly with *Life* magazine. Commuters, shoppers, Times Square at night, much else from city at its peak. Captions by John von Hartz. 181pp. 9¼ x 10¾.   23585-8 Pa. $12.95

INDIAN SIGN LANGUAGE, William Tomkins. Over 525 signs developed by Sioux and other tribes. Written instructions and diagrams. Also 290 pictographs. 111pp. 6⅛ x 9¼.   22029-X Pa. $3.95

CATALOG OF DOVER BOOKS

ANATOMY: A Complete Guide for Artists, Joseph Sheppard. A master of figure drawing shows artists how to render human anatomy convincingly. Over 460 illustrations. 224pp. 8⅜ x 11¼. 27279-6 Pa. $11.95

MEDIEVAL CALLIGRAPHY: Its History and Technique, Marc Drogin. Spirited history, comprehensive instruction manual covers 13 styles (ca. 4th century thru 15th). Excellent photographs; directions for duplicating medieval techniques with modern tools. 224pp. 8⅜ x 11¼. 26142-5 Pa. $12.95

DRIED FLOWERS: How to Prepare Them, Sarah Whitlock and Martha Rankin. Complete instructions on how to use silica gel, meal and borax, perlite aggregate, sand and borax, glycerine and water to create attractive permanent flower arrangements. 12 illustrations. 32pp. 5⅜ x 8½. 21802-3 Pa. $1.00

EASY-TO-MAKE BIRD FEEDERS FOR WOODWORKERS, Scott D. Campbell. Detailed, simple-to-use guide for designing, constructing, caring for and using feeders. Text, illustrations for 12 classic and contemporary designs. 96pp. 5⅜ x 8½. 25847-5 Pa. $3.95

SCOTTISH WONDER TALES FROM MYTH AND LEGEND, Donald A. Mackenzie. 16 lively tales tell of giants rumbling down mountainsides, of a magic wand that turns stone pillars into warriors, of gods and goddesses, evil hags, powerful forces and more. 240pp. 5⅜ x 8½. 29677-6 Pa. $6.95

THE HISTORY OF UNDERCLOTHES, C. Willett Cunnington and Phyllis Cunnington. Fascinating, well-documented survey covering six centuries of English undergarments, enhanced with over 100 illustrations: 12th-century laced-up bodice, footed long drawers (1795), 19th-century bustles, 19th-century corsets for men, Victorian "bust improvers," much more. 272pp. 5⅝ x 8¼. 27124-2 Pa. $9.95

ARTS AND CRAFTS FURNITURE: The Complete Brooks Catalog of 1912, Brooks Manufacturing Co. Photos and detailed descriptions of more than 150 now very collectible furniture designs from the Arts and Crafts movement depict davenports, settees, buffets, desks, tables, chairs, bedsteads, dressers and more, all built of solid, quarter-sawed oak. Invaluable for students and enthusiasts of antiques, Americana and the decorative arts. 80pp. 6½ x 9¼. 27471-3 Pa. $8.95

HOW WE INVENTED THE AIRPLANE: An Illustrated History, Orville Wright. Fascinating firsthand account covers early experiments, construction of planes and motors, first flights, much more. Introduction and commentary by Fred C. Kelly. 76 photographs. 96pp. 8¼ x 11. 25662-6 Pa. $8.95

THE ARTS OF THE SAILOR: Knotting, Splicing and Ropework, Hervey Garrett Smith. Indispensable shipboard reference covers tools, basic knots and useful hitches; handsewing and canvas work, more. Over 100 illustrations. Delightful reading for sea lovers. 256pp. 5⅜ x 8½. 26440-8 Pa. $7.95

FRANK LLOYD WRIGHT'S FALLINGWATER: The House and Its History, Second, Revised Edition, Donald Hoffmann. A total revision–both in text and illustrations–of the standard document on Fallingwater, the boldest, most personal architectural statement of Wright's mature years, updated with valuable new material from the recently opened Frank Lloyd Wright Archives. "Fascinating"–*The New York Times.* 116 illustrations. 128pp. 9¼ x 10¾. 27430-6 Pa. $12.95

PHOTOGRAPHIC SKETCHBOOK OF THE CIVIL WAR, Alexander Gardner. 100 photos taken on field during the Civil War. Famous shots of Manassas Harper's Ferry, Lincoln, Richmond, slave pens, etc. 244pp. 10⅝ x 8¼. 22731-6 Pa. $9.95

FIVE ACRES AND INDEPENDENCE, Maurice G. Kains. Great back-to-the-land classic explains basics of self-sufficient farming. The one book to get. 95 illustrations. 397pp. 5⅜ x 8½. 20974-1 Pa. $7.95

SONGS OF EASTERN BIRDS, Dr. Donald J. Borror. Songs and calls of 60 species most common to eastern U.S.: warblers, woodpeckers, flycatchers, thrushes, larks, many more in high-quality recording. Cassette and manual 99912-2 $9.95

A MODERN HERBAL, Margaret Grieve. Much the fullest, most exact, most useful compilation of herbal material. Gigantic alphabetical encyclopedia, from aconite to zedoary, gives botanical information, medical properties, folklore, economic uses, much else. Indispensable to serious reader. 161 illustrations. 888pp. 6½ x 9¼. 2-vol. set. (USO) Vol. I: 22798-7 Pa. $9.95
Vol. II: 22799-5 Pa. $9.95

HIDDEN TREASURE MAZE BOOK, Dave Phillips. Solve 34 challenging mazes accompanied by heroic tales of adventure. Evil dragons, people-eating plants, blood-thirsty giants, many more dangerous adversaries lurk at every twist and turn. 34 mazes, stories, solutions. 48pp. 8¼ x 11. 24566-7 Pa. $2.95

LETTERS OF W. A. MOZART, Wolfgang A. Mozart. Remarkable letters show bawdy wit, humor, imagination, musical insights, contemporary musical world; includes some letters from Leopold Mozart. 276pp. 5⅜ x 8½. 22859-2 Pa. $7.95

BASIC PRINCIPLES OF CLASSICAL BALLET, Agrippina Vaganova. Great Russian theoretician, teacher explains methods for teaching classical ballet. 118 illustrations. 175pp. 5⅜ x 8½. 22036-2 Pa. $5.95

THE JUMPING FROG, Mark Twain. Revenge edition. The original story of The Celebrated Jumping Frog of Calaveras County, a hapless French translation, and Twain's hilarious "retranslation" from the French. 12 illustrations. 66pp. 5⅜ x 8½. 22686-7 Pa. $3.95

BEST REMEMBERED POEMS, Martin Gardner (ed.). The 126 poems in this superb collection of 19th- and 20th-century British and American verse range from Shelley's "To a Skylark" to the impassioned "Renascence" of Edna St. Vincent Millay and to Edward Lear's whimsical "The Owl and the Pussycat." 224pp. 5⅜ x 8½. 27165-X Pa. $5.95

COMPLETE SONNETS, William Shakespeare. Over 150 exquisite poems deal with love, friendship, the tyranny of time, beauty's evanescence, death and other themes in language of remarkable power, precision and beauty. Glossary of archaic terms. 80pp. 5³⁄₁₆ x 8¼. 26686-9 Pa. $1.00

BODIES IN A BOOKSHOP, R. T. Campbell. Challenging mystery of blackmail and murder with ingenious plot and superbly drawn characters. In the best tradition of British suspense fiction. 192pp. 5⅜ x 8½. 24720-1 Pa. $6.95

THE WIT AND HUMOR OF OSCAR WILDE, Alvin Redman (ed.). More than 1,000 ripostes, paradoxes, wisecracks: Work is the curse of the drinking classes; I can resist everything except temptation; etc. 258pp. 5⅜ x 8½. 20602-5 Pa. $5.95

SHAKESPEARE LEXICON AND QUOTATION DICTIONARY, Alexander Schmidt. Full definitions, locations, shades of meaning in every word in plays and poems. More than 50,000 exact quotations. 1,485pp. 6½ x 9¼. 2-vol. set.
Vol. 1: 22726-X Pa. $17.95
Vol. 2: 22727-8 Pa. $17.95

SELECTED POEMS, Emily Dickinson. Over 100 best-known, best-loved poems by one of America's foremost poets, reprinted from authoritative early editions. No comparable edition at this price. Index of first lines. 64pp. 5³⁄₁₆ x 8¼. 26466-1 Pa. $1.00

CELEBRATED CASES OF JUDGE DEE (DEE GOONG AN), translated by Robert van Gulik. Authentic 18th-century Chinese detective novel; Dee and associates solve three interlocked cases. Led to van Gulik's own stories with same characters. Extensive introduction. 9 illustrations. 237pp. 5⅜ x 8½. 23337-5 Pa. $7.95

THE MALLEUS MALEFICARUM OF KRAMER AND SPRENGER, translated by Montague Summers. Full text of most important witchhunter's "bible," used by both Catholics and Protestants. 278pp. 6⅝ x 10. 22802-9 Pa. $12.95

SPANISH STORIES/CUENTOS ESPAÑOLES: A Dual-Language Book, Angel Flores (ed.). Unique format offers 13 great stories in Spanish by Cervantes, Borges, others. Faithful English translations on facing pages. 352pp. 5⅜ x 8½. 25399-6 Pa. $8.95

THE CHICAGO WORLD'S FAIR OF 1893: A Photographic Record, Stanley Appelbaum (ed.). 128 rare photos show 200 buildings, Beaux-Arts architecture, Midway, original Ferris Wheel, Edison's kinetoscope, more. Architectural emphasis; full text. 116pp. 8¼ x 11. 23990-X Pa. $9.95

OLD QUEENS, N.Y., IN EARLY PHOTOGRAPHS, Vincent F. Seyfried and William Asadorian. Over 160 rare photographs of Maspeth, Jamaica, Jackson Heights, and other areas. Vintage views of DeWitt Clinton mansion, 1939 World's Fair and more. Captions. 192pp. 8⅞ x 11. 26358-4 Pa. $12.95

CAPTURED BY THE INDIANS: 15 Firsthand Accounts, 1750-1870, Frederick Drimmer. Astounding true historical accounts of grisly torture, bloody conflicts, relentless pursuits, miraculous escapes and more, by people who lived to tell the tale. 384pp. 5⅜ x 8½. 24901-8 Pa. $8.95

THE WORLD'S GREAT SPEECHES, Lewis Copeland and Lawrence W. Lamm (eds.). Vast collection of 278 speeches of Greeks to 1970. Powerful and effective models; unique look at history. 842pp. 5⅜ x 8½. 20468-5 Pa. $14.95

THE BOOK OF THE SWORD, Sir Richard F. Burton. Great Victorian scholar/adventurer's eloquent, erudite history of the "queen of weapons"–from prehistory to early Roman Empire. Evolution and development of early swords, variations (sabre, broadsword, cutlass, scimitar, etc.), much more. 336pp. 6⅛ x 9¼. 25434-8 Pa. $9.95

AUTOBIOGRAPHY: The Story of My Experiments with Truth, Mohandas K. Gandhi. Boyhood, legal studies, purification, the growth of the Satyagraha (nonviolent protest) movement. Critical, inspiring work of the man responsible for the freedom of India. 480pp. 5⅜ x 8½. (USO)   24593-4 Pa. $8.95

CELTIC MYTHS AND LEGENDS, T. W. Rolleston. Masterful retelling of Irish and Welsh stories and tales. Cuchulain, King Arthur, Deirdre, the Grail, many more. First paperback edition. 58 full-page illustrations. 512pp. 5⅜ x 8½.   26507-2 Pa. $9.95

THE PRINCIPLES OF PSYCHOLOGY, William James. Famous long course complete, unabridged. Stream of thought, time perception, memory, experimental methods; great work decades ahead of its time. 94 figures. 1,391pp. 5⅜ x 8½. 2-vol. set.
Vol. I: 20381-6 Pa. $13.95
Vol. II: 20382-4 Pa. $14.95

THE WORLD AS WILL AND REPRESENTATION, Arthur Schopenhauer. Definitive English translation of Schopenhauer's life work, correcting more than 1,000 errors, omissions in earlier translations. Translated by E. F. J. Payne. Total of 1,269pp. 5⅜ x 8½. 2-vol. set.
Vol. 1: 21761-2 Pa. $12.95
Vol. 2: 21762-0 Pa. $12.95

MAGIC AND MYSTERY IN TIBET, Madame Alexandra David-Neel. Experiences among lamas, magicians, sages, sorcerers, Bonpa wizards. A true psychic discovery. 32 illustrations. 321pp. 5⅜ x 8½. (USO)   22682-4 Pa. $9.95

THE EGYPTIAN BOOK OF THE DEAD, E. A. Wallis Budge. Complete reproduction of Ani's papyrus, finest ever found. Full hieroglyphic text, interlinear transliteration, word-for-word translation, smooth translation. 533pp. 6½ x 9¼.
21866-X Pa. $11.95

MATHEMATICS FOR THE NONMATHEMATICIAN, Morris Kline. Detailed, college-level treatment of mathematics in cultural and historical context, with numerous exercises. Recommended Reading Lists. Tables. Numerous figures. 641pp. 5⅜ x 8½.
24823-2 Pa. $11.95

THEORY OF WING SECTIONS: Including a Summary of Airfoil Data, Ira H. Abbott and A. E. von Doenhoff. Concise compilation of subsonic aerodynamic characteristics of NACA wing sections, plus description of theory. 350pp. of tables. 693pp. 5⅜ x 8½.   60586-8 Pa. $14.95

THE RIME OF THE ANCIENT MARINER, Gustave Doré, S. T. Coleridge. Doré's finest work; 34 plates capture moods, subtleties of poem. Flawless full-size reproductions printed on facing pages with authoritative text of poem. "Beautiful. Simply beautiful."–*Publisher's Weekly.* 77pp. 9¼ x 12.   22305-1 Pa. $7.95

NORTH AMERICAN INDIAN DESIGNS FOR ARTISTS AND CRAFTSPEOPLE, Eva Wilson. Over 360 authentic copyright-free designs adapted from Navajo blankets, Hopi pottery, Sioux buffalo hides, more. Geometrics, symbolic figures, plant and animal motifs, etc. 128pp. 8⅜ x 11. (EUK)   25341-4 Pa. $8.95

SCULPTURE: Principles and Practice, Louis Slobodkin. Step-by-step approach to clay, plaster, metals, stone; classical and modern. 253 drawings, photos. 255pp. 8⅛ x 11.
22960-2 Pa. $11.95

THE INFLUENCE OF SEA POWER UPON HISTORY, 1660–1783, A. T. Mahan. Influential classic of naval history and tactics still used as text in war colleges. First paperback edition. 4 maps. 24 battle plans. 640pp. 5⅜ x 8½. 25509-3 Pa. $14.95

THE STORY OF THE TITANIC AS TOLD BY ITS SURVIVORS, Jack Winocour (ed.). What it was really like. Panic, despair, shocking inefficiency, and a little heroism. More thrilling than any fictional account. 26 illustrations. 320pp. 5⅜ x 8½. 20610-6 Pa. $8.95

FAIRY AND FOLK TALES OF THE IRISH PEASANTRY, William Butler Yeats (ed.). Treasury of 64 tales from the twilight world of Celtic myth and legend: "The Soul Cages," "The Kildare Pooka," "King O'Toole and his Goose," many more. Introduction and Notes by W. B. Yeats. 352pp. 5⅜ x 8½. 26941-8 Pa. $8.95

BUDDHIST MAHAYANA TEXTS, E. B. Cowell and Others (eds.). Superb, accurate translations of basic documents in Mahayana Buddhism, highly important in history of religions. The Buddha-karita of Asvaghosha, Larger Sukhavativyuha, more. 448pp. 5⅜ x 8½. 25552-2 Pa. $12.95

ONE TWO THREE . . . INFINITY: Facts and Speculations of Science, George Gamow. Great physicist's fascinating, readable overview of contemporary science: number theory, relativity, fourth dimension, entropy, genes, atomic structure, much more. 128 illustrations. Index. 352pp. 5⅜ x 8½. 25664-2 Pa. $8.95

ENGINEERING IN HISTORY, Richard Shelton Kirby, et al. Broad, nontechnical survey of history's major technological advances: birth of Greek science, industrial revolution, electricity and applied science, 20th-century automation, much more. 181 illustrations. ". . . excellent . . ."–*Isis*. Bibliography. vii + 530pp. 5⅜ x 8¼. 26412-2 Pa. $14.95

DALÍ ON MODERN ART: The Cuckolds of Antiquated Modern Art, Salvador Dalí. Influential painter skewers modern art and its practitioners. Outrageous evaluations of Picasso, Cézanne, Turner, more. 15 renderings of paintings discussed. 44 calligraphic decorations by Dalí. 96pp. 5⅜ x 8½. (USO) 29220-7 Pa. $4.95

ANTIQUE PLAYING CARDS: A Pictorial History, Henry René D'Allemagne. Over 900 elaborate, decorative images from rare playing cards (14th–20th centuries): Bacchus, death, dancing dogs, hunting scenes, royal coats of arms, players cheating, much more. 96pp. 9¼ x 12¼. 29265-7 Pa. $12.95

MAKING FURNITURE MASTERPIECES: 30 Projects with Measured Drawings, Franklin H. Gottshall. Step-by-step instructions, illustrations for constructing handsome, useful pieces, among them a Sheraton desk, Chippendale chair, Spanish desk, Queen Anne table and a William and Mary dressing mirror. 224pp. 8⅛ x 11¼. 29338-6 Pa. $13.95

THE FOSSIL BOOK: A Record of Prehistoric Life, Patricia V. Rich et al. Profusely illustrated definitive guide covers everything from single-celled organisms and dinosaurs to birds and mammals and the interplay between climate and man. Over 1,500 illustrations. 760pp. 7½ x 10⅛. 29371-8 Pa. $29.95

Prices subject to change without notice.

Available at your book dealer or write for free catalog to Dept. GI, Dover Publications, Inc., 31 East 2nd St., Mineola, N.Y. 11501. Dover publishes more than 500 books each year on science, elementary and advanced mathematics, biology, music, art, literary history, social sciences and other areas.